The Unitary Executive and the Modern Presidency

Joseph V. Hughes Jr. and Holly O. Hughes Series on the Presidency and Leadership

A list of all titles in this series is available at the end of the book.

The Unitary Executive and the Modern Presidency

Edited by Ryan J. Barilleaux and Christopher S. Kelley

Texas A&M University Press
COLLEGE STATION

First edition

This paper meets the requirements
of ANSI/NISO Z39.48-1992
(Permanence of Paper).
Binding materials have been chosen for durability.

LIBRARY OF CONGRESS CATALOGING-IN-PUBLICATION DATA

The unitary executive and the modern presidency / edited by Ryan J. Barilleaux
and Christopher S. Kelley. — 1st ed.
p. cm. — (Joseph V. Hughes Jr. and Holly O. Hughes series on
the presidency and leadership)
Includes index.
ISBN-13: 978-1-60344-173-5 (cloth : alk. paper)
ISBN-10: 1-60344-173-5 (cloth : alk. paper)
ISBN-13: 978-1-60344-190-2 (pbk. : alk. paper)
ISBN-10: 1-60344-190-5 (pbk. : alk. paper)
1. Executive power—United States. 2. Executive-legislative relations—United States.
3. United States—Politics and government—20th century. 4. United States—Politics
and government—21st century. I. Barilleaux, Ryan J., 1957– II. Kelley, Christopher S.,
1964– III. Series: Presidency and leadership (Unnumbered)
JK516.U54 2010
352.230973—dc22

2009047682

To the memory of my brother,
Ira Barilleaux Jr.
—*RJB*

To my daughters,
Megan & Zoe,
who are boundless sources
of inspiration.
—*CSK*

CONTENTS

PREFACE AND ACKNOWLEDGMENTS

This book is the product of a panel convened on the titular subject at the annual meeting of the American Political Science Association (APSA), held in Philadelphia in 2006. The theme of the convention? Power reconsidered.

Our panel, focusing on the unitary executive in a separated system, assembled a group of political scientists to undertake a critical examination of the theory of presidential power referred to so often by Pres. George W. Bush. At that time—as is still largely the case today—the only substantive research on the unitary executive theory was being done by legal scholars, key among them Steven Calabresi, a former Justice Department attorney in the Reagan administration and self-described "father of the unitary executive."

The legal scholars seemed interested only in discussions of whether the unitary executive was indeed supported by the founding fathers at the Federal Convention of 1787, as well as whether it was implemented by nineteenth-century presidents. Furthermore, the popular conception of the unitary executive theory seemed to focus only on its use by George W. Bush, with little attention to the theory's tenets or antecedents. Our panel sought to explain what the theory was, how and why the Reagan administration came to embrace it, and finally, how those presidents who followed Reagan—including Bill Clinton, a Democrat—used it. We also wanted to tie the theory to the larger literature on unilateral presidential action, which has become a popular explanation of presidential power following Watergate.

The panel discussion had strong attendance, and there was real excitement about extending the discussion beyond the APSA convention and including more individuals than those on the panel. Thus was born this book.

Initially our hope was to include both political scientists and legal scholars, especially those who have been defenders of the theory itself. We also wanted to take a step forward to bridge the gap between political scientists and legal scholars, who too often write and meet apart from one another.

Our view was that we all shared a common interest in building a greater understanding of our subject—presidential power—and should strive to work together rather than apart. We received tentative commitments by some legal scholars, but they ultimately chose not to participate. Nevertheless, the contributors to this volume have produced what we believe is an important examination of a controversial subject that addresses an audience larger than just those scholars who already study the president's constitutional powers.

This project has truly been a group effort. All of the contributors produced solid essays and did so in the time limits we established, and they have been patient as we have moved the manuscript through the production process. We also owe a debt of thanks to those who served on the APSA panel but did not contribute an essay for this volume, including Nancy Kassop, David Adler, and Robert Spitzer. In addition, we are grateful for the support and patience of those at Texas A&M University Press—in particular, Mary Lenn Dixon, editor-in-chief—and of Jim Pfiffner, the Hughes Series editor, who enthusiastically took on this project. Finally, we appreciate the comments of the anonymous reviewers for Texas A&M University Press, whose careful reading of the manuscript made the final product much stronger. Any errors in this book are entirely our own.

Introduction

What Is the Unitary Executive?

RYAN J. BARILLEAUX AND CHRISTOPHER S. KELLEY

The presidential nomination process of 2008 included questions and news reports about an issue that has not been present during a presidential election cycle since the 1976 cycle—questions and concerns involving the limits of executive power.[1] This is because the Bush administration vigorously advanced a little understood theory of presidential power known as the unitary executive.

In a meeting before the editorial board at the *Boston Globe,* Senator Hillary Clinton (D-N.Y.) had this to say about the behavior of President Bill Clinton: "I think you have to restore the checks and balances and the separation of power, which means reining in the presidency." Clinton also said she "did not subscribe to the 'unitary executive' theory that argues the Constitution prevents Congress from passing laws limiting the president's power over executive branch operations."[2]

The Unitary Executive Goes Public

The unitary executive theory has become inextricably linked with the Bush administration in large part because of the attention it received in 2006, first during the Supreme Court confirmation hearings for Judge Samuel Alito and then Bush's frequent use of the signing statement for bills that Congress approved and sent to the Oval Office.

The Alito confirmation hearings drew interest to the theory in large part due to Judge Alito's support for it. A *Wall Street Journal* article in January 2006 declared "Judge Alito's View of the Presidency: Expansive Powers."[3] The article focused on Alito's tenure in the Reagan administration Justice Department and described how he was one of a number of conservative legal scholars who developed a theory of presidential power designed to help presidents protect their constitutional powers and to "go it alone" when facing a recalcitrant Congress. The article also discussed how the George W. Bush administration had been using the term repeatedly in a variety of public documents, which included the signing statement, the executive order, and the proclamation.

It was not until a few months later that the unitary executive theory and the Bush administration would become intertwined, when a series of media reports described how President Bush had been using the signing statement to nullify hundreds of provisions of law—and using the unitary executive as his defense. The media reports uncovered a pattern of his making sweeping challenges to various provisions of legislation and defending such actions under the auspices of a prerogative to "supervise the unitary executive branch." For example, in President Bush's signing of the John Warner National Defense Authorization Act for fiscal year 2007, he challenged sixteen different provisions "in a manner consistent with the President's constitutional authority to supervise the unitary executive branch."[4]

The media could have made Bush's use of the signing statement a learning opportunity for the general public, but it failed to do so. Instead, any discussion of the unitary executive was either linked to the Bush administration and described in terms that either belittled it (e.g., "the so-called unitary executive theory" or "the obscure theory of the unitary executive") or cast it in terms of an imperial presidency. The larger questions, such as precisely what the theory was and where it originated, were left unexplored. This leaves us with two different issues under consideration. First, what is the nature of the theory as it was intended by its founders as well as its understanding by Presidents Reagan, G. H. W. Bush, and Clinton? Second, did the George W. Bush administration embrace the theory according to its principles or did the administration use the theory as a disguise for the execution of a different kind of presidential power? We briefly discuss these points by way of introducing the contributions to this book.

Key Principles of the Unitary Executive

The unitary executive theory originated in the Reagan administration, which came to office at a time when there was great suspicion directed toward presidents and their exercise of power. Because of the Nixon administration and Watergate, the Congress, the press, and the American public perceived any unilateral move by the president as suspicious. The

Reagan administration needed a constitutional explanation for those times when it would act unilaterally, and thus it embraced the unitary executive as a constitutional theory of presidential power.

The theory draws from three sources within Article II of the Constitution. The first is the "vesting" clause, which differs from similar clauses in Articles I and III. In those two articles, the "vesting" power is divided or qualified. In Article I, the "legislative" power exercised by the Congress is limited to those powers listed within Article I. In Article III, the "judicial" power is divided between the Supreme Court and inferior courts. Article II simply says that the "executive power is granted to" the president. Thus, "unitarians" (proponents of the unitary executive) take this vesting to mean both the executive powers explicitly granted in Article II and so-called "prerogative" powers, which exist outside the limits of Article II. Furthermore, unitarians believe that the whole of executive power rests with the president, which usually means unitarians resist the creation of "independent" agencies or the use of executive power by individuals who are not "executive officers."

The second source of the theory is the "oath" clause of Article II, which acts as a shield to protect presidents from enforcing laws they *independently* determine to be unconstitutional. This particular clause is at the heart of the controversy involving the Bush administration's use of the signing statement to challenge provisions of law that the president believes are unconstitutional. While there were several contentions that George W. Bush was making a novel claim of power, and considerable criticism of how often Bush relied upon it after signing bills into law, the claim of the presidential privilege to issue signing statements was not unique to the forty-third president.

The privilege of making an independent judgment about the constitutionality of law was written into the design of the Constitution. James Madison argued in the *Federalist Papers* that the "several departments being perfectly co-ordinate by the terms of their common commission, none of them, it is evident, can pretend to an exclusive or superior right of settling the boundaries between their respective powers."[5]

Walter Dellinger, who led the Justice Department's Office of Legal Counsel (OLC) during the Clinton administration, echoed Madison in a memorandum he wrote to White House counsel Abner Mikva in 1994: "The President has enhanced responsibility to resist unconstitutional provisions that encroach upon the constitutional power of the Presidency." Dellinger argued that absent a clear ruling by the Supreme Court, the "oath" clause obligated the president to "shoulder the responsibility of protecting the constitutional role of the presidency."[6]

The third and final source to the unitary executive theory of power is the "take care" clause, which requires the president, with assistance from inferior executive branch officers, to ensure that the laws are faithfully executed. Michael Herz argues that this clause ensures that presidents will not only execute the law personally but also monitor the executive branch agencies to ensure that the laws, as understood by the president, are faithfully executed.[7]

Presidents are obligated to make sure that policy is executed as they wish it to be because the president is the only politically accountable individual in the executive branch. Elena Kagan, a former domestic policy advisor in the Clinton administration, argues that "when Congress delegates discretionary authority to an agency official, because that official is subordinate to the President, it is so granting discretionary authority (unless otherwise specified) to the President."[8]

Because the Congress cannot monitor everything that happens inside the executive branch, and because the give and take of the legislative process often leaves important policy vague or undefined, the "take care" clause gives presidents a great deal of room to pull important policy closer to their own position.

The Origins of the Unitary Executive Theory

Some unitarians claim that the unitary executive theory was established at Philadelphia in the summer of 1787 and put into practice in the George Washington administration.[9] However, the explicit defense of unilateral presidential power dates to the Reagan administration in general and to the OLC within the Reagan Justice Department specifically.

When the Reagan administration came to office in 1981, it was a low point for presidential power. The lies exposed as a result of Vietnam and then Watergate left little support for presidential power inside or outside of government. In reaction to these events, Congress became aggressive in asserting its powers, with executive authority cast into suspicion as a remnant of the discredited "imperial presidency" associated with Lyndon Johnson and Richard Nixon. This poisoned environment ruined the presidencies of Gerald Ford and Jimmy Carter and would have likely done the same to Ronald Reagan had he and his key advisors not come to government with a plan to revive and bolster presidential power.

Among the key components to rejuvenating the presidency was the development of a constitutional theory of presidential power with muscle. Thus, conservatives inside the Reagan Justice Department, as well as conservative organizations such as the Heritage Foundation and the Federalist Society (an organization started by many of the same lawyers in the Reagan Justice Department), went to work constructing the unitary executive theory and defending it at conferences and in law journals. In addition, they urged the president to mention the term when issuing public pronouncements in an effort to "reinterpret the scope of executive power and the limits to congressional authority," particularly where the presidency and the Congress clashed.[10]

President Reagan used the term six times during his tenure and President George H. W. Bush used it forty-one times in public pronouncements such as proclamations, executive orders, and presidential signing statements.[11] The theory itself was formally unveiled in a 1992 *Harvard Law Review* article by Steven Calabresi, an attorney in the OLC during the Reagan administration. It was entitled "The Structural Constitution: Unitary Executive, Plural Judiciary."[12]

The Unitary Executive and the George W. Bush Administration

The George W. Bush administration made the term "unitary executive" almost a household expression. From 2001 through 2007, the administration mentioned the term in signing statements, executive orders, or other public pronouncements 145 times.[13]

When the Bush administration came to office in 2001, it had every intention of putting the theory into practice. After the bitterly divisive 2000 election, conventional wisdom held that Bush would need to be contrite and look for consensus if he wished to salvage his presidency. Yet the administration acted in a decidedly different manner. Many think that President Bush did not start flexing executive power until after the 9/11 attacks, when his poll numbers were in the eightieth and ninetieth percentiles, but the record of his administration shows evidence of "flexing" from those first days of his presidency.

At the outset of his tenure, Bush placed a two-month hold on all the rules passed in the waning days of the Clinton administration in order to give his people a chance to review them.[14] He issued an executive order establishing the Office of Faith-Based Initiatives when the Congress refused to do so.[15] Less than a month after his inauguration he issued a series of executive orders designed to undercut the power of organized labor.[16] President Bush also attempted to terminate an office the Clinton administration had established to deal with AIDS and race. He unilaterally ordered a limit on federal funding of embryonic stem-cell research, and he asserted executive privilege to protect information that was sought by the Republican-controlled House Judiciary Committee dealing with the Justice Department under former Clinton administration attorney general Janet Reno.[17]

On the international stage, candidate Bush promised a more humble, less arrogant foreign policy. When he became president, however, he withdrew the United States from the Anti-Ballistic Missile (ABM) Treaty with Russia, commenced funding of the controversial "Star Wars" missile defense program of the 1980s, and upset many nations—including American allies—by withdrawing from the Kyoto Protocol on climate change. Then came the 9/11 attacks, followed by the Bush Doctrine of preemptive attack, and it was clear that unilateralism was as much a part of domestic politics as it was of foreign policy.[18]

It seems clear that the point person most responsible for President Bush's aggressive brand of unilateralism was Vice President Richard Cheney, who long had been a strong supporter of expanding the power of the presidency.[19] Cheney had served in the Nixon administration's Office of Economic Opportunity and later the White House, but it was his experience as President Ford's chief of staff that had a profound effect on his view of separation of powers at the end of the twentieth century.

In the aftermath of Nixon's resignation, the new president faced hostility from Congress, the public, and the press. During the Ford administration, Congress passed legislation—often over the president's veto—that restrained the powers of the presidency. By the end of the 1970s, President Ford argued that the "pendulum has swung so far that you could almost say we have moved from an imperial Presidency to an imperiled Presidency. Now we have a Congress that is broadening its powers too greatly." Cheney described this period of time as a "low point of presidential authority."[20]

As the Bush administration took office in January 2001, it was clear that Cheney would not let history repeat itself. While most spoke of consensus, Cheney urged the president to govern as if he had been handed a mandate: "Even after we went through all of that, he [Bush] never wanted to allow the closeness of our election to in any way diminish the power of the presidency, lead him to make a decision that he needed to somehow trim his sails, and be less than a fully authorized, if you will, commander-in-chief, leader of our government, President of the United States."[21] The vice president and his staff took it upon themselves to ensure that not only would President Bush be successful as a president but also that the powers of the office would expand. This expansion would halt a slide that, as Cheney saw it, began with Watergate and threatened effective government. Cheney told the *Washington Post*'s Dana Milbank, "I have repeatedly seen an erosion of the powers and the ability of the President of the United States to do his job."[22] Cheney and his chief of staff, David Addington, were at the forefront of the administration's initiatives to advance presidential power.

On the surface, it would appear that the Bush administration was faithful to the principles of the unitary executive. For example, President Bush was diligent in using the signing statement to defend the oath he swore to uphold the Constitution and the Office of the Presidency. Through the end of 2008, President Bush had issued 171 signing statements that challenged 1,168 provisions of law. When all of the challenges made by every president before George W. Bush are added together, the total comes to just under 600 challenges. This figure means that President Bush nearly doubled the number of challenges made by all previous presidents. Moreover, a look at what the president objected to presents a clearer picture of how the unitary executive theory comes into play.

The empirical record is instructive. Neil Kinkopf and Peter Shane have created an index of signing statements issued by George W. Bush, complete with a count of the areas where the administration challenged Congress. Among the major challenges are recommendations violations (212), bicameralism and presentment violations (235), foreign policy prerogative violations (147), appointments clause violations (31), protection of information (170), and commander-in-chief violations (76).[23]

President Bush was also diligent in exercising the "take care" powers by directing a great deal of energy into the supervision of lower-level executive branch officers. From the start, he charged the Office of Management and Budget (OMB) with ensuring that all regulations were vetted through a cost-benefit prism. Each executive branch agency was required to justify to the Office of Information and Regulatory Affairs (OIRA—an office within the OMB) the benefits of any rule that would subtract $100 million or more from the U.S. economy.

Furthermore, in an extraordinary action taken in January 2007, President Bush amended a Clinton-era order whereby "policy officers" would be placed in the regulatory agencies to give the administration "overt presence" in the development of regulations.[24] Prior to this move, pressure from the White House was esoteric—agency personnel understood they were being "watched," although there was no direct intervention. Now there was no question but that the White House was directly monitoring agency rulemaking.

While George Bush's actions seem consistent with the tenets of the unitary executive theory, the reality is that the manner in which the White House acted elicited a negative reaction even from some unitarians. This reaction begs the question of whether the Bush administration was really following the unitary executive theory of power or whether it subscribed to some other theory of presidential power.

Harold Krent, the dean of Chicago-Kent College of Law, argues that many of the actions taken by the Bush administration in both domestic and international politics have not been in accord with the unitary executive theory. Rather, the Bush administration's actions seemed to be more consistent with a "super-sized" unitary executive.[25] Bush, Krent argues, attempted to maximize and centralize power inside the Office of the Presidency, making irrelevant the need for lower-level executive branch officers. Moreover, Bush apparently failed to recognize areas where the president and Congress share power, and he seemed to have little respect for judicial decisions that ran counter to the wishes of the president or even the vice president. For Krent, this is not the unitary executive properly understood but rather "unilateralism," and it more aptly describes the kind of power the Bush administration exercised.

It is our hope that this book makes these two issues separate—the unitary executive and how it has evolved, and the Bush administration's rejection of the unitary executive theory (which had been embraced by his immediate predecessors, Republican and Democrat alike) in favor of presidential unilateralism.

The book's main text is divided into two parts. First, we present a historical overview of the unitary executive—where it came from and why it was developed. Our hope is to provide the reader with a context for understanding the Bush presidency—something that has been lacking in the popular discussions of theory. Second, we focus on the Bush administration's defense of its actions as being unitarian, something that has garnered criticism even from a chief proponent of the unitary executive. Charlie Savage of the *Boston Globe* wrote that "Steven Calabresi, a co-founder of the Federalist Society (recognized as the intellectual father of the unitary executive theory) . . . watched with astonishment" the way in which the Bush administration misused and misconstrued the theory.[26]

The contributors and their chapters are arranged as follows: we open with Louis Fisher, who challenges those unitarians who attempt to argue that the unitary executive theory was put into practice the moment that George Washington took office. In particular, Fisher focuses on the argument offered by Steven Calabresi and Christopher Yoo, who date the unitary executive to the Constitutional Convention.[27] Fisher criticizes the two for being selective with their evidence to defend a unitary presidency, for example, their reference to the 1926 *Myers* decision without also mentioning the 1935 *Humphrey's* decision, which significantly qualified the former.[28] Fisher notes that in the 1986 *Bowsher* decision, which invalidated portions of the Gramm-Rudman deficit control measures and is considered by unitarians to be a nod toward their position, the Supreme Court justices took great pains to make clear that they had no intention of qualifying or overriding the decision in *Humphrey's*.[29]

Next, Ryan Barilleaux and David Zellers trace the precursor to the birth of the unitary executive—presidential unilateralism in the Ford and Carter presidencies. The conventional wisdom posits the origin of the unitary executive in the Reagan administration. The conventional wisdom, however, misses an important component to the theory's origins. It was Ford and Carter who came immediately after Nixon and who were on the front lines of the assault upon the prerogatives of the presidency. Those two presidents were forced to devise methods to gain "leverage" over political forces both inside and outside the executive branch. This leverage, according to the authors, employed presidential persuasion as well as constitutional powers to expand the powers of the presidency. Thus, the authors conclude that once Reagan took office in 1981, his immediate predecessors had already built up a reservoir of power and precedents that made it easier for his administration to justify unilateral actions based upon past practice.

Melanie Marlowe traces the development of presidential review of the regulatory policymaking process, which began with the Nixon administration and continued in earnest during the Reagan years. Presidential involvement in the regulatory process is an instrumental part of the unitary executive. In particular, presidential involvement is designed to enhance the accountability placed on the president for policy that comes from the White House. Marlowe argues that whatever we think about the constitutional legitimacy surrounding a role for the president, because of persistent involvement since Reagan's tenure in office, review of regulatory policy has become an established power that presidents currently enjoy and will not relinquish any time soon.

Christopher S. Kelley rounds out part I, focusing his chapter on the Clinton administration's contribution to the development of the signing statement. Kelley's chapter broadens the conventional understanding of the unitary executive theory, which basically views Republican presidencies as the greatest proponents of the unitary executive. Kelley examines Clinton's defense of presidential prerogatives by way of OLC opinions that aggressively defended both the legitimate use of the presidential signing statement and the presidential obligation to refuse enforcement of any law the chief executive determines is not constitutional. Kelley highlights a number of signing statements that not only challenged unconstitutional provisions of law but also, and more importantly, made sure that the challenges were carried out. Kelley also looks at another important tenet of the unitary executive theory—the control over the executive branch—and how Clinton, by way of an important executive order, continued the practice of the Reagan and subsequent Bush administrations of inserting the president into the regulatory process at the expense of the Congress.

Part II focuses on particular actions by the George W. Bush administration and its attempt to defend these actions by invoking a constitutional defense of the unitary executive.

Michael A. Genovese describes the theory of the unitary executive and how the Bush administration used it to justify claims of power. Genovese's chapter provides insight into why many of the "fathers" of the unitary executive—individuals such as Steven Calabresi—have been critical of the Bush administration's defense of the theory. Genovese argues that when the Bush administration exhausted claims of expansive executive power, it finally turned to the unitary executive as justification for its use of power.

Mitchel A. Sollenberger and Mark J. Rozell look at the energy task force episode early in Bush's first term. They tie the controversy into the Bush administration's defense of the unitary executive. In the administration's brief to the Supreme Court, it hinged its argument on two tenets of the unitary executive: the constitutional right of presidents to receive confidential advice and their right to make, for Congress's consideration, whatever recommendations they see fit. As Sollenberger and Rozell argue, the Supreme Court bought the administration's argument, establishing a precedent for "judicial deference to executive authority." This chapter provides an interesting insight to Fisher's argument. Fisher argues that the current unitarians have consistently overstated, or excluded, key Supreme Court decisions supporting the arguments of the theory. And that is true, in many cases. However, as Sollenberger and Rozell demonstrate, the Supreme Court of today and the future is far more deferential—and willing—to agree with some, if not all, of the key parts of the theory. One reason for this change may be the professional résumés of the current members of the federal judiciary. On the Supreme Court alone several justices, including Chief Justice John Roberts, were members of the Office of Legal Counsel during the post-Watergate period. These individuals were thus at the fore of the theory's development.

Richard M. Pious looks at the controversy involving the warrantless wiretaps that intercepted calls from both noncitizens and citizens and that many believed violated the law. In addition, the Bush administration had a program in place to spy on its own intelligence agencies in order to identify those who leaked sensitive information to the press. The Bush administration, however, defended the action through its own interpretation of the commander-in-chief power granted in Article II. Pious argues that, in doing so, the Bush administration created a system of "parallel governance" whereby the president can rely upon statutory and constitutional powers as the need arises. Pious also details Congress's complicity in the administration's actions, arguing that it did not hold the administration responsible for breaches in law. In what Pious refers to as "soft prerogative" power, he argues that when the administration faced a confrontation with the Congress over prerogative, it would "work to obtain authorization that would legitimize its activities" through legislation. The legislation, in most cases, would be broad grants of authority, enabling the administration to obtain its goals anyway.

Bryan W. Marshall and Patrick J. Haney focus squarely on the complicity of Congress in allowing the president to expand the power of the presidency at the expense of the Congress. Whether it was the post-9/11 vote by Congress to authorize the president to use whatever means he decided to combat the terrorists internationally or the vote in 2002 to allow the president to use force against Iraq, on each occasion Congress voted to remove itself from its obligation to ensure that the president was not abusing his authority and instead chose to watch the presidential abuse of power "from the cheap seats." Thus, Marshall and Haney conclude that no criticism of the Bush administration's unitarian advances can be complete without also considering how Congress opted out.

The volume concludes with a discussion of what the future is likely to hold for the unitary executive theory specifically and presidential power more generally. Given the dynamics of power in Washington in the decades since Watergate, it is likely that assertive actions by the White House will continue. In that case, it is all the more important to have a good understanding of the ideas that underlie contemporary presidential assertiveness, the precedents that have been set by George W. Bush and his predecessors, and the potential that the unitary executive theory holds for influencing presidential behavior in the future.

Notes

1. See David Nather, "New Handshake, Same Grip," *CQ Weekly*, December 17, 2007, 3702–15; Charlie Savage, "Candidates on Executive Power: A Full Spectrum, They Assess Use of Signing Statements," *Boston Globe*, December 22, 2007, A1; and Bob Egelko, "Candidates' View[s] of War Court Differ on U.S.'s Global Duty," *San Francisco Chronicle*, January 2, 2008, A1. Each news story was based on surveys sent to each of the candidates regarding their views of presidential power, or, in the case of Egelko, the candidate's view of international institutions.

2. Quoted in Marcella Bombardieri, "Clinton Vows to Check Executive Power," *Boston Globe*, October 11, 2007, A18.

3. Jess Bravin, "Judge Alito's View of the Presidency: Expansive Powers," *Wall Street Journal*, January 5, 2006, A1.

4. George W. Bush, "Statement on Signing the John Warner National Defense Authorization Act for Fiscal Year 2007," *Weekly Compilation of Presidential Documents*, October 17, 2007, 1836–37.

5. James Madison, "Method of Guarding against the Encroachments of Any One Department of Government by Appealing to the People through a Convention," *The Federalist Papers*, no. 49, http://Thomas.loc.gov/home/histdox/fed_49.html (accessed October 29, 2007).

6. Walter Dellinger, "Presidential Authority to Decline to Execute Unconstitutional Statutes," Memorandum for the Honorable Abner J. Mikva, Counsel to the President, November 2, 1994, http://www.usdoj.gov/olc/nonexcut.htm (accessed October 28, 2007).

7. Michael Herz, "Imposing Unified Executive Branch Statutory Interpretation," *Cardozo Law Review* 15, no. 1–2 (October 1993): 252–53.

8. Elena Kagan, "Presidential Administration," *Harvard Law Review* 114, no. 8 (June 2001): 2327.

9. See Steven G. Calabresi and Christopher S. Yoo, *The Unitary Executive: Presidential Power from Washington to Bush* (New Haven: Yale University Press, 2008).

10. Phillip J. Cooper, "George W. Bush, Edgar Allan Poe, and the Use and Abuse of Presidential Signing Statements," *Presidential Studies Quarterly* 35, no. 3 (August 2005): 531, DOI: 10.1111/j.1741–5705.2005.00262.x

11. Bravin, "Judge Alito's View of the Presidency," A1.

12. Steven Calabresi, "The Structural Constitution: Unitary Executive, Plural Judiciary," *Harvard Law Review* 105, no. 6 (1992).

13. Data were obtained by accessing the *Weekly Compilation of Presidential Documents* and searching for "unitary executive" by year. In some cases, the term appeared multiple times within the same document, as is the case with Bush's signing statements. Dataset is on file with the authors.

14. Cyril T. Zaneski, "Rule Breakers," *Government Executive,* January 1, 2002, http://govexec.com/features/0102/0102s4.htm (accessed April 10, 2005).

15. George W. Bush, "Executive Order 13,199—Establishment of White House Office of Faith-Based and Community Initiatives," *Federal Register* 66, no. 21 (January 29, 2001).

16. George W. Bush, "Executive Order 13,201—Notification of Employee Rights Concerning Payment of Union Dues or Fees," *Federal Register* 66, no. 36 (February 17, 2001); "Executive Order 13,202—Preservation of Open Competition and Government Neutrality towards Government Contractors' Labor Relations on Federal and Federally Funded Construction Projects," *Federal Register* 66, no. 36 (February 17, 2001); "Executive Order 13,203—Revocation of Executive Order and Presidential Memorandum Concerning Labor-Management Partnerships," *Federal Register* 66, no. 36 (February 17, 2001); "Executive Order 13,204—Revocation of Executive Order on Nondisplacement of Qualified Workers under Certain Contracts," *Federal Register* 66, no. 36 (February 17, 2001).

17. Christopher S. Kelley, "Rethinking Presidential Power—The Unitary Executive and the George W. Bush Presidency," paper prepared for the annual meeting of the Midwest Political Science Association, Chicago, April 7–10, 2005, 24.

18. Alexis Simendinger, "Results-Oriented President Uses Levers of Power," *Government Executive Magazine,* http://www.govexec.com/story_page.cfm?filepath=/dailyfed/0102/012502nj2.htm&oref=search (accessed May 26, 2009).

19. See, for example, Barton Gellman, *Angler: The Cheney Vice Presidency* (New York: Penguin, 2008).

20. Ford quoted in Marvin Stone, "Presidency: Imperial or Imperiled?" *U.S. News & World Report,* January 15, 1979, 88; Cheney quoted in Barton Gellman and Jo Becker, "Protecting the President's Power," June 26, 2007, http://blog.washing-

tonpost.com/cheney/sidebars/cheney_on_presidential_power/index.html (accessed December 15, 2007).

21. Cheney quoted in Bob Woodward, "Cheney Upholds Power of the Presidency," *Washington Post,* January 20, 2005, A07.

22. Cheney quoted in Dana Milbank, "In Cheney's Shadow, Counsel Pushes the Conservative Cause," *Washington Post,* October 11, 2004, A21.

23. Neil Kinkopf and Peter Shane, "Index of Presidential Signing Statements: 2001–2007," *American Constitution Society,* October 2007, 174, http://www.acslaw.org/node/5309 (accessed January 4, 2008).

24. William J. Clinton, "Executive Order 12,866: Regulatory and Review," *Federal Register* 58, no. 190 (October 4, 1993); George W. Bush, "Executive Order 13,422: Further Amendments to Executive Order 12,866 on Regulatory Planning and Review," January 18, 2007, http://www.whitehouse.gov/news/releases/2007/01/20070118.html (accessed January 9, 2008).

25. Harold J. Krent, "From a Unitary to Unilateral Presidency," *Boston University Law Review* 88, no. 2 (2008).

26. Charlie Savage, "Reaganites Reconsider," *The Nation,* September 24, 2007, http://www.thenation.com/docprint.mhtml?i=20070924&s=savage (accessed January 9, 2008).

27. Calabresi and Yoo, *The Unitary Executive.*

28. *Myers v. United States,* 272 U.S. 52, 135 (1926); *Humphrey's Executor v. United States,* 295 U.S. 602 (1935).

29. *Bowsher v. Synar,* 478 U.S. 714 (1986).

PART I

AN OVERVIEW OF THE UNITARY EXECUTIVE

The Unitary Executive

Ideology versus the Constitution

LOUIS FISHER

Scholars in recent decades have promoted the theory of the unitary executive. According to their constitutional model, all executive powers are centered in the president and thus subject to that executive's direct command and control.[1] The model not only concentrates power in the presidency but attempts to insulate the president from checks and constraints from other branches. As one study claimed, the development of the unitary executive from 1789 to 1945 "helped remake the institution of the presidency into the primary institution for mobilizing and implementing political will" and set the stage "for the imperial presidency that would dominate modern times."[2] John Yoo promotes a variation of this theory by describing the president as the "unitary, rational actor."[3] Although the framers looked to the president to provide responsibility, accountability, and unity, the model of the unitary executive was never adopted or intended, nor does it have any wholesale application today either in theory or practice.

The Founders and Some Exceptions to Executive Power

During congressional debate in 1789 on establishing the first three executive departments (Foreign Affairs, Treasury, and War), lawmakers agreed that each department would be headed by a secretary appointed by the president with the advice and consent of the Senate. In that manner Congress stated a preference for a single executive to head the departments over the competing model of a multimember board.[4] Presidential accountability was underscored when Congress acknowledged that department heads could be removed by the president.[5] However, recognizing the president's freedom to remove department heads did not extend to every subordinate executive official.

Steven Calabresi and Christopher Yoo sum up the first half century of the federal government with these words: "no one could doubt the President's constitutional power to control the *entire* executive branch (including the Treasury Department) and the actions of *all* of his subordinates."[6] The examples offered in this section and the next, on ministerial duties, demonstrate that the generalization Calabresi and Yoo offer is far too broad and fails to address important exceptions to the unitary model that are well known.

AUTONOMY FOR THE COMPTROLLER

When James Madison discussed the tenure of the comptroller of the Treasury, he said it was necessary "to consider the nature of this office." Its properties were not "purely of an Executive nature," he explained. "It seems to me that they partake of a Judiciary quality as well as Executive; perhaps the latter obtains in the greatest degree." Because of the mixed nature of the office, "there may be strong reasons why an officer of this kind should not hold his office at the pleasure of the Executive branch of the Government."[7]

Given the fact that the comptroller was just being created for the new Treasury Department, how did Madison know enough about the office to understand its duties and nature? The answer lies in the decision of the Continental Congress in 1781 to create the superintendent of finance, auditors, and the comptroller. The latter official functioned as a quasi-judicial officer who was responsible for the settlement of public accounts and on all appeals "shall openly and publicly hear the parties, and his decision shall be conclusive."[8]

Madison wanted to preserve the comptroller's independence, even from the president. His concerns were written into law in 1795 when Congress made the comptroller's decision on certain claims "final and conclusive."[9] Actions by the comptroller were eventually challenged in court as a violation of due process of law. The *Murray's Lessee* case (1856) involved Samuel Swartwout, a collector of customs for the port of New York from 1830 to 1838. During that period he kept large amounts of revenue for personal speculation. After the government discovered shortages in his account, a "warrant of distress" was issued to recover the funds. Acting under an 1820 statute, the office of the first comptroller certified the condition of the account to the agent of the Treasury, who then issued the warrant against the delinquent officer. The statute authorized the marshal to execute the warrant by entering into the district of the officer to collect the necessary amount. The marshal could post notices in the town announcing the sale of the officer's goods and property.[10]

Swartwout argued that the statute was unconstitutional because it allowed executive officers to discharge judicial duties. The Supreme Court admitted that the actions against delinquent officers bore some resemblance to judicial power. However, largely on the strength of early British law and congressional legislation in 1798, 1813, and 1815, the Court concluded unanimously that the statute of 1820 satisfied due process.[11] This type of adjudicatory duty within the executive branch would remain detached from presidential scrutiny and control, unless it could be shown that the executive official was not faithfully executing the law. Only under those conditions could the president intervene.

POST OFFICE DEPARTMENT

Also during these early years, the Post Office Department was never considered to be as closely connected to the president as the departments of Foreign Affairs, Treasury, and War were. The statute creating the Post Office Department in 1789 did not designate it as an "executive department," even though other legislation passed that year made the postmaster general "subject to the direction of the President of the United States in performing the duties of his office, and in forming contracts for the transportation of the mail."[12] During debates in 1790, members of Congress were divided on the question of whether to delegate the power to designate post roads to the president or the postmaster general or to reserve it for Congress. Those who argued against the first option warned that revenue would be centered in the hands of the executive, combining purse and sword and thus leading to the destruction of liberties in America. They also maintained that such delegation was unconstitutional because the Constitution expressly reserved the power to establish post roads to Congress.[13]

By 1792, Congress had decided to retain for itself the power to designate post roads. The statute authorized the postmaster general (not the president) to enter into contracts and make appointments. It also deleted language making the postmaster general subject to the direction of the president. Financial autonomy was ensured by allowing the Post Office to operate from postal revenues, with the balance to be returned to the Treasury.[14]

President George Washington not only understood but accepted the independence of the Post Office during this period. Although the Constitution expressly states that the president "shall nominate," subject to the advice and consent of the Senate, he acquiesced to the decision of Congress to keep the Post Office at a distance from the president. Washington wrote on January 6, 1790, "I have uniformly avoided interfering with any appointments which do not require my official agency, and the Resolutions and Ordinances establishing the Post Office under the former Congress, and which have been recognized by the present Government, giving power to the Postmaster General to appoint his own Deputies, and making him accountable for their conduct, is an insuperable objection to my taking any part in this matter."[15]

THE WHISKEY REBELLION

In collecting evidence to support the unitary executive model, Calabresi and Yoo discuss President Washington's actions during the Whiskey Rebellion of 1794. So great was his reach, they say, that he "sought help subject to presidential guidance and direction from *state* as well as *federal* officials in their enforcement of federal law during the Whiskey Rebellion . . . . Washington invoked his duties under the Take Care Clause in asking state courts and executives to use their weight and influence to bring the rebels to justice." His proclamation charged and required "all Courts, Magistrates and Offices" to exert their powers to restore peace, and he "assumed command of the state militias even though those troops nominally fell under the jurisdiction of the states."[16] To Calabresi and Yoo, this was an impressive display of executive power. As described by Calabresi and Yoo, Washington appeared to have exerted full control not only over federal agencies but state officials as well, including state judges. However, a careful reader will note that Washington was asking state officials to help "in their enforcement of federal law" and that he acted under the "take care" clause. What federal law was he was enforcing? Calabresi and Yoo do not say. When one reads the statute, it appears that, far from exercising any independent presidential power, Washington was doing what presidents are supposed to do: carry out the policy that Congress had enacted into law.

Legislation in 1792 had provided that whenever the United States "shall be invaded, or be in imminent danger of invasion from any foreign nation or Indian tribe," the president may call forth the state militias "to repel such invasions and to suppress insurrections."[17] The statute introduced a novel way of monitoring and checking presidential action. Whenever the laws of the United States were violated and their execution obstructed in any state, "by combinations too powerful to be suppressed by the ordinary course of judicial proceedings, or by the powers vested in the marshals by this act," the president would have to be first notified of that fact by an associate justice of the Supreme Court or by a federal district judge. Only after such notice could the president call forth the militia of the state to suppress the insurrection.[18]

Carefully adhering to the statute, Washington provided Justice James Wilson with evidence to verify the rebellion in western Pennsylvania and received back from Wilson a certification that ordinary legal means were insufficient to execute national law. Washington called forth the militias of four states to put down the rebellion. District Judge Richard Peters joined Alexander Hamilton and District Attorney William Rawle in accompanying the troops.[19] This process offers no support for the model of a unitary executive, which would allow presidents, unchecked, to place federal and state officers under their command and control.

Ministerial Duties

The heads of executive departments function only in part as political agents of the president. They also perform legal duties assigned to them by Congress. Even the departments initially labeled as executive in character, such as Foreign Affairs and War, served Congress as well as the president. Statutory duties assigned to them were to be carried out faithfully, notwithstanding contrary policies selected by the president.

This dual role was recognized by Chief Justice John Marshall in *Marbury v. Madison* (1803). He spoke about two types of duties for the secretary of state: ministerial and discretionary. The first duty, as a public ministerial officer of the United States, extended to the nation and its citizens. Congress, operating through statutes, could direct the secretary to carry out certain activities. The second duty, as an executive official and advisor, was to the president alone. When a secretary of state performs "as an officer of the United States," he or she is "bound to obey the laws." In this capacity the secretary acts "under the authority of law, and not by the instructions of the president. It is a ministerial act which the law enjoins on a particular officer for a particular purpose."[20]

This distinction between these two executive duties is reflected in a number of court cases and opinions issued by attorneys general. In one case, Postmaster General Amos Kendall, in the Jackson administration, refused to pay the claim of an individual who had contracted to carry the mail and sought compensation for his services. Congress directed that the amount be paid, as did the circuit court for the District of Columbia. The Supreme Court agreed that the postmaster general could not refuse a payment authorized by law. Payment of the claim constituted a "purely ministerial" act for which there could be no discretion. Neither the president nor the postmaster general possessed any authority to deny or control a ministerial act. Although the executive power is vested in the president, "it by no means follows, that every officer in every branch of that department is under the exclusive direction of the President." It would be an "alarming doctrine," said the Court, that Congress could not impose on any executive officer any duty it thinks proper, "which is not repugnant to any rights secured and protected by the constitution; and in such cases, the duty and responsibility grow out of and are subject to the control of the law, and not to the direction of the President."[21]

Attorneys general viewed ministerial acts the same way. In 1854, Attorney General Caleb Cushing stated that when laws "define what is to be done by a given head of department, and how he is to do it, there the President's discretion stops; but if the law require an executive act to be performed, without saying how or by whom, it must be for him to supply the direction."[22] Many attorneys general have advised presidents about the substantial political and legal constraints that limit their ability to intervene in departmental matters. Even when the president has the power to control the decision of a department head, intervention may be imprudent and of doubtful legality. Although it is theoretically correct that department heads shall discharge their administrative duties in such manner as the president may direct, it was conceded by Attorney General Edward Bates that it is "quite impossible for the President to assume the actual direction of the multifarious business of the departments."[23]

Beyond these questions of judgment and practicality, on many occasions an attorney general will tell the president that the White House has no *legal* right to interfere with administrative decisions. President James Monroe asked whether he could alter the decision made by the auditors and comptrollers in the Treasury Department. The advice from Attorney General William Wirt was blunt: "It appears to me that you have no power to interfere. . . . If the laws, then, require a particular officer by name to perform a duty, not only is that officer bound to perform it, but no other officer can perform it without a violation of the law; and were the President to perform it, he would not only be not taking care that the laws were faithfully executed, but he would be violating them himself."[24]

The same principle appears in many other opinions issued by attorneys general.[25] Congress may distribute ministerial functions of government among various bureau chiefs and executive officials, without regard to hierarchical principles of public administration. Neither the president nor any department head "could, by any degree of laborious industry, revise and correct all the acts of his subordinates. And if he could, as the law now stands, it would be as illegal as unwise."[26] If a president agreed to take appeals in one case and review a subordinate's decision, "it is apparent that it would lie in every case and from all the Executive Departments, and soon you would be overwhelmed with the details of administration."[27] Another attorney general observed that the president is responsible for seeing that administrative officers faithfully perform their duties, "but the statutes regulate and prescribe these duties, and he has no more power to add to, or subtract from, the duties imposed upon subordinate executive and administrative officers by the law, than those officers have to add or subtract from his duties."[28]

During the impoundment disputes in the Nixon administration, federal courts regularly relied on the concept of ministerial duties to rule against the administration and force the release of funds. In case after case the judiciary found that the allocation or obligation of funds constituted a ministerial action, permitting no discretion or judgment on the part of an administrator. Some decisions pointed out that discretion could be exercised up to a certain point but no further. For example, in 1972 Secretary of Agriculture Earl Butz declared that fifteen counties in Minnesota were eligible for emergency loans. A federal judge ruled that although the act of declaration was discretionary, once the secretary designated the counties eligible for assistance it was incumbent upon the department to accept loan applications and process them.[29] Ministerial duties also apply to the president. In 1974 an appellate court held that President Nixon had violated the law by refusing to carry out a statute on federal pay. When he refused to submit a statutorily required alternative pay plan, he violated the law.[30]

Quasi-Judicial Duties

Department officers who discharge quasi-judicial functions have had independent status from the start, whether they are comptrollers and auditors in the Treasury Department or reviewers of pensions and other claims. For example, in 1890 Congress established within the Department of Treasury the Board of General Appraisers to review the acts of appraisers of merchandise and collectors of duties. The board's decision on cases submitted to it was final and conclusive within the department, although appeals could be taken to the federal courts.[31] It would have been impermissible for the president or one of his assistants to intervene in the board's deliberations, given the judicial nature of its work.

In 1926, Congress created the U.S. Customs Court to supersede the board. Although not changing the powers, duties, or personnel of the board, the statute established it as an Article I legislative court. Congress made the Customs Court a constitutional judicial body in 1956, and in 1980 legislation replaced the Customs Court with the Court of International Trade.[32] A similar evolution appears with the handling of federal claims: these were assigned initially in 1855 to the Court of Claims, which gave advisory opinions to guide Congress in legislating private bills and later was authorized to make binding judgments. The White House had no authority or grounds to interfere with this administrative process. Legislation in 1953 made the Court of Claims an Article III constitutional court, in 1932 Congress returned it to the status of an Article I legislative court, and in 1992 Congress changed its name to the U.S. Court of Federal Claims.[33]

The tax court also illustrates how Congress can place certain adjudicative functions within the executive branch and insulate them from presidential or White House influence. Legislation in 1924 created the Board of Tax Appeals. Although the secretary of the treasury was directed to furnish the board with appropriate quarters, staff, and supplies, the board was described in the statute as "an independent agency in the executive branch of the Government."[34] Congress changed the name in 1942 to the Tax Court of the United States and in 1969 converted it to an Article I legislative court.[35] At all times Congress expected the court to operate independently of presidential influence.

In *Myers v. United States* (1926), Chief Justice William Howard Taft upheld the president's removal power in a sweeping opinion that generally delights adherents of the unitary executive. Taft struck down a statute that had limited the president's power to remove a postmaster. According to some scholars, "It is interesting to note that the conclusion that the Constitution of 1787 established a unitary executive has found general acceptance among courts," and they cite *Myers* for that proposition.[36] Yet Taft's opinion focused only on officials who carried out purely executive duties. He said that other administrative duties, such as those of an adjudicatory nature, deserved to be treated differently. Taft's cautionary words pull the rug out from the unitary executive school. He plainly recognized that certain ministerial and adjudicatory duties are outside the president's control and that only after the executive official designated by law to decide the matter has exercised judgment can the president review the decision to ensure that the law had been faithfully executed. The passage below highlights both ministerial and adjudicatory duties:

> The ordinary duties of officers prescribed by statute come under the general administrative control of the President by virtue of the general grant to him of the executive power, and he may properly supervise and guide their construction of the statutes under which they act in order to secure that unitary and uniform execution of the laws which Article II of the Constitution evidently contemplated in vesting general executive power in the President alone. . . . Of course there may be duties so peculiarly and specifically committed to the discretion of a particular officer as to raise a question whether the President may overrule or revise the officer's interpretation of his statutory duty in a particular instance. Then there may be duties of a quasi-judicial character imposed on executive officers and members of executive tribunals whose decisions after hearing affect interests of individuals, the discharge of which the President cannot in a particular case properly influence or control. But even in such a case he may consider the decision after its rendition as a reason for removing the officer, on the ground that the discretion regularly entrusted to that officer by statute has not been on the whole intelligently or wisely exercised. Otherwise he does not discharge his own constitutional duty of seeing that the laws be faithfully executed.[37]

At certain stages in an agency proceeding, intervention by Congress or the president may violate basic principles of administrative law. Particularly sensitive are adjudicatory proceedings of an agency. Executive branch employees who handle adjudicatory matters have a special right to independence in making their decisions. Department heads recognize the limitations that prevent them from interfering with decisions by administrative law judges (ALJs).[38] Similarly, congressional interference with an agency adjudicatory proceeding may be of damaging character and constitute an improper intrusion. Questions by a Senate subcommittee in 1955 were so probing that Edward F. Howrey, chairman of the Federal

Trade Commission, announced that he would have to disqualify himself from a pending case.[39]

Independent Commissions

The unitary executive model challenges the right of Congress to create "independent commissions" that operate with some autonomy from presidential control. The Reagan administration made repeated efforts in court to have these commissions declared unconstitutional but was singularly unsuccessful in advancing this legal theory.

The independent regulatory commission differs from the conventional administrative agency in two ways. First, it is designed by statute to operate in a more detached manner than an executive agency. Second, the responsibility for carrying out the law falls on a group of administrators (a multimember staff) rather than on a single executive. It is quite true that presidents (particularly those who serve two terms) can gain control over an independent commission because of their appointments, but the commission nonetheless maintains an independence that is not available to an executive department.

Congress used three techniques to secure the independence of regulatory commissions. The terms of commissioners are staggered to insulate them from presidential transitions, the president's power to remove commissioners is limited by specific statutory grounds, and restrictions are placed on the number of commissioners who may belong to the same political party. Both Congress and the president have at their disposal a number of political tools to control the commissions, but unless and until those powers are exercised, the commissions exercise substantial independence.

The Interstate Commerce Commission (ICC), created by Congress in 1887, is the forerunner and prototype of the independent regulatory commission. Congress modeled the ICC after railroad commissions that had been operating in more than twenty states. Reformers believed that commissions, unlike legislators, could readily accumulate the highly technical and expert knowledge needed to effectively supervise the railroad corporations. With the railroad industry changing rapidly, the commission form seemed a more flexible instrument for regulation than the enactment of statutes that would have to be amended periodically to keep pace with technological changes.

Initially the state railroad commissions functioned as fact-finding and advisory bodies, operating as agents of the legislatures. In that sense they resembled claims courts that were located in the executive branch but were meant to serve Congress, not the president. Gradually the railroad commissions assumed the character of permanent bodies, discharging duties that might have been entrusted to the executive department.[40]

The ICC was followed by other independent regulatory commissions: the Federal Reserve System in 1913, the Federal Trade Commission (FTC) in 1914, the Federal Power Commission in 1920, and five agencies that appeared in the 1930s: the Securities and Exchange Commission (SEC), the Federal Communications Commission, the Civil Aeronautics Board, the National Labor Relations Board, and the Federal Maritime Commission. Some of these agencies were destined to disappear; other administrative bodies took their place or were assigned new statutory duties.

The rise of independent commissions forced the Supreme Court in 1935 to rethink and qualify what Chief Justice Taft had said in *Myers*. The specific issue before the Court that year was whether Congress could limit the president's power to remove a member of the Federal Trade Commission to three criteria set forth in the statute: inefficiency, neglect of duty, or malfeasance in office. The Court concluded that the FTC was an independent, nonpartisan body of experts charged not with political or executive duties but operated predominantly as a quasi-judicial and quasi-legislative agency.[41] When Congress provides for the appointment of officers whose functions are largely of legislative and judicial quality, it may specify the grounds for removal, and the president has no constitutional grounds to remove the officers for other reasons. The Court emphasized that the postmaster at issue in *Myers* was restricted to executive—not legislative or judicial—functions.

In his argument to the Court, Solicitor General Stanley Reed insisted that if the Court was of the opinion that the FTC statute deprived the president of the power to remove a commissioner except for one or more of the causes stated, the provision was unconstitutional. Rejecting the idea that the FTC was a judicial tribunal, Reed said it was not necessary to consider whether the president's power to remove a judge from a non-Article III court may be restricted by Congress.[42] He was referring to the various courts established by Congress to consider such matters as claims, duty appraisal, and taxes.

A unanimous Court rejected Reed's position that Congress had no constitutional power to limit the president's power to remove FTC commissioners. The legislative history convinced the Court that the FTC was to enjoy an independence unlike that of the agency it replaced: the Bureau of Corporations, located within the Department of Commerce. The commission was not to be "subject to anybody in the government but . . . only to the people of the United States." Congress intended it to be free from "political domination or control" and "separate and apart from any existing department of the government—not subject to the orders of the President." To hold that commissioners could continue in office "at the mere will of the President, might be to thwart, in large measure, the very ends which Congress sought to realize by definitely fixing the term of office."[43]

The Court confined *Myers* to this "narrow point": the president had constitutional power "to remove a postmaster of the first class, without the advice and consent of the Senate as required by act of Congress." A postmaster was "an executive officer restricted to the performance of executive duties" and was not charged with any duties "related to either the legislative or judicial power." The theory in *Myers* is that a postmaster "is merely one of the units in the executive department and, hence, inherently subject to the exclusive and illimitable power of removal by the Chief Executive, whose subordinate and aid[e] he is." By contrast, the FTC "cannot in any proper sense be characterized as an arm or an eye of the executive. Its duties are performed without executive leave and, in the contemplation of the statute, must be free from executive control." The commission functions "in part quasi-legislatively and in part quasi-judicially."[44] The 1935 decision has been reinforced by other rulings.[45]

During the Reagan administration, the Justice Department decided it was time to press the unitary executive model and reverse such decisions as *Humphrey's Executor.*[46] In its brief in the case challenging the constitutionality of the Gramm-Rudman deficit reduction statute, the department argued that independent commissions are inconsistent with the framers' deliberate choice of "a unitary Executive in order to promote a sense of personal responsibility and accountability to the people in the execution of the laws—and thereby to ensure vigorous administration of the laws and protection of the liberty, property, and welfare of the people."[47] There is a measure of accuracy to this language, but not to the extent of ensuring that the president has personal control over every activity in the executive branch. The framers never adopted hierarchy and centralization as the prime and overriding values.

When the Gramm-Rudman case was argued before the Supreme Court, attorneys defending the statute warned the justices that the Reagan administration wanted to invalidate all of the independent regulatory agencies.

Solicitor General Charles Fried dismissed these contentions as mere "scare tactics." The courtroom filled with laughter when Justice Sandra Day O'Connor replied, "Well, Mr. Fried, I'll confess you scared me with it."[48]

Chief Justice Warren Burger assigned himself the task of writing the majority opinion that struck down Gramm-Rudman. His colleagues advised him not to cast any doubt about the constitutionality of independent commissions, and yet his first draft did precisely that, prompting the justices to insist that he rewrite the final opinion to steer clear of posing any challenge to *Humphrey's Executor.*[49] When the Court released its decision, it specifically stated in a footnote that it did not intend to unravel the tangled skein of independent commissions. It denied that its decision on Gramm-Rudman "requires casting doubt on the status of 'independent' agencies because no issues involving such agencies are presented here." A concurrence by Justice John Paul Stevens, joined by Justice Thurgood Marshall, nailed down the point. They said it was "well settled" that Congress may delegate legislative power to independent agencies. In his dissent, Justice Byron White criticized the majority's "distressingly formalistic" view of separation of powers and concluded that Congress could vest a broad range of executive functions in officers who "are free from the partisanship that may be expected of agents wholly dependent upon the President." In another dissent, Justice Harry Blackmun interpreted *Humphrey's Executor* to allow executive power to be carried out by officers who do not serve "at the President's pleasure."[50]

Theodore Olson, former head of the Office of Legal Counsel in the Reagan administration, filed a suit that challenged the constitutionality of the FTC. The suit argued that the commission's enforcement functions must be carried out by officers who are subject to the supervisory control of the president and who serve at the pleasure of the president.[51] The merits of the case were not addressed because of procedural questions about jurisdiction and ripeness.[52] In a subsequent case, however, a federal appellate court upheld the SEC against the challenge that its exercise of civil enforcement actions violated separation of powers. The plaintiffs argued that the president is given sole and exclusive control over the execution of the laws. That thesis was firmly tossed aside by the appellate court: "It is a matter of fundamental law that the Constitution assigns to Congress the power to designate duties of particular officers. The President is not obligated under the Constitution to exercise absolute control over our government executives. The President is not required to execute the laws; he is required to take care they be executed faithfully."[53]

Advocates of the unitary executive model insist that the Constitution makes the president personally responsible for the coherence and uniformity of executive branch actions and that any interference with that role impermissibly undermines the accountability that the framers placed in the president. Any departure from that model, they warn, opens the door to "special interests" and their control over independent commissions. Yet organized groups from the private sector are not fastidious about who they try to influence. They solicit assistance from any branch of government, including the executive branch, that is in a position to help. The idea that the president can be personally cognizant and involved in every agency decision, even with the assistance of aides, has never been persuasive, particularly with the size of the federal government today. An observation by Judge Henry J. Friendly in 1962 is still on target: "It is indulging in fantasy to speak of 'the President' as formulating policy pronouncements for the agencies himself. The spectacle of a chief executive, burdened to the limit of endurance with decisions on which the very existence of mankind may depend, personally taking on the added task of determining to what extent newspapers should be allowed to own television stations or whether railroads should be allowed to reduce rates only to or somewhat below the truck level, is pure mirage."[54] In 1979 Judge Friendly nevertheless supported a recommendation by the American Bar Association for closer presidential control over regulatory activities, including those in the independent agencies. How this proposal would work in practice has never been pinned down. But even if an independent commission were transferred to one of the existing executive departments, there would remain the need to ensure that its adjudicatory functions be off limits to presidential or White House influence.

The Independent Counsel Case

When the Supreme Court upheld the constitutionality of the independent counsel statute in *Morrison v. Olson* (1988), it further limited Chief Justice Taft's decision in *Myers.* Taft had acknowledged that his protection of the president's removal power was restricted to administrative officers carrying out discretionary executive matters, not ministerial or quasi-judicial duties. That point was strengthened in such cases as *Humphrey's Executor. Morrison* took it a step further by upholding limits on the president's power to supervise the executive duty to prosecute.

One of the questions for the Court was whether Congress could restrict the attorney general's power to remove the independent counsel only to those instances in which "good cause" could be shown. Did that interfere "with the President's exercise of his constitutionally appointed functions" and impermissibly reduce the president's "ability to control the prosecutorial powers wielded by the independent counsel"?[55] Writing for the Court, Chief Justice William Rehnquist distinguished the independent counsel statute from *Myers,* which concerned an effort by Congress to require the Senate's advice and consent for the removal of certain postmasters. The independent counsel statute, however, did not involve "an attempt by Congress itself to gain a role in the removal of executive officials other than its established power of impeachment and conviction." Congress left the removal power with the attorney general, subject to good cause. In that sense, the removal provisions of the independent counsel statute were more analogous to *Humphrey's Executor* than to *Myers.*[56]

Those who brought the case against the independent counsel statute insisted that *Humphrey's Executor* "did not involve officials who performed a 'core executive function,'" such as prosecution by law enforcement officials. For them, the proper reference point was *Myers,* not *Humphrey's Executor.* The Court conceded that *Humphrey's Executor* had carved out an exception for "quasi-legislative" and "quasi-judicial" duties but now stated that "the determination of whether the Constitution allows Congress to impose a 'good cause'-type restriction on the President's power to remove an official cannot be made to turn on whether or not that official is classified as 'purely executive.'"[57]

The appropriate guide was not to select "rigid categories" (executive, legislative, judicial) to determine the president's removal power "but to ensure that Congress does not interfere with the President's exercise of the 'executive power' and his constitutionally appointed duty to 'take care that the laws be faithfully executed' under Article II." The Court concluded that the procedures in the independent counsel statute, including good-cause removal, did not "impede the President's ability to perform his constitutional duty." It did not see "how the President's need to control the exercise of that discretion is so central to the functioning of the Executive Branch as to require as a matter of constitutional law that the counsel be terminable at will by the President."[58]

Those who write about the unitary executive make a point of emphasizing that presidents from 1789 to the present time have vigorously and consistently resisted all congressional efforts to curtail their "control over law execution." From the First Congress to now, "*Presidents have consistently asserted their authority to execute the law.*"[59] Obviously that is not so. No legislative intrusion into presidential executive duties offends unitary executive advocates more than the independent statute. How did it become law? It did not happen over the veto of a president; it was President Jimmy Carter who signed it and praised its objectives. When it expired and had to be reauthorized, it was President Reagan himself who signed it into law. When it expired and had to be revived, Reagan signed it again. When the law again expired and the Republicans decided that, with Bill Clinton in office, it would be a dandy thing to have on the books, Clinton signed it. If presidents were really stand-up leaders determined to protect their unitary powers, they should have exercised their veto. It never happened.

Legislative Vetoes

In *INS v. Chadha* (1983) the Supreme Court struck down the "legislative veto," a mechanism that Congress had exercised for more than a half century to monitor and control executive agency decisions. Under this procedure, Congress delegated legislative power broadly but reserved to itself the authority to reject certain actions without having to pass another law. The typical means of disapproval relied either on a concurrent resolution (passed by both houses) or a simple resolution (passed by either house). Neither of those measures goes to the president for signature or veto. It was primarily on that ground—the "presentment" clause—that the Court found the legislative veto invalid. It also decided that one-house legislative vetoes violated the constitutional requirement of bicameralism. Writing for the Court, Chief Justice Burger said that whenever congressional action has the "purpose and effect of altering the legal rights, duties and relations of persons" outside the legislative branch, Congress must act through both houses in a bill presented to the president.[60]

Anyone familiar with the growth of the legislative veto and the reason for its existence would have understood that the Court's decision was far too doctrinaire, theoretical, and impractical. Executive agencies and Congress over the years had crafted an accommodation that offered benefits to each side. Agencies gained greater discretionary authority to handle emerging and unanticipated problems; Congress could monitor and control these mid-course corrections without having to pass another law. Regardless of what the Court decided, the legislative veto would continue, in one form or another. I made that prediction in 1982, when challenges to the legislative veto were in the lower courts. I wrote, "But with or without the legislative veto, Congress will remain knee-deep in administrative decisions, and it is inconceivable that any court or any president can prevent this. Call it supervision, intervention, interference or plain meddling, Congress will find a way." I pointed out that Congress and the agencies had worked out an agreement on "reprogramming": the shifting of funds from one program to another within the same appropriations account. This flexibility was highly valued by agencies, but they had to agree that major reprogrammings "must be approved by the committees (or subcommittees) with jurisdiction over the program."[61]

Those who believe that the Supreme Court has the last word on the meaning of the Constitution assumed that this particular constitutional dispute had been disposed of. Those, like myself, who believe that the Court is merely one of many participants in the making and shaping of constitutional law expected the legislative veto to continue in one form or another, and continue it has. I estimate that the number of new legislative vetoes enacted after *Chadha* is well above five hundred. *Chadha* did away with legislative vetoes in the form of one-house and two-house vetoes, but committee and subcommittee vetoes remain vital mechanisms for accommodating the needs of agencies and Congress.[62]

What is interesting about the continuation of committee-review procedures after *Chadha* is that they appear not merely in statutory provisions (objected to regularly by presidents in their signing statements) but in agency budget manuals as well. That is, despite constitutional objections raised by presidents and the Justice Department, executive departments and agencies have found it both practicable and necessary to expressly recognize in their written guidelines that certain types of administrative actions must be presented to designated committees (and subcommittees) for their review and approval.

Here are some examples. The Department of Defense (DOD) regularly produces the most detailed instructions on reprogramming, spelling out the procedures and thresholds to both notify committees and obtain their approval. DOD directives explain that under certain circumstances, approval is needed from the Appropriations, Armed Services, and Intelligence committees.[63] Other agency documents are less elaborate. The budget execution manual for the Department of Energy explains that congressional controls over reprogramming depend on the "approved program baseline and are generally delineated in the department's base table and related documentation." Congress requires the department to "ensure that the appropriate committees are promptly and fully notified whenever a necessary change to the approved program baseline is required." Notifications of such changes are provided to Congress through submission of formal reprogramming proposals, "and the Department shall comply with subsequent directions in the responses from the Congressional committees."[64] Stated here is the requirement to not merely notify the committees but to comply with their directions. Failure to honor this understanding "will not only violate the trust and latitude granted the Department, but could translate into stringent statutory constraints and limitations imposed on the Department by Congress."[65]

Reprogramming instructions drafted by the Department of Transportation (DOT) are explicit about committee prior approval: "Reprogrammings submitted to Congress must not be implemented until DOT is officially notified to proceed with the proposed actions by both the House and Senate Appropriations Subcommittees."[66] Similar language appears in the budget manual for the Treasury Department. Adjustments to the financial plan are considered normal and expected, but Congress "has established limitations on amounts and major program changes that can be reprogrammed without formal approval by the Appropriations Subcommittees."[67] Dollar thresholds are spelled out to indicate the type of reprogrammings that require subcommittee approval. A sample letter from the Treasury Department to an appropriations subcommittee begins, "This letter requests approval for a reprogramming in. . . ."[68]

Committee or subcommittee approval may be implied in some cases. The budget manual for the U.S. Geological Survey provides that reprogramming proposals submitted to the Appropriations committees "for prior approval shall be considered approved after 30 days if the Committee has posed on objection."[69] My understanding, after talking to agency staffers and committee members for decades, is that if the agency does not hear within the prescribed period of time, it does not move forward. Instead, it calls the committee or subcommittee and asks whether there are any objections. The proposed reprogramming is not implemented until explicit committee approval is granted.

Committee controls over agency actions have a long history. They have proved to be a helpful device in permitting the delegation of discretionary authority to the agencies while at the same time retaining close legislative review and control. *Chadha* has not eliminated the types of committee-agency agreements that guide the reprogramming process and other executive actions. These committee vetoes have not been litigated and subjected to judicial review and possible invalidation, nor is there any indication that someone is likely to gain standing to bring these committee vetoes into court.

Advocates of the unitary executive focus on what presidents say in their signing statements. It is no doubt true that presidents are quite consistent in the years after *Chadha* in indicating in their signing statements that a committee veto included in a bill is contrary to *Chadha* and will not be considered legally binding. It is equally true, and far more important, that agencies nonetheless continue to seek approval from their review committees. Instead of looking solely at what presidents *say*, it would be useful for scholars of the unitary executive to look at what agencies *do*. It would help eliminate descriptions about some sort of idealized and centralized world that does not exist.

Conclusions

Elements of the unitary executive model appear as dicta in the Gramm-Rudman case. The Supreme Court agreed, with language in *Humphrey's Executor* that enshrined a pure and doctrinaire form of separation of powers that essentially eliminated the more important value of checks and balances: "The fundamental necessity of maintaining each of the three general departments of government entirely free from the control or coercive influence, direct or indirect, of either of the others, has often been stressed and is hardly open to serious question."[70] In fact, it is hardly open to serious question that such a formulation has nothing to do with express provisions in the Constitution, the framers' intent, or the operation of government over the last two centuries. Congress was obviously not "entirely free" from the control or coercive influence of the Court when it declared the legislative veto or the Gramm-Rudman statute unconstitutional. The president is subject to the control and coercive influence of Congress when it passes laws and conducts investigations, and Congress is subject to the control and coercive influence of presidents when they exercise the veto and attempt to withhold documents.

The Gramm-Rudman decision also indulged in a fairy-tale description of the Constitution by announcing that once Congress "makes its choice in enacting legislation, its participation ends. Congress can thereafter control the execution of its enactment only indirectly—by passing new legislation."[71] No one who pays even cursory attention to the news media can accept that description of the federal government. The Court itself has acknowledged that Congress has the constitutional power to investigate executive agencies, issue subpoenas to obtain agency documents and testimony, and hold executive officials in contempt. Continued participation by Congress does not require the passage of laws. In 1988, the Court moved closer to reality by stating that "we have never held that the Constitution requires that the three Branches of Government 'operate with absolute independence.'"[72] A year later it again embraced a pragmatic, functional understanding of separation of powers, noting that the framers "did not require—and indeed rejected—the notion that the three Branches must be entirely separate and distinct."[73]

Presidential unity and accountability were important values to the framers, but they looked even more intently to a vigorous system of checks and balances to minimize the inevitable abuses of power that would occur. Early in the development of the national government important precedents were developed to keep certain agency decisions at arm's length from the president, and those exceptions have continued to grow with independent commissions, agency adjudication, Article I courts, and the kinds of agency-committee accommodations regularly practiced with the reprogramming of funds. Those well-established activities and agreements present durable and constitutional limits to the unitary executive model.

Notes

This chapter draws from a paper presented at the annual meeting of the American Political Science Association, Philadelphia, August 30–September 3, 2006. Dr. Fisher's analysis is his own and does not necessarily reflect the views of the Library of Congress.

1. Christopher S. Yoo, Steven G. Calabresi, and Anthony J. Colangelo, "The Unitary Executive in the Modern Era, 1945–2004," *Iowa Law Review* 90 (2004): 601; Christopher S. Yoo, Steven G. Calabresi, and Laurence D. Nee, "The Unitary Executive during the Third Half-Century, 1889–1945," *Notre Dame Law Review* 80 (2004): 1; Steven G. Calabresi and Christopher Yoo, "The Unitary Executive during the Second Half-Century," *Harvard Journal of Law and Public Policy* 26 (2003): 668; Steven G. Calabresi and Christopher S. Yoo, "The Unitary Executive during the First Half-Century," *Case Western Reserve Law Review* 47 (1997): 1451; Steven G. Calabresi and Saikrishna B. Prakash, "The President's Power to Execute the Laws," *Yale Law Journal* 104 (1994): 541; Steven G. Calabresi and Kevin H. Rhodes, "The

Structural Constitution: Unitary Executive, Plural Judiciary," *Harvard Law Review* 105 (1992): 1153.

2. Yoo, Calabresi, and Nee, "Unitary Executive during the Third Half-Century," 109.

3. John Yoo, *The Powers of War and Peace: The Constitution and Foreign Affairs after 9/11* (Chicago: University of Chicago Press, 2005), 20. Yoo's full statement is that "the demands of the international system promote vesting the management of foreign affairs in a unitary, rational actor. . . . [A] unitary rational actor remains an ideal to guide foreign policy."

4. The value of a single executive gained appreciation during the Continental Congress. Louis Fisher, *President and Congress* (New York: Free Press, 1972), 6–16, 253–70.

5. Louis Fisher, *Constitutional Conflicts between Congress and the President* (Lawrence: University Press of Kansas, 1997), 50–53.

6. Calabresi and Yoo, "Unitary Executive during the First Half-Century," 1559 (original emphasis).

7. *Annals of Cong.* 1 (June 27, 1789): 611–12.

8. For history of the comptroller during the Continental Congress, see Louis Fisher, "The Administrative World of *Chadha* and *Bowsher,*" *Public Administration Review* 47 (1987): 213, 214–15.

9. *Stats at Large of USA* 1 (1795): 442, sec. 4.

10. *Stats at Large of USA* 3 (1820): 592.

11. *Murray's Lessee v. Hoboken Land and Improvement Co.,* 18 Howard 272 (1856).

12. *Stats at Large of USA* 1 (1789): 70.

13. Henry Barrett Learned, *The President's Cabinet* (New Haven: Yale University Press, 1912), 232–35; Leonard D. White, *The Federalists* (New York: Free Press, 1948), 226–27.

14. *Stats at Large of USA* 1 (1792): 232–34; White, *The Federalists,* 176–77.

15. *The Writings of George Washington,* ed. John C. Fitzpatrick (Washington, D.C.: Government Printing Office, 1939), 30:490.

16. Calabresi and Yoo, "The Unitary Executive during the First Half-Century," 1484 (original emphasis).

17. *Stats at Large of USA* 1 (1792): 264, sec. 1.

18. Ibid., sec. 2.

19. Louis Fisher, *Presidential War Power,* 2nd ed. (Lawrence: University Press of Kansas, 2004), 22–23.

20. 5 U.S. 137, 157 (1803).

21. *Kendall v. United States,* 37 U.S. 522, 610 (1838). For other ministerial duties

directed by the courts, see *United States v. Schurz,* 102 U.S. 378 (1880); *Butterworth v. Hoe,* 112 U.S. 50 (1884); *United States v. Price,* 116 U.S. 43 (1885); *United States v. Louisville,* 169 U.S. 249 (1898); and *Clackamus County, Ore., v. McKay,* 219 F.2d 479, 496 (D.C. Cir. 1954), vacated as moot, 349 U.S. 909 (1955).

22. *Opinions of the Attorney General* 6 (1854): 326, 341. See also *Decatur v. Paulding,* 39 U.S. 497, 516 (1840); *Reeside v. Walker,* 52 U.S. 272, 290 (1850); and *United States v. Guthrie,* 58 U.S. 284 (1854).

23. *Opinions of the Attorney General* 10 (1863): 527, 527–28.

24. *Opinions of the Attorney General* 1 (1823): 624, 625.

25. E.g., *Opinions of the Attorney General* 1 (1824): 636; 1 (1824): 678; 1 (1825): 705; 1 (1825): 706; 2 (1831): 480; 2 (1832): 507; 2 (1832): 544; 4 (1846): 515; 5 (1851): 287; 11 (1864): 14; and 13 (1869): 28.

26. *Opinions of the Attorney General* 11 (1864): 14, 15.

27. *Opinions of the Attorney General* 18 (1884): 31, 32.

28. *Opinions of the Attorney General* 19 (1890): 685, 686–87.

29. *Berends v. Butz,* 357 F.Supp. 143, 151 (D. Minn. 1973).

30. *National Treasury Employees Union v. Nixon,* 492 F.2d 587 (D.C. Cir. 1974).

31. *U.S. Statutes at Large* 26 (1890): 131, 136–38, sec. 12–15

32. *U.S. Statutes at Large* 44 (1926): 669; 70 (1956): 532; 94 (1980): 1727.

33. *Stats at Large of USA* 10 (1855): 612; 14 (1863): 765; 14 (1866): 9; *U.S. Statutes at Large* 22 (1883): 485; 23 (1885): 283; 24 (1887): 505; 67 (1953): 226; 96 (1982): 27; 106 (1992): 4516.

34. *U.S. Statutes at Large* 43 (1924): 336–38.

35. *U.S. Statutes at Large* 56 (1942): 957; 83 (1969): 730.

36. Yoo, Calabresi, and Nee, "The Unitary Executive during the Third Half-Century," 4 n.14.

37. 272 U.S. 52, 135 (1926).

38. E.g., *Nash v. Califano,* 613 F.2d 10 (2d Cir. 1980).

39. *Pillsbury Company v. Federal Trade Commission,* 354 F.2d 952, 954–56, 963–64 (5th Cir. 1966).

40. Robert E. Cushman, *The Independent Regulatory Commissions* (New York: Oxford University Press, 1941), 21–34.

41. *Humphrey's Executor v. United States,* 295 U.S. 602 (1935).

42. Ibid., 616, 617.

43. Ibid., 625 (first, second, and third quotes from a Senate report), 626 (fourth quote).

44. Ibid., 626 (first quote); 627 (second, third, and fourth quotes); 628 (fifth and sixth quotes).

45. *Morgan v. Tennessee Valley Authority,* 28 F.Supp. 732 (E.D. Tenn. 1939);

Morgan v. Tennessee Valley Authority, 115 F.2d 990 (6th Cir. 1940), cert. denied, 312 U.S. 701 (1941); *Wiener v. United States,* 357 U.S. 349 (1958); *Morrison v. Olson,* 487 U.S. 654 (1988).

46. Morton Rosenberg, "Congress's Prerogative over Agencies and Agency Decisionmakers: The Rise and Demise of the Reagan Administration's Theory of the Unitary Executive," *George Washington Law Review* 57 (1989): 627.

47. "Brief for the United States," *Bowsher v. Synar,* Supreme Court of the United States, October Term, 1985, 21.

48. *160 Landmark Briefs and Arguments of the Supreme Court of the United States: Constitutional Law,* ed. Philip B. Kurland and Gerhard Casper (Washington, D.C.: University Publications of America, 1987), 604.

49. Bernard Schwartz, "An Administrative Law 'Might Have Been'—Chief Justice Burger's *Bowsher* v. *Synar* Draft," *Administrative Law Review* 42 (1990): 221.

50. *Bowsher v. Synar,* 478 U.S. 714 (1986), 725 n.4 ("casting doubt" quote), 757 ("well settled" quote), 762 (White's quote), 777 (Blackmun's quote).

51. "Complaint," *Ticor Title Ins. Co. v. FTC* (D.D.C. September 26, 1985), 6.

52. *Ticor Title Ins. Co. v. FTC,* 814 F.2d 731 (D.C. Cir. 1987); *Ticor Title Ins. Co. v. FTC,* 625 F.Supp. 747 (D.D.C. 1986).

53. *S.E.C. v. Blinder, Robinson & Co., Inc.,* 855 F.2d 677, 682 (10th Cir. 1988), cert. denied, 489 U.S. 1033 (1989).

54. Henry J. Friendly, *The Federal Administrative Agencies* (Cambridge, Mass.: Harvard University Press, 1962), 154.

55. 487 U.S. at 685 (1988).

56. Ibid., 686.

57. Ibid., 688 (first quote), 689 (remaining quotes).

58. Ibid., 689–90 (first and second quotes), 691 (third quote), 691–92 (fourth quote).

59. Calabresi and Yoo, "The Unitary Executive during the First Half-Century," 1457 (first quote), 1459–60 (second quote, original emphasis).

60. *INS v. Chadha,* 462 U.S. 919, 952 (1983).

61. Louis Fisher, "Congress Can't Lose on Its Veto Power," *Washington Post,* February 21, 1982, D1, D5 (quotes).

62. For an analysis of the staying power of legislative vetoes ten years after *Chadha,* see Louis Fisher, "The Legislative Veto: Invalidated, It Survives," *Law & Contemporary Problems* 56 (autumn 1993): 273.

63. U.S. Department of Defense, "Reprogramming of DOD Appropriated Funds," *DOD Financial Management Regulation,* vol. 3, chap. 6 (August 2000).

64. U.S. Department of Energy, Budget Execution Manual, DOE M 135.1–1 (9–30–95), at V-1, para. 1a(1).

65. Ibid., V-2, para. 1a(2).

66. U.S. Department of Transportation, Reprogramming Guidance, May 2005, 1, para. 3.

67. U.S. Treasury Department, Strategic Management Manual, March 29, 2001, chap. 6-30, p. 1.

68. Ibid., chap. 6–32, pp. 1, 5 (quote).

69. U.S. Geological Survey Manual, March 6, 1998, 327.1—Funds Control, p. 6, para. 12B(4).

70. *Bowsher v. Synar,* 478 U.S. at 725 (quoting from *Humphrey's Executor v. United States,* 295 U.S. 602, 629 [1935]).

71. 478 U.S. at 733–34.

72. *Morrison v. Olson,* 487 U.S. 654, 693–94 (1988) (quoting from *United States v. Nixon,* 418 U.S. 693, 707 [1974]).

73. *Mistretta v. United States,* 488 U.S. 361, 380 (1989).

Executive Unilateralism in the Ford and Carter Presidencies

RYAN J. BARILLEAUX AND DAVID ZELLERS

The assertion of executive power by the administration of George W. Bush has been a subject of much contention and the source of an intense amount of political heat. Even a cursory dip into the Internet reveals numerous articles, blogs, and quotes on the "extreme" and "unprecedented" nature of Bush's unilateral executive actions, from warrantless wiretaps to signing statements and the use of other direct powers. To read much of the current and recent debate, one might conclude that George Bush grabbed hold of a vague and underdeveloped principle—unilateral presidential action—and used it as no chief executive had ever done before.

While the issue of whether President Bush's actions were extreme is a legitimate subject for political debate, the question of whether they are unprecedented is an important one and an empirical one. Consequently, presidential scholars have worked to provide a clearer perspective on the unilateral presidency than one can find in current polemics. They have certainly pointed to the roots of assertive presidential unilateralism in recent administrations, with much attention being given to the Reagan era. In the debate that surrounded the confirmation of Judge Samuel Alito to the Supreme Court, the nominee's work for the Reagan Justice Department and the theories of executive power he advanced in internal memoranda received much scrutiny. Likewise, Christopher Kelley and others have pointed to the efforts of Attorney General Edwin Meese to have presidential signing statements included as part of the official legislative history of bills signed by the president.[1] It is demonstrably the case that the actions of the Bush administration are not completely unprecedented.

Despite this interest in the roots of today's unilateralism, little attention has been paid to the executive unilateralism of Presidents Gerald Ford and Jimmy Carter. Because the Ford-Carter era was marked by congressional assertiveness and a general perception of presidential weakness—it has been characterized as the time of a "post-imperial presidency," an "imperiled presidency," and a "no-win presidency"—there has been little investigation of the actions of these presidents to assert executive power, act autonomously, and shape policy through direct means. Yet actions such as Ford's pardon of Richard Nixon and Jimmy Carter's abrogation of the mutual defense treaty with Taiwan are widely known, and they were unilateral in nature.

Why does the record of the Ford-Carter period matter to presidential power in the twenty-first century? There are at least three answers. First, many of the claims made about George W. Bush's use of executive power are based on the notion that his actions are unprecedented. Precedent is crucial to understanding the American presidency, and it is an empirical question whether precedents exist for some current or recent executive action. Second, much of the debate about the use of unilateral power in recent years is based on the idea that presidential unilateralism is characteristic of only certain administrations, such as those of Richard Nixon, Ronald Reagan, and George W. Bush. Again, this is an empirical matter, and our understanding of contemporary uses of presidential power requires that we have a solid understanding of its past uses. Third, the record of the Ford-Carter years can illuminate how presidents employ the powers at their disposal, both those explicitly granted and those that are contested.

Presidents Ford and Carter served during a time of considerable change in American politics. Their presidencies took place during a decade that saw the office rise to the zenith of its power before plummeting to an apparent nadir. Gerald Ford was forced to deal with an opposition Congress and make decisions that would heal the nation but injure his own political standing. Jimmy Carter faced a challenge not from an opposition Congress but from a battle between the president's goals and the political and institutional realities that he faced. Each man labored to govern against considerable political odds, and each relied in part on unilateral executive actions to advance his agenda.

To what extent did Ford and Carter employ unilateral presidential power? What role does unilateral power play in the conduct of the presidency? Those questions are the focus of this work. Our purpose is to examine unilateral executive actions by these presidents in order to shed light on the foundations of George W. Bush's aggressive assertions of unilateral power. If there are precedents for unilateral executive action to be found in the "post-imperial" era of Ford and Carter, then the powers claimed by Bush will be more fully understood. The actions of these "post-imperial" presidents can help to draw the underlying power of the American presidency into sharper relief. They can improve our understanding of the presidency in our own time.

We examine ten categories of unilateral executive actions for Ford and Carter: vetoes, pardons and clemency actions, presidential signing statements, executive orders, proclamations, claims of executive privilege, executive agreements, national security directives (given different names in the Ford and Carter administrations), uses of force, and other unilateral actions. Our evidence is drawn from the public record of the *Public Papers of the Presidents,* documents from the Ford and Carter presidential libraries, declassified documents, and other sources (see tables 1 and 2, as well as endnotes). These categories provide a wide-ranging view of unilateral power in the years of the "imperiled" presidency and contribute to a better understanding of the political history of the presidency since the resignation of Richard Nixon.

The actions of Presidents Ford and Carter must also be examined in a larger context, that of the role of unilateral executive power in the conduct of the presidency. Assertions of unilateral power have the hallmarks of the George W. Bush presidency and are among the most controversial aspects of his tenure. The empirical record of the Ford-Carter years can shed the most light on the Bush presidency if they are examined in light of presidential power properly understood.

Unilateral Action and the Nature of Presidential Power

The American presidency is certainly no stranger to unilateral action. From George Washington's Proclamation of Neutrality and Lincoln's conduct of the Civil War to Richard Nixon's use of impoundment, American chief executives have asserted the power to act in defense of what they consider the national interest.

Are such assertions of unilateral power signs of presidential strength or weakness, and do they serve the president's purposes or ultimately undermine them? The answer is not a simple one. On one hand, the prevailing view of presidential power, as expressed in Richard Neustadt's classic *Presidential Power and the Modern Presidents,* holds that "presidential power is the power to persuade." What matters, he contends, is the personal influence of the incumbent president. Unilateral actions by the chief executive (what Neustadt calls "command") can be self-defeating because they can instigate a backlash against the power of the Oval Office. Consequently, the "power to persuade is the power to bargain."[2] From this perspective, presidents make unilateral assertions of power because they have failed to bargain successfully; they are signs that the president lacks influence over other political actors.

From a different perspective, the one employed here, unilateral executive action can be seen as an instrument of power because it increases the president's leverage in dealings with other actors. One presidential action, such as a veto or executive order, can demonstrate resolve, shape events, and press other actors to compromise with the chief executive. Indeed, Franklin Roosevelt, one of the heroes in Neustadt's conception of presidential power, frequently employed the veto to increase his leverage in dealing with Congress. Presidential power need not be seen as either persuasion or command. Presidents seek to advance their goals, meet the responsibilities imposed by their office, and influence the course of national politics and policy. The means that a president has available to do these things, and the chief executive's likelihood of success, depend on the president's leverage.

Presidential leverage refers to everything that the chief executive can bring to bear in support of an objective and to whether the combination of presidential resources is sufficient to overcome the opposition to the objective. In some cases, presidential leverage may be great merely because the president's constitutional authority is unchallengeable (even if controversial), such as when Presidents Clinton and George H. W. Bush pardoned high-profile offenders shortly before leaving office. In other cases, leverage may be great because political circumstances pave the way for broad executive influence; after the terrorist attacks of September 11, 2001, President George W. Bush was able to gain overwhelming congressional approval of the USA PATRIOT Act, confirmation of his (previously) controversial choice for ambassador to the United Nations, and a sweeping resolution endorsing any and all means to respond to the attacks of that day.

Presidential leverage is rooted in the Constitution and law; supported by the institutional props of staff, executive units, and party organizations; and moderated through the dynamics of presidential strategy and skill, public opinion, interest-group and partisan politics, the media, and events and circumstances. When the president has clear constitutional or legal authority to act, leverage is great and can be overcome only by powerful opposing forces militating against the chief executive's chosen course.

When the chief executive's goals can be achieved only through the agency of others, such as an act of Congress, the president has less leverage. In general, the president has greater leverage in foreign affairs than domestic issues and greater leverage in times of crisis than in times of quiescence.

Presidents can increase their leverage in several ways. They can add to the institutional power of the office through actions that set precedents for expansions of that power. The instrument for these expansions is venture constitutionalism, which comprises actions that assert new or expanded presidential authority under the Constitution. Such actions, if accepted or acquiesced to by Congress, the country, or the courts, lay down precedents for future chief executives.[3]

Another way to increase leverage is through skillful maneuvering and action that is an attempt not only to persuade but also to employ both executive power and politicking to increase the president's chances for success. In 1995, Bill Clinton confronted the 104th Congress and shut down the government rather than agree to a budget bill passed by the Republican majority. Through a combination of his constitutional power and successful identification of the Republican Congress as the culprit in the shutdown, Clinton was able to increase his leverage and extract compromises from his political adversaries. All of this came only months after the 1994 midterm elections, in which Democratic majorities in both the House and Senate were defeated and pollsters learned that voters would have removed Clinton from office if they had had the chance. The following year, Clinton won reelection over his Republican opponent. His actions combined "persuasion" and "command" to increase presidential leverage.

Presidents can also increase their leverage by successful appeals for public support. In 1981, Ronald Reagan delivered a televised address to the nation asking for public support of his first budget, which faced possible defeat in the Democratic-majority House of Representatives. The following day, Capitol Hill was flooded with telephone calls, telegrams, and letters urging Congress to support the president; some of these appeals were spontaneous, while others were orchestrated by operatives in the Republican National Committee. Combined with old-fashioned bargaining between the president and members of Congress, the appeal for public support increased Reagan's leverage enough to overcome Democratic opposition.

Presidents Ford and Carter each employed unilateral executive actions to enhance their leverage. The record of their presidencies reveals much about the power of the office.

TABLE 1

Unilateral executive actions in the Ford administration

Type of action	*Number*	*Significant examples*
Vetoes[a]	Regular/Pocket/% success	Several appropriations bills, to force Congress to restrain spending
	48 18 75%	Common Situs Picketing bill, December 1975
Pardons & clemency[b]	409	Pardon of Richard Nixon, September 1974
		Clemency program for Vietnam-era draft evaders, 1974–1976
Signing statements[c]	130	Statement on signing Bill Amending Child Support Provisions of the Social Security Act (August 1975)—declared that the president would treat a one-chamber legislative veto over standards for program implementation as a "request for information about the proposed standards in advance of their promulgation"
		Statement on signing the Japan-U.S. Friendship Act (October 1975)—declared that members of Congress could serve only as nonvoting members of Japan-U.S. Friendship Commission, despite text of law providing for members of Congress on the commission
		Statement on signing the Foreign Assistance and Related Programs Appropriations Act (July 1976)—declared that the president would not concur in giving House and Senate Appropriations committees a legislative veto over certain funds for foreign aid
		Statement on signing the Dept. of Defense Appropriation Act (February 1976)—declared that the president would treat a provision he deemed unconstitutional as a "complete nullity"

Executive orders[d]	169	11,821—required all legislative proposals, regulations, and rules emanating from the executive branch to include a statement certifying inflationary impact of the proposed action 11,850—reserved to the president authority to allow use of riot control agents in foreign military operations 11,905—clarified authority and responsibilities of U.S. intelligence agencies and prohibited them from participating in any assassination plots
Proclamations[e]	175	4313—announced a program for the return of Vietnam-era draft evaders and military deserters
Claims of executive privilege[f]	several	Refused to allow Secretary of State Kissinger to comply with subpoena issued by the House Select Committee on Intelligence requesting all documents relating to U.S. covert actions since January 1961 (November 1975) Refused to turn over to the House Committee on Interstate and Foreign Commerce documents related to a request by the FBI to the American Telephone and Telegraph Company (AT&T) for the warrantless wiretap of U.S. citizens for national security purposes (February 1976)
Executive agreements[g]	677	Final act of the Conference on Security and Cooperation in Europe—a.k.a. the "Helsinki Accord" on human rights in Eastern Europe and the Soviet Union, August 1975
National security directives[h] (National Security Decision Memoranda—NSDMs)	84	NSDM 280—authorized plan for underground nuclear tests and assigned "highest national priority" to those tests scheduled for completion before Threshold Test Ban Treaty was to take effect in 1976 (August 1974) NSDM 286—ordered long-term reduction in U.S. forces in Thailand (February 1975) NSDM 305—terminated U.S. restrictions on third countries trading with Cuba (September 1975) NSDM 345—authorized U.S. development and acquisition of "non-nuclear anti-satellite capability" to "nullify certain militarily important Soviet space systems" (January 18, 1977—two days before leaving office)

Type of action	*Number*	*Significant examples*
Uses of force[i]	5	Vietnam, evacuation of U.S. personnel, 1975
		Cambodia, evacuation of U.S. personnel, 1975
		Mayaguez incident, 1975
		Lebanon, evacuation of U.S. personnel, 1976
		Korea, U.S. forces dispatched after two Americans killed, 1976
Other executive actions	several	Appointed Alexander Haig as NATO supreme commander, September 1974
		Completed U.S.-Soviet accord on nuclear arms control, Vladivostok, November 1974
		Established blue ribbon panel on CIA activities, January 1975
		Opposed (thus effectively blocking) federal bailout of New York City, October 1975
		Completed four foreign trips, 1974–1976
		Negotiated Egyptian-Israeli agreement on Sinai peninsula, September 1975
		Signed Peaceful Nuclear Explosions Treaty, 1976

Sources for Table 1

[a]"The American Presidency Project," http://www.presidency.ucsb.edu/ws/ (accessed February 9, 2007).

[b]"Presidential Clemency Actions, 1789–2001," http://jurist.law.pitt.edu/pardonspres1.htm (accessed February 9, 2007).

[c]Christopher S. Kelley, "The Unitary Executive and the Presidential Signing Statement" (PhD diss., Miami University, Ohio, 2003), 192.

[d]"Administration of Gerald R. Ford (1974–1977)," http://www.archives.gov/federal-register/executive-orders/ford.html (accessed February 9, 2007).

[e]"Proclamations," http://www.presidency.ucsb.edu/proclamations.php (accessed February 9, 2007).

[f]Louis Fisher, *The Politics of Executive Privilege* (Durham, N.C.: Carolina Academic Press, 2004), 43, 116–17, 246–48; and Mark Rozell, *Executive Privilege* (Baltimore: Johns Hopkins University Press, 1994), 84–96.

[g]Lyn Ragsdale, *Vital Statistics on the Presidency* (Washington, D.C.: Congressional Quarterly, 1996), 311.

[h]"Ford Administration National Security Decision Memoranda," Gerald R. Ford Presidential Library, http://www.fordlibrarymuseum.gov/library/document/nsdmnssm/nsdm.htm (accessed February 9, 2007).

[i]Ragsdale, *Vital Statistics,* 330.

Gerald Ford and Executive Unilateralism

When Gerald Ford entered the presidency in August 1974, he assumed an office at the low point in its power and prestige. Richard Nixon had been driven from the White House by the Watergate scandal, and Ford took office with few of the political advantages that usually bolster a new president. He was not widely known to the nation, having served only a few months as vice president; he had not conducted a campaign for the presidency to build political support; he had not won an election; and he had been appointed to the vice presidency upon the resignation of the scandal-plagued Spiro Agnew. He did benefit from a reservoir of goodwill from Congress and a public grateful for a respite from the agonies of Watergate, but Ford's pardon of Nixon cost him public and congressional support and contributed to a devastating setback for his party in the November 1974 midterm congressional elections.

Under these circumstances, the prospects for the exercise of executive power by President Ford seemed dim. Congress, especially after the pardon and the 1974 midterms, was determined to assert its power. It voted in 1975 to cut off funding for the Vietnam War, to prohibit the administration from intervening in the civil war in Angola, and to investigate the Central Intelligence Agency, and it showed a general impatience with the presidency. Despite Ford's long service in Congress and personal friendships with members of both parties, the Democratic-controlled Congress was "hostile to his policies."[4]

Ford made overt gestures toward building and maintaining good relations with Congress. Within days of assuming the presidency, he told legislators in a joint session, "I don't want a honeymoon with you. I want a good marriage."[5] He set aside several hours each week to meet with members of Congress, showed respect for legislators and the legislative body, and voluntarily appeared before a congressional committee in 1974 to defend his pardon of Richard Nixon. In many ways, especially those noted above, he displayed a deferential attitude toward the House and Senate.

Nevertheless, Ford exercised unilateral executive power across a number of fronts (see table 1). He used the veto extensively, wielded pardon and clemency power in two high-profile areas, issued executive orders and national security directives, tested the newly enacted War Powers Resolution, and employed signing statements to shape the implementation of acts of Congress. He did not refrain from using executive power to shape policy, even in the face of congressional assertiveness.

VETOES AS AN INSTRUMENT OF PRESIDENTIAL POWER

Reflecting on his presidency several years after leaving office, Gerald Ford told an interviewer,

> I set a record for the number of vetoes while I was in the White House. I think during two-and-a-half years of my presidency I vetoed sixty-seven or sixty-eight [*sic*] measures and most of them were upheld even by a Democrat House and Senate. One thing that most people don't realize is—a veto is not a negative action. Now the press generally calls it a negative action. But it is an affirmative action by president to reflect views of all the people in the country. When [a] Senator or member of the House votes for a piece of legislation it is for his state or for his district. The veto is action taken by the chief executive to reflect views of the public as a whole.[6]

In all, Ford vetoed sixty-six measures passed by Congress—forty-eight by conventional veto and another eighteen by means of a pocket veto (which, coming at the end of a congressional session, cannot be overridden). As his comments to the interviewer make clear, Ford viewed the veto as an instrument of presidential power.

He used it, as have most presidents, to block legislation he believed was contrary to the national interest. This was the case in the matter of such measures as the Common Situs Picketing bill, which Congress passed in December 1975. That bill was particularly important because it contained key provisions that had been crafted by his own secretary of labor, John Dunlop, as part of a deal with labor and business leaders. Despite his earlier encouragement of Dunlop to construct a business-labor compromise that formed the heart of the bill, Ford concluded that the central provisions were bad policy. He vetoed the bill at the price of opposition from organized labor in the 1976 campaign and went so far as to explain and defend his decision in his memoirs.[7]

Ford primarily employed the veto, however, as a weapon with which to force Congress to restrain federal spending. Indeed, Ford's use of the veto in this fashion was explicitly a strategic move, which he undertook on the advice of Alan Greenspan, chair of the Council of Economic Advisers.[8] As James Cannon, Ford's assistant for domestic affairs, summarized the results of this approach, "Ford was not in office long enough to stop the nation's headlong plunge into national debt, but he did show that a president could slow it down. . . . Except for unemployment compensation, which went up because of the recession, total federal outlays in the last Ford budget were lower than in the previous year."[9] In defense of this strategy, Ford told Cannon, "I felt it was the constitutional mandate for the President of the United States, as *the* person who represented everybody, that this executive tool had to be used to prevent the Congress from making unwise judgments."[10]

PARDONS AND CLEMENCY

One area in which the Constitution gives the president broad unilateral power is in the matter of pardons and clemency. Save for cases of impeachment, the president's power to reduce or remove penalties for federal crimes—even to the extent of granting blanket amnesty for a broad class of offenders—is virtually unlimited. Gerald Ford employed this power in two high-profile ways during his presidency.

The first of these exercises was Ford's "full, free, and absolute pardon" of Richard Nixon for "all offenses against the United States" during his tenure as president.[11] This action was an explicitly unilateral exercise of presidential power, carried out over the objections of some of his staff as well as those members of Congress Ford informed of his decision before he announced it to the nation. Ford granted the pardon only a month after assuming office, surprising a nation that had until then given him broad support. He refused to delay the pardon, as Senator Barry Goldwater, House Majority Leader Thomas "Tip" O'Neill, and others suggested that he do, until a more politically auspicious time (such as after the 1974 midterm congressional elections or even the 1976 presidential election) or until Nixon was indicted or even convicted for his Watergate crimes.[12] Ford made what he thought was the correct decision and announced it as soon as his mind was made up. He paid a high price for that decision—his job approval rating plummeted and anti-Nixon Democrats in Congress protested loudly—but he did not flinch.

Nor did Ford back down from his plan for earned clemency for Vietnam-era draft resisters and deserters. Shortly after assuming office, he appeared before the national convention of the Veterans of Foreign Wars to announce his plan for "earned reentry . . . into an atmosphere of hope, hard work, and mutual trust" for draft evaders, and he called on the veterans to assist him.[13] Employing his constitutional power, he allowed those young men who had fled to Canada to avoid the military draft, or even deserted the military in order to avoid serving in Vietnam, to earn clemency. Despite criticism from conservatives (that he was coddling cowards and turncoats) and from many in the affected group (that he was hypocritical for pardoning Nixon but not draft evaders), Ford carried out his plan.

Gerald Ford saw the primary mission of his presidency as working to heal the nation in the wake of Watergate and Vietnam. To emphasize that point, he even entitled his memoirs *A Time to Heal.* But to advance these twin goals, he turned to unilateral actions of presidential clemency that neither Congress nor public opinion could undo.

SIGNING STATEMENTS

Presidents have long made statements—both orally and in writing—upon signing acts of Congress, but only in the era of George W. Bush have these signing statements received significant attention as instruments by which presidents have sought to shape policy. Nevertheless, the forty-third president is not the first chief executive to employ signing statements as an instrument of power, nor was Gerald Ford.

President Ford issued 130 signing statements during his time in office. Most of these were largely rhetorical in nature, but Ford also used them to make statements of policy, in many cases admonishing Congress to show restraint in spending or government regulation. Significantly, however, Ford also used these statements to indicate how he would implement a law that Congress had enacted and that he had signed.

Through 1974 and most of 1975, Ford's policy-oriented comments in signing statements tended to be hortatory in nature. He would identify a provision of a law that he found problematic, then call on the legislative body to work with the executive to improve the law or federal policy in that area. For example, in signing the Forest and Rangeland Renewable Resources Planning Act of 1974—which he did only ten days after assuming office—he announced, "I would be less than candid if I did not admit that certain provisions of this act disturb me. . . . But the benefits of this legislation far outweigh any potential drawbacks, and I am confident that the Congress and the executive branch, working together, can and will manage, develop, and improve our priceless natural legacy of forests and rangelands."[14] The action he found most objectionable was the legislative veto. In May 1975, he signed the Amtrak Improvement Act of 1975 despite a one-chamber legislative veto provision. He called the provision "an unconstitutional exercise of congressional power" and expressed concern about the "increasing frequency with which Congress passes legislation containing such provisions."[15]

In other cases, the president would call on Congress to amend or even repeal an objectionable provision in a law. In January 1975, Ford identified several problematic provisions in the Social Services Amendments of 1974 and recommended that "these defects should be corrected in the next Congress."[16] In still other cases, Ford put members of Congress on notice that he would not seek funds to implement a policy or program that he opposed. On signing the Federal Fire Prevention and Control Act of 1974, the president identified one requirement he found objectionable and told Congress, "I will not seek appropriations to implement this particular provision of the bill."[17]

Beginning in the summer of 1975, Ford used signing statements to inform Congress that he would ignore unconstitutional provisions or instruct his administration to treat those provisions as merely advisory. In August, upon signing a bill amending child support provisions of the Social Security Act, he drew a line over the legislative veto (explicitly reminding Congress that he had warned legislators about such provisions in his signing statement on the Amtrak bill that May). Again declaring the legislative veto unconstitutional, he instructed the secretary of health, education, and welfare to "treat this provision of H.R. 7710 simply as a request for information" rather than a requirement that the administration meet certain proposed standards for congressional review.[18] He issued comparable instructions to his administration in response to other bills containing similar provisions.

By 1976, Ford's assertion of unilateral power to interpret laws had reached its height. In February, responding to yet another legislative veto imposed by Congress, he spoke in blunt language. In this case, the Defense Appropriation Act sought to give the Appropriations and Armed Services committees in each chamber a veto over the U.S. Army's procurement of ammunition. The president reminded Congress that such a provision was unconstitutional and proclaimed that he would treat it as "a complete nullity. I cannot concur in this legislative encroachment upon the constitutional powers of the executive branch."[19] He no longer couched his unilateralism in the language of cooperation—he was now willing to explicitly assert the unilateral authority to defy Congress. He had arrived at a use of the signing statement that has come to be associated with later presidents.

EXECUTIVE ORDERS

Ford issued 169 executive orders while in office, and these covered a range of policy and management issues. In some cases, he did use these orders to engage in unilateral exercises of power, as two examples illustrate. Executive Order 11,821 (signed November 27, 1974) required all legislative proposals, regulations, and rules emanating from the executive branch to include a statement certifying the inflationary impact of the proposed action. This order followed Richard Nixon's precedent of requiring "quality of life reviews" for proposed federal regulations and would serve as a further precedent for the administrative clearance process instituted by Ronald Reagan and maintained by his successors.[20]

Executive Order 11,905 (signed February 18, 1976) is probably the most well known of Ford's orders. Not only did it clarify the authority and responsibilities of U.S. intelligence agencies but it also explicitly provided that "no employee of the United States Government shall engage in, or conspire to engage in, political assassination."[21] This ban was reiterated by Ronald Reagan, in Executive Order 12,333 (signed December 4, 1981), although in October 2001 the *Washington Post* reported that President George W. Bush had signed an "intelligence finding" that the prohibition did not apply in wartime and that political assassination might thus be used against al-Qaida leaders.[22]

PROCLAMATIONS

Like all presidents, Gerald Ford issued a large number of proclamations, 175 in all. Most of these were ceremonial in nature, flowing from the president's role as chief of state. These included proclamations of Mother's Day, American Heart Month, National Farm Safety Week, and other noble but symbolic occasions and purposes. Several proclamations invoked the president's power to impose, defer, or cancel certain trade restrictions. Proclamations of this type, however, were not really unilateral in nature: they were based on grants of power to the chief executive from Congress, mostly through the Trade Expansion Act of 1962.[23]

Ford did issue two proclamations exercising unilateral power, both related to his Vietnam draft-evader clemency program. The first (4313, issued September 16, 1974), outlined the principles and terms for the program, setting an initial deadline for an affected person to present himself to a U.S. attorney before January 31, 1975.[24] The second (4345, issued January 30, 1975) extended the deadline for participation in the program to March 1, 1975.[25] In both proclamations, it was clear that the program was the president's own; he was acting solely on his Article II authority to grant reprieves and pardons.

CLAIMS OF EXECUTIVE PRIVILEGE

Gerald Ford's desire for a "good marriage" with Congress did not mean that he was willing to give the legislature all the information that it wanted from the executive. Indeed, Ford invoked executive privilege on several occasions to withhold information from Congress, and two examples illustrate his willingness to resort to unilateralism for purposes of national security.

The first example involved the president's refusal to allow Secretary of State Henry Kissinger to comply with a November 1975 subpoena from the House Select Committee on Intelligence to provide documents related to covert actions. Ford invoked executive privilege to stop the committee's attempt to issue a contempt citation against Kissinger, and in the end the president allowed a member of the National Security Council staff members to read verbatim from the relevant documents rather than provide them to the panel.[26]

In the second instance, President Ford went even further to withhold information from Congress. In this case, a subcommittee of the House Committee on Interstate and Foreign Commerce in 1976 requested information from the American Telephone and Telegraph Company (AT&T) regarding a program of warrantless wiretaps of citizens for reasons of national security. Not only did the president tell the subcommittee chair that divulging such information was contrary to national security, but he also acted to prevent AT&T from complying with the subcommittee's request on its own. When the company declared itself willing to provide the requested information, the Ford administration took AT&T to court to prevent the disclosure, invoking executive privilege. The federal district court accepted the administration's claim but was overturned by the D.C. Circuit Court, which admonished the executive and legislative branches to compromise. The issue was unresolved for the remainder of Ford's time in the White House because he continued to insist on executive privilege, but in 1978 an agreement between the subcommittee and the Carter Justice Department settled the matter.[27]

These examples are significant for several reasons. First, they reveal that President Ford regarded executive privilege as a real and effective executive prerogative. Second, they demonstrate that he saw national security, and the president's responsibility for it, as trumping congressional powers and other constitutional restrictions. Third, not only was Ford willing to fight for executive privilege in court but the issue about which he was willing to fight was a program of warrantless wiretaps of American citizens. This means that Ford rather broadly interpreted the power of the U.S. government to act in pursuit of national security.

EXECUTIVE AGREEMENTS

Gerald Ford followed the practice of post–World War II presidents in signing many executive agreements, a total of 677 in all. Of these, the most famous was the Final Act of the Conference on Security and Cooperation in Europe, better known as the Helsinki Accord. This agreement, concluded in August 1975, has been seen as a "*critical contribution to the development of human rights movements in Eastern Europe and the Soviet Union.*"[28] The document, which contained language committing its signatories (including most Warsaw Pact states) to observe human rights, was dismissed by critics as lacking in enforcement mechanisms. But dissidents in the Soviet Union and elsewhere used the Helsinki Accord as a shield beneath which they could establish committees to monitor implementation of the agreement, thus beginning the human-rights movements that would eventually contribute to the fall of communism.[29]

NATIONAL SECURITY DIRECTIVES

President Ford made many decisions in the area of national security policy, and eighty-four of these were formally recorded in National Security Decision Memoranda (NSDMs). These instruments were used to delineate American foreign policy regarding a particular issue or region of the world, to record presidential approval of security-related research programs, or to order changes in official national security policy. For example, NSDM 280 (signed November 28, 1974) authorized a program of underground nuclear testing for fiscal year 1975 (subsequent NSDMs would cover later years) and declared it to be of the "highest national priority" that testing be accomplished before the Threshold Test Ban Treaty was set to take effect in 1976.[30]

Other NSDMs demonstrate even more clearly President Ford's willingness to act unilaterally in national security affairs. NSDM 286 (signed February 7, 1975) order long-term reductions in American troop levels in Thailand, while through NSDM 305 (signed September 15, 1975) the president unilaterally terminated U.S. restrictions on third countries trading with Cuba.[31] Only two days before leaving office in 1977, Ford authorized a research program to develop non-nuclear anti-satellite technology to "nullify certain militarily important Soviet space systems."[32] He was thus willing to assert executive power as he believed necessary.

USES OF FORCE

Gerald Ford came to the presidency as opposition to "presidential war" was reaching its peak. In 1973, Congress had passed the War Powers Resolution over Richard Nixon's veto, with the intention of preventing future military commitments like the one in Vietnam. By December 1974, it likewise moved to legislate an end to American participation in the war in Indochina. Ford complied with the strictures imposed by Congress, but only up to a point. Indeed, he engaged in the use of force five times while in office: three times to evacuate American personnel from dangerous situations (Vietnam and Cambodia in 1975, and Lebanon as it descended into civil war in 1976); once to rescue the crew of the USS *Mayaguez* in 1975; and once to bolster U.S. troops in South Korea following the killings of two American military personnel in 1976.

Each of these actions was an example of the president exercising unilateral power because in none of these cases did Ford request or receive congressional approval. Ford made a general attempt to comply with the reporting provisions of the War Powers Resolution but pointed out after the *Mayaguez* incident (which occurred during a congressional recess) that it was physically impossible to inform all relevant members of Congress, as prescribed by the resolution, of the American military action that would be taken. In fact, he thought it "naive" that members of Congress would try to insist on presidential consultation—rather than just reporting—before almost any military action.[33]

OTHER EXECUTIVE ACTIONS

Like any American president, Ford also engaged in an assortment of activities that drew upon his constitutional powers and that were essentially unilateral in nature. He participated in several diplomatic endeavors, including four foreign trips, negotiating the Vladivostok accord (which set the stage for future arms-control agreements) with the Soviet Union (1974), signing the Peaceful Nuclear Explosions Treaty (1976), and helping to broker a 1975 agreement between Egypt and Israel regarding the Sinai peninsula. He also appointed a blue-ribbon commission, headed by Vice President Nelson Rockefeller, to investigate CIA activities (1975), hoping to head off a congressional investigation. And he made clear his refusal to support a federal bailout for New York City (October 1975), which was headed for bankruptcy, thus effectively killing a plan to offer the city assistance.

One of the best examples of Ford's unilateralism in office was his appointment of General Alexander Haig as NATO supreme commander in the fall of 1974. Haig had become Nixon's chief of staff following the resignation of H. R. Haldeman in the wake of the Watergate scandal, and Ford wanted to ease Haig out in order to install his own staff team. Haig was controversial because of his association with Watergate, and some in Congress and the media thought that Haig had gone too far to protect Nixon. Ford considered naming Haig, a career officer, as Army chief of staff, but that position required Senate confirmation. Instead, he named him to command NATO forces, an appointment he could make without congressional support. Indeed, many of Haig's critics in Congress tried to pressure Ford into submitting Haig's name to the Senate anyway, but the president ignored them and dispatched the general to Europe.[34]

GERALD FORD'S UNILATERALISM

Gerald Ford came to the presidency from a career in Congress, and he had spent his career mastering a congressional perspective on politics and government. Nevertheless, as president he accepted and developed an executive perspective on the separation of powers. He made sincere efforts to restore good relations between the White House and Capitol Hill, but he also exercised unilateral power when he thought it necessary and in the national interest. Even in a period that is regarded as the nadir of executive power, Gerald Ford—without the conventional political bases of presidential power—engaged in executive unilateralism.

Some observers have argued that Ford's reliance on unilateralism, such as his use of vetoes to restrain spending, was a result of the acrimony created by his pardon of Richard Nixon. While the pardon certainly generated a hostile reaction from the Democratic Congress, there is no reason to think that the same Congress would have been otherwise inclined to support Ford's budget goals or accept his position on the legislative veto. Even in the aftermath of the pardon, Ford's use of executive unilateralism helped him to develop a record that almost won the 1976 presidential election.

Jimmy Carter and Executive Unilateralism

The presidential campaign of 1976 saw Jimmy Carter cast himself in the role of the Washington outsider; he would not be one to play the same game as others had before him. In positioning himself as an outsider Carter was able to seize upon the growing public sentiment that Washington was a cesspool of scandals, lies, and corruption. The timing of his run for president could not have been better, coming on the heels of the resignations in disgrace of both Vice President Agnew and President Nixon. While he won as an outsider and often took an outsider's approach to many aspects of the office, Carter nevertheless employed many of the same unilateral tools of the presidency that his predecessors had used.

During the campaign of 1976, Carter had expressed a desire to have an open presidency. In a May 1976 interview with Bill Moyers, Carter leveled several criticisms at the secrecy and closed nature of government. When asked what the lessons of the previous decades had been, Carter insisted that one solution was "to strip away the secrecy of government in every possible way we can, to open up deliberations of the executive and legislative branches." Carter's desire for openness should not be mistaken for weakness in government. In the same interview he also said, "I don't object to a strong, aggressive Congress. A strong, aggressive Supreme Court. And a strong, aggressive President—if what goes on in our government is known by, debated by, questioned by, controlled by the people in this country."[35]

Carter did not face the same political challenges that his predecessor had. The Democratic-controlled Congress that had swept into power in 1974 was now firmly in place. The challenge to Carter was how to deal with his own party and competing interests within its coalition. Like Gerald Ford, Jimmy Carter relied on unilateral executive power to address his own policy preferences as well as to maintain the power of his office (see table 2). Carter made extensive use of executive orders, proclamations, and executive agreements in order to meet the goals set forth by the administration.

VETOES AS AN INSTRUMENT OF PRESIDENTIAL POWER

Jimmy Carter used the veto a total of thirty-one times, including thirteen regular vetoes and eighteen pocket vetoes. He was very successful in his use of the veto, with an 84 percent success rate. For example, in 1978 he used the instrument to address his disapproval of a defense appropriation bill (H.R. 10929). His veto message listed a number of concerns with the bill as it stood; for example, although the bill called for greater military preparedness and research, it eliminated the planned purchase of a nuclear-powered aircraft carrier.[36] Carter's aim was not to build an aircraft carrier but to ensure that general naval construction continued and that spending priorities were aimed at defense capability and readiness, especially those forces committed to NATO. Ultimately this veto would be sustained.

Another important Carter veto was of a bill to extend the public debt limit (H.R. 7428). Carter's reason for vetoing this bill was that

TABLE 2

Unilateral executive actions in the Carter administration

Type of action	*Number*	*Significant examples*
Vetoes[a]	Regular/Pocket/ % success 13 18 84.6%	Several appropriations bills, to address spending priorities Debt Limit Extension Bill, June 1980
Pardons and clemency[b]	566	Pardon of Selective Service Act violators (1964–1973), January 1977 Commutation of sentence for G. Gordon Liddy, April 1977 Commutation of Sentence for Patricia Campbell Hearst, February 1979
Signing statements[c]	247	Statement on signing the War Powers Bill (December 1977)—expresses "serious concern" regarding a provision that would allow Congress to terminate a national emergency by concurrent resolution; states that this feature may be unconstitutional Statement on signing the Amtrak Improvement Act of 1978 (October 1978)—announces the president will permit the secretary of transportation to use discretionary waiver to waive "buy American" provisions in order to ensure meeting obligations of international agreements Statement on signing Dept. of State, etc., Appropriations Bill (August 1979)—declares that the president will regard section 108 (mandating opening or closing of certain U.S. consulates) as "a recommendation and not a requirement" Statement on signing of the Panama Canal Act of 1979 (September 1979)—states that the administration sees the treaty as self-executing and therefore not requiring any further legislative action Statement on signing Defense Authorization Act of 1981 (September 1980)—declares that a legislative veto contained in section 302(b) is unconstitutional and will be treated as a "report-and-wait" provision

Executive orders[d]	320	11,967—relating to the amnesty granted to violators of the Selective Service Act from August 4, 1964, to March 28, 1973 (January 1977) 12,036—outlines the duties and responsibilities of and restrictions on U.S. intelligence activities (January 1978) 12,041—amends the Generalized System of Preferences (February 1978)
Proclamations[e]	335	4495—Termination of Natural Gas Emergency (April 1977) 4702—Import of Petroleum and Petroleum Products from Iran (November 1979)
Claims of executive privilege[f]	several	Refused a congressional request for documents related to a decision not to support water dam projects (April 1977) Refused to turn over documents to the House Subcommittee on Environment, Energy, and Natural Resources until the White House could fully review the documents and decide *not* to invoke executive privilege (April 1980)
Executive agreements[g]	1021	Agreement with Australia regarding the peaceful use of nuclear energy pursuant to the requirements of the Nuclear Non-Proliferation Act of 1979 (July 1979)
Presidential Directives[h] (PDs)	63	PD7—review of U.S. position in SALT II negotiations (March 1977) PD24—Telecommunications Protection Policy (November 1977) PD52—U.S. policy toward Cuba (October 1979) PD59—codified "counterforce" targeting of nuclear weapons as supplement to "assured destruction" targeting (July 1980) PD62, 63—National Strategy & Persian Gulf Security Framework, as a response to Soviet aggression in Afghanistan (January 15, 1981)
Uses of force[i]	2	Zaire, logistical support, 1978 Iran, unsuccessful helicopter mission to rescue hostages (1980)

Type of action	*Number*	*Significant examples*
Other executive actions	several	Camp David Peace Accords (1978) Dissolution of defense treaty with Taiwan (1979) Full diplomatic recognition of People's Republic of China (1979) Parallel unilateral policy declarations on nuclear weapons (1977, 1980) Carter Doctrine and covert arms for Afghan mujahedeen (1980) Boycott of 1980 Summer Olympics in Moscow (1980)

Sources for Table 2

[a]"The American Presidency Project," http://www.presidency.ucsb.edu/ws/ (accessed February 17, 2007).

[b]"Presidential Clemency Actions, 1789–2001," http://jurist.law.pitt.edu/pardonspres1.htm (accessed February 17, 2007).

[c]Christopher S. Kelley, "The Unitary Executive and the Presidential Signing Statement" (PhD diss., Miami University, Ohio, 2003), 192.

[d]"Administration of Jimmy Carter (1977–1981)," http://www.archives.gov/federal-register/executive-orders/carter.html (accessed February 17, 2007).

[e]"Proclamations," http://www.presidency.ucsb.edu/proclamations.php (accessed February 17, 2007).

[f]Louis Fisher, *The Politics of Executive Privilege* (Durham, N.C.: Carolina Academic Press, 2004), 43, 116–17, 246–48; Mark Rozell, *Executive Privilege* (Baltimore: Johns Hopkins University Press, 1994), 84–96.

[g]Lyn Ragsdale, *Vital Statistics on the Presidency* (Washington, D.C.: Congressional Quarterly, 1996), 311.

[h]"Presidential Directives (PD) and Presidential Review Memoranda (PRM)," Jimmy Carter Presidential Library, http://www.jimmycarterlibrary.org/documents/pddirectives/pres_directive.phtml (accessed February 17, 2007). PDs were foreign policy directives equivalent to National Security Decision Memoranda (NSDMs) in the Ford administration.

[i]Ragsdale, *Vital Statistics*, 330.

an amendment attached to the bill sought to restrict the president's program for the oil import conservation fee.[37] Carter had made several prior statements indicating that any attempt to end the oil import conservation fee would be met with a veto; the administration saw the conservation fee as part of its larger strategy of energy policy. Carter took a hard line with this issue; the oil conservation fee was just one part of an energy policy that had political implications throughout the 1980 campaign. Ultimately, the debt limit bill would be passed but without the amendment attached, thus giving the president a victory in asserting his prerogatives through executive power.

PARDONS AND CLEMENCY

Jimmy Carter issued more than five hundred pardons as president, including a number of high-profile actions. One of his first acts as president was to issue a blanket amnesty to individuals who had evaded the Vietnam-era draft. This blanket pardon resolved early concerns over the measures taken by President Ford in regard to draft violators. Carter's pardon had the effect of "restoring . . . full political, civil, and other rights" to those persons who, from August 4, 1964, through March 28, 1973, had violated the "Military Selective Service Act, or any regulation thereunder."[38]

The president also used his power to commute sentences during his term. Nixon administration staffer and Watergate conspirator G. Gordon Liddy received a commutation that reduced his sentence and changed the date of his parole eligibility. Liddy had originally been given a twenty-year sentence, which was reduced to eight years. The commutation was based on "a comparison of Mr. Liddy's sentence with those of all others convicted in Watergate related prosecutions."[39] Another high-profile commutation was that of Patricia Campbell Hearst, who had been sentenced to prison for her involvement with the Symbionese Liberation Army after her kidnapping by the same group. (Hearst would ultimately be given a full pardon by President Clinton in January 2001, and she credited Carter's commutation for helping her ultimately gain the full pardon.[40])

SIGNING STATEMENTS

President Carter used signing statements to applaud positive legislative work as well as chastise the Congress when legislation did not meet the White House's expectations or fall in line with its preferences. Carter's language in the signing statements did not undergo the same evolution of increasing sternness that Ford's had. Many of his signing statements offered thanks and congratulations to members of Congress upon the signing of legislation; when Carter expressed concern regarding a bill's provisions or asserted executive prerogatives he did so in a cordial and direct manner.

An example of a concern expressed by Carter comes from the signing statement accompanying H.R. 7738, an act that dealt with the powers of the president in time of war, in which Carter stated that, "in approving the bill, I must note my serious concern over the provision in Section 207(b), which would allow Congress to terminate a national emergency declared by the President by concurrent resolution. Provisions such as these raise profound constitutional questions, since Article I, Section 7, of the Constitution requires that congressional action having the force of law be presented to the President for his signature or veto."[41] The statement goes on to assert that the power to execute laws is exclusive to the president and that such a provision may be unconstitutional. The language in the statement is direct and concise and provides a firm legal background for the concern expressed by Carter.

Carter also used signing statements to emphasize the president's obligation to ensure that the government lives up to its agreements with other countries. In a 1978 statement on signing the Amtrak Improvement Act of 1978, he asserted, "I am also concerned over the 'Buy American' provision in this bill. S. 3040 would require that Amtrak's purchase of goods costing over $1 million be limited to those mined, produced or manufactured in the United States. However, there are provisions in the legislation permitting the Secretary of Transportation to waive these 'Buy American' requirements under certain conditions. I expect the Secretary to exercise his discretionary waiver authority in a manner that is consistent with the public interest, including our obligations under international agreements."[42] This statement is important for a number of reasons. First, it provides guidance for administration officials in their role of assisting the president in executing the laws. Second, it asserts the power of the president in foreign relations, specifically the assurance that the United States will live up to international agreements. Finally, this statement demonstrates Carter's use of nonconfrontational language in signing statements (which belies his administration's otherwise testy relationship with Congress). His goal appears to have been to use the signing statement to protect executive unilateralism without coming to blows with the legislative body.

EXECUTIVE ORDERS

Executive orders have been one of the most commonly employed tools of unilateral executive power. Carter issued 320 executive orders, and they covered a wide range of policy areas. On his first day in office, Carter used an executive order to implement his blanket pardon for violators of the Selective Service Act. In Executive Order 12,041 (February 1978), he instituted changes in the Generalized System of Preferences as they related to the developing world. One of the most important executive orders Carter issued was number 12,036 (January 1978). This order defined the organization of foreign intelligence-gathering activities; it was similar in structure and intent to Ford's Executive Order 11,905 (which famously prohibited U.S. involvement in assassination plots). These examples serve to illustrate the flexibility of the executive order and the way presidents can use it to address an array of executive prerogatives.

PROCLAMATIONS

Proclamations are often ceremonial acts by a president, but they can also be used as substantive policy tools. During the hostage crisis in Iran, the president used Proclamation 4702 (November 1979) to restrict the importation of petroleum and petroleum-related products from Iran. This proclamation was one of a number of early diplomatic measures employed to deal with the crisis. The intent of the proclamation was to "eliminate the dependence of the United States on Iran as a source of crude oil."[43]

CLAIMS OF EXECUTIVE PRIVILEGE

In the shadow of Watergate and the congressional investigations that followed, the phrase *executive privilege* had an almost radioactive characteristic to it. The Carter administration never invoked executive privilege in the traditional sense; it did, however, take actions that served the same purpose without actually invoking the term *executive privilege.*

One of the earliest political battles the administration faced arose from the president's objection to the construction of several federal water projects, an activity traditionally funded by Congress. The White House refused a congressional request for documents relating to the decision not to fund the projects; when the White House claimed the documents were privileged, the Audubon Society filed suit to obtain the papers in question. Carter was confident in his assertion of executive privilege and approved it, but ultimately the issue was resolved when the Department of Interior and the Audubon Society settled the matter out of court.[44] The introduction of a nongovernment actor in this situation could have created a very unstable situation for the president, but the settlement allowed the administration to avoid a larger problem.

Another use of executive privilege was in response to the House Subcommittee on Commerce, Consumer, and Monetary Affairs investigation of foreign investments in the United States. The subcommittee requested documents from the Department of Treasury, which the secretary refused to hand over; the committee balked at any refusals or restrictions. The counsel for Treasury urged the president to use a "governmental privilege" if Congress issued a subpoena for the documents, but the matter was resolved through negotiations and executive privilege was never actually invoked.[45]

This sort of negotiation served the administration well in its attempts to avoid invoking executive privilege. Carter saw the use of executive privilege as a tool of last resort, a view consistent with his pronounced desire for open administration.[46] Nevertheless, the Carter administration was neither averse to withholding documents nor opposed to withholding testimony from administration officials. A letter from Lloyd Cutler (counsel to the president) to Representative Samuel S. Stratton (D-N.Y.) in 1980 addressed the issue of individual testimony: "The Congress has always respected the privilege of the President to decline the requests that the President himself or his immediate White House advisers appear to testify before congressional committees."[47] Indeed, Carter did not fear using the principle of executive privilege to protect his administration, but he preferred to avoid invoking the term and its echoes of the past.

EXECUTIVE AGREEMENTS

Carter used executive agreements in two ways: as an instrument of better foreign relations and as a means for complying with legislation. An example of this second use was a 1979 agreement between the United States and Australia pertaining to the use of nuclear energy. The Nuclear Non-Proliferation Act of 1978 required the president to "renegotiate existing peaceful nuclear cooperation agreements to obtain new provisions set forth in the Act."[48] This was the first of a series of agreements Carter would make in accordance the nuclear legislation.

The executive agreement was also used by President Carter in conjunction with the Fishery Conservation and Management Act of 1976. Carter made a series of agreements, the first being with the European Economic Community, and further encouraged the provisions of the agreement to be incorporated into the Fishery Conservation Zone Transition Act.[49]

Executive agreements are not always used to seal a deal, but they can be used to further the diplomatic process. The United States and Canada entered into an executive agreement in 1977 to permit studies on the possibility of a pipeline from Alaska through Canada to the lower forty-eight states. The text of the agreement stated that it "does not constitute Canadian approval of construction of a transit pipeline across its territory. Upon completion of studies in progress, the Government of Canada will announce whether or not it is willing to permit construction of a transit pipeline of Alaskan gas."[50] This particular type of use of an executive agreement helped to formalize the diplomatic process between the administration and foreign governments and to ensure continuity of ongoing projects and agreements.

NATIONAL SECURITY DIRECTIVES

One of the semantic changes that came about during the Carter administration was the renaming of National Security Decision Memoranda (NSDMs) as Presidential Directives (PDs). Beyond semantics, a number of the Carter PDs are notable because of the changes they made to American strategic policy overall. One of the most fundamental shifts in national defense policy during the Carter administration was the retargeting of nuclear weapons to deal with counterforce targeting. PD 59 dealt with the policy for deploying nuclear weapons; the directive makes it clear that the United States would maintain a policy of deterrence and that the use of nuclear weapons would be in conjunction with general purpose forces and not a substitute for them.[51]

Carter also issued two important PDs in his final days in office. Presidential Directives 62 and 63 were part of the implementation of the "Carter Doctrine" of addressing the possibility of Soviet aggression in the Persian Gulf region. PD 63 also addressed the escalating war between Iran and Iraq. It stated that measures were to be taken to ensure the security of the Straits of Hormuz and laid out a number of provisions for strengthening military power and diplomatic ties in the greater Middle East and Horn of Africa.[52] These final directives from the Carter presidency continue to serve as cornerstones of American policy in the Middle East.

USES OF FORCE

Carter refrained from using force through much of his presidency, and there were only two significant military episodes during his tenure. The first was a mission to provide logistical support to the government of Zaire in response to an invasion of the country by Katangan rebels supported by Cuba.[53] Carter ordered the U.S. Air Force to transport Moroccan soldiers into Zaire to assist the government's fight against the insurgents, and the rebellion was crushed.

The second—and more famous incident—was the 1980 mission to save the American hostages held by Iran since the previous year. This undertaking, known as Operation Eagle Claw, is one of the best-known covert actions—and failures of action—in American military history. The rescue mission, undertaken by an elite unit known as the Delta Force, was aborted while in progress. President Carter wrote of the failed mission in his memoirs: "I am still haunted by memories of that day—our high hopes for success, the incredible series of mishaps, the bravery of our rescue team, the embarrassment of failure, and above all, the tragic deaths in the lonely desert. I actually slept a couple of hours, and then got up early to prepare my television broadcast, which would explain to the American people what had occurred."[54] Both of these missions were unilateral presidential actions, and the hostage rescue mission was a tightly held secret until it was aborted.

OTHER EXECUTIVE ACTIONS

Carter also undertook a number of unilateral actions that do not fit neatly into the other categories. Most of these dealt with challenges in the area of foreign policy.

One of the greatest accomplishments of American foreign policy in the twentieth century came with the 1978 signing of the Camp David Peace Accords between Israel and Egypt. This agreement represented the beginning of a more active role for the United States in Middle Eastern affairs, specifically in the Arab-Israeli peace process.

Another set of unilateral actions by Carter pertained to China policy. In 1979 he extended full diplomatic recognition to the People's Republic of China, completing the American embrace of the PRC begun with Richard Nixon's historic "opening to China" in 1972. Concomitant with this recognition, Carter abrogated the mutual defense treaty that the United States had had with Taiwan (although Congress passed and Carter signed the Taiwan Relations Act that year to guarantee protection of the island). While Carter's critics could not stop recognition of the PRC, Senator Barry Goldwater (R-Ariz.) did sue the president over his authority to terminate the Taiwan treaty. In *Goldwater v. Carter* (1979), the Supreme Court upheld Carter's action.[55]

Carter also came to employ executive unilateralism in innovative ways. Twice, he bypassed Congress on nuclear arms control by issuing (in tandem with the Soviet Union) parallel unilateral policy declarations (PUPDs) on arms control. The first, in 1977, provided for the extension of the SALT I treaty, which was due to expire. The second, in 1980, implemented the SALT II treaty despite the fact that the president had asked a hostile Senate to suspend consideration of the treaty. These PUPDs—parallel statements issued by the United States and the Soviet Union to declare a mutual policy without a signed agreement—enabled Carter (and his successors) to circumvent congressional opponents (and the Arms Control and Disarmament Act of 1961) and make arms-control policy unilaterally.[56] Subsequently, both Ronald Reagan and George H. W. Bush would rely on Carter's precedents to maintain presidential dominance over nuclear arms-control policy.

Carter also exerted his executive power as a national leader during the Soviet invasion of Afghanistan. The president's decision to boycott the 1980 Summer Olympics in Moscow was one of the most controversial decisions of his entire presidency. Carter made the bold decision to announce the planned boycott days before the Iowa caucuses for the 1980 presidential election and a short time before the opening of the 1980 Winter Olympic Games in Lake Placid, New York. While the president had no formal power over the American Olympic delegation, his role as national leader is evident here. In this case, the executive powers of the presidency extended beyond those codified in the Constitution and law.

JIMMY CARTER'S UNILATERALISM

Jimmy Carter came to the presidency as an outsider who proclaimed that he would do things differently than his predecessors had. As it turned out, he discovered that achieving his policy goals and dealing with various problems required employing many of the same kinds of unilateral powers that Gerald Ford and others had exercised. At key points in his presidency, Carter relied on executive unilateralism to govern and to advance his policy goals. By the time he left Washington in January 1980, his staff was advising the incoming Reagan team to devote some time and attention to exploring the outer reaches of the president's constitutional powers.[57]

Conclusion

In 1974, Richard Pious commented on a particularly widespread popular belief by asking "Is presidential power 'poison'?" The 1970s saw Richard Nixon expand the Vietnam War into Cambodia, impound funds appropriated by Congress, open diplomatic negotiations with China, and conclude the SALT I treaty with Moscow, and then it witnessed the collapse of the Nixon presidency over Watergate. Congress, emboldened in its resolve to take on the "imperial presidency" thanks to the influx of Democrats in its ranks after the 1974 midterm elections, seemed uninterested in deferring to executive power. It ordered an end to the war in Vietnam and prohibited the Ford administration from intervening in the civil war in Angola in 1975. Congress was so determined to demonstrate its independence and power that some scholars described the period as one with "foreign policy by Congress."[58] In domestic policy, Congress passed the Budget and Impoundment Act of 1974 to outlaw impoundment and strengthen its role in the budget process. As a result of these and other actions, the post-Watergate period seemed to be a time of legislative government in the United States.

In the face of such assertiveness, the presidency was seen as being at a low point in its power and prestige. Commentators searched for terms to describe the turn of events, calling the presidency "post-imperial," "tethered," and even "impossible." In this context, Gerald Ford and Jimmy Carter were widely interpreted as good men facing insurmountable obstacles to success and the use of presidential power. One of us went so far as to describe the period as an "interregnum."[59]

Hindsight is often much clearer, however, than contemporary observations, and it is apparent that the Ford-Carter years were not unrelieved periods of executive weakness. Certainly, Ford and Carter faced tough odds in their efforts to govern, but they were neither wholly unsuccessful nor weak. Both presidents employed unilateral executive power, even in the face of congressional opposition. Both presidents found ways to gain leverage in dealing with Congress and had greater influence over policy than they are often given credit for. Most important, both presidents asserted unilateral presidential powers that enhanced their own autonomy and served as key precedents for unilateral actions by their successors.

Given the empirical record reviewed in this study, one might view the Ford-Carter era as a kind of prehistory of the Reagan-Clinton-Bush presidencies. Contrary to the widespread notion that the Ford and Carter administrations were chastened presidencies, distinct from the assertive unilateralism of the early twenty-first century, those years were a time in which the White House sought autonomy for presidential action.

This quest for autonomy took two major forms. In the first form, Presidents Ford and Carter relied on well-established presidential powers to act independently or to restrain Congress. Ford used his veto power to confront Congress over spending, pardon Richard Nixon, and provide a clemency program for Vietnam-era draft evaders, and he issued executive orders to ban assassinations as an instrument of American foreign policy. Carter also employed the veto to confront Congress over spending priorities, granted amnesty to draft evaders, and issued executive orders to shape policy on intelligence and trade, as well as to halt oil imports from Iran in response to the hostage crisis in Iran.

In the second form of autonomy, Presidents Ford and Carter employed unilateral powers based on more contestable sources of authority. Each employed signing statements to proclaim that he would regard some provision in an act of Congress as advisory to the president and not binding on the executive. Each made claims of executive privilege, issued foreign policy directives, and ordered the use of force when he thought it necessary. Moreover, each of these presidents undertook other unilateral actions that did not fall neatly into the established categories of presidential authority. Carter, for example, insisted on a U.S. boycott of the 1980 Summer Olympics in Moscow, although he lacked any real authority to do so.[60] Despite the gloss on the Ford-Carter period as one of executive weakness, each president was willing to employ both conventional and less conventional means of unilateral executive powers to shape policy.

In light of this view of Ford and Carter, the unilateralism of the George W. Bush presidency can be seen as part of a larger story rather than an anomalous episode. The political history of the post-Watergate presidency is one of almost continuous striving by presidents to enhance and secure autonomy in policymaking. In response to the events of September 11, 2001, George W. Bush was particularly aggressive in asserting executive autonomy, but he was not breaking with some long-standing tradition of executive restraint. Rather, the record of the Ford and Carter years demonstrates that George W. Bush built on precedents laid down in that time. Perhaps neither Ford nor Carter would have agreed with the way in which their precedents have been appropriated by Bush (indeed, Jimmy Carter has been a critic of the Bush presidency), but that is the nature of precedent: one cannot always control how it is used.

To what extent did Ford and Carter employ unilateral executive power? The answer is that they did so more than we often realize, that they did so both to promote their goals and to protect the interests of the presidency, and that they did so in ways that set the post-Watergate presidency on a path toward greater autonomy and independence from Congress.

What do the Ford-Carter years say about the nature of presidential power? The answer here is that presidential power is not just a function of personal power, as Neustadt would argue, but that it also includes the various institutional powers and resources at the disposal of the chief executive. These resources include the president's ability to act unilaterally, whether in well-established ways (vetoes, pardons) or innovative ones (signing statements, PUPDs). Executive unilateralism is more than a sign of failed bargaining; it can enhance the president's leverage in the near term and contributes to expanded institutional power in the future.

The Ford-Carter years also suggest that the Obama presidency is likely to be marked by continued use of executive unilateralism. President Obama may want to distinguish himself from his immediate predecessor, but there is no reason to believe that he will not employ conventional and less conventional unilateral actions to advance his agenda. The record of Presidents Ford and Carter suggest that President Obama, like these incumbents from the era of the "post-imperial presidency," will employ a variety of means to enhance his autonomy and promote his policy goals. Whether the means are well established or innovative, the president can increase his leverage in the pulling and hauling of America's separated system.

Notes

1. Christopher S. Kelley, "The Unitary Executive and the Presidential Signing Statement" (PhD diss., Miami University, Ohio, 2003).

2. Richard E. Neustadt, *Presidential Power and the Modern Presidents* (New York: Free Press, 1990), 28, 32. See also Raymond Tatalovich and Thomas S. Engeman, *The Presidency and Political Science* (Baltimore: Johns Hopkins University Press, 2003).

3. See Ryan J. Barilleaux, "Venture Constitutionalism and the Enlargement of the Presidency," in *Executing the Constitution: Putting the Presidency Back into the Constitution,* ed. Christopher S. Kelley (Albany: State University of New York Press, 2006), 37–52.

4. David Nather and Martin Kady II, "Gerald Ford, 38th President, Mourned by Nation," http://www.nytimes.com/cq/2006/12/27/cq_2064.html (accessed February 8, 2007).

5. Gerald R. Ford, "Address to a Joint Session of Congress, August 12, 1974," http://www.presidency.ucsb.edu/ws/?pid=4694 (accessed February 8, 2007).

6. Gerald Ford, quoted in "Presidential Conversations on the Constitution," http://www.whyy.org/tv12/presidents/issues.html#vp (accessed February 13, 2007).

7. Gerald R. Ford, *A Time to Heal* (New York: Harper and Row, 1979), 341–44, 412.

8. John Robert Greene, *The Presidency of Gerald R. Ford* (Lawrence: University Press of Kansas, 1995), 77.

9. James Cannon, *Time and Chance* (New York: HarperCollins, 1994), 403.

10. Quoted in ibid., 403 (original emphasis).

11. Barry Werth, *31 Days: The Crisis That Gave Us the Government We Have Today* (New York: Doubleday, 2006), 221. See also Ford, *A Time to Heal,* 179.

12. Werth, *31 Days,* 316–19.

13. Ford, *A Time to Heal,* 142.

14. Gerald Ford, "Statement on Signing the Forest and Rangeland Renewable Resources Planning Act of 1974," August 18, 1974, http://www.presidency.ucsb.edu/ws/?pid=4443 (accessed January 25, 2007).

15. Gerald Ford, "Statement on Signing the Amtrak Improvement Act of 1975," May 26, 1975, http://www.presidency.ucsb.edu/ws/print.php?pid=4937 (accessed February 6, 2007).

16. Gerald Ford, "Statement on Signing the Social Services Amendments of 1974," January 4, 1975, http://www.presidency.ucsb.edu/ws/?pid=4783 (accessed February 6, 2007).

17. Gerald Ford, "Statement on Signing the Federal Fire Prevention and Control Act of 1974," October 29, 1974, http://www.presidency.ucsb.edu/ws/?pid=4517 (accessed February 6, 2007).

18. Gerald Ford, "Statement on Signing a Bill Amending Child Support Provisions of the Social Security Act," August 11, 1975, http://www.presidency.ucsb.edu/ws/print.php?pid=5168 (accessed February 6, 2007).

19. Gerald Ford, "Statement on Signing the Department of Defense Appropriation Act, 1976," February 10, 1976, http://www.presidency.ucsb.edu/ws/index.php?pid=6277 (accessed February 13, 2007).

20. See Ryan J. Barilleaux, *The Post-Modern Presidency: The Office after Ronald Reagan* (New York: Praeger, 1988), 85–86.

21. Gerald Ford, "Executive Order 11,905," February 18, 1976, http://www.presidency.ucsb.edu/ws/index.php?pid=59348 (accessed February 15, 2007).

22. Kristin Eichensehr, "On the Offensive: Assassination Policy under International Law," http://hir.harvard.edu/articles/1149/ (accessed February 15, 2007).

23. Gerald Ford, "Proclamation 4410—Termination of Temporary Quantitative Limitation on the Importation into the United States of Certain Beef and Veal from Canada," December 31, 1975, http://www.presidency.ucsb.edu/ws/index.php?pid=920 (accessed February 14, 2007).

24. Gerald Ford, "Proclamation 4313—Announcing a Program for the Return of Vietnam Era Draft Evaders and Military Deserters," September 16, 1974, http://www.presidency.ucsb.edu/ws/index.php?pid=4714 (accessed February 14, 2007).

25. Gerald Ford, "Proclamation 4345—Program for the Return of Vietnam Era Draft Evaders and Military Deserters," January 30, 1975, http://www.presidency.ucsb.edu/ws/index.php?pid=23803 (accessed February 14, 2007).

26. Louis Fisher, *The Politics of Executive Privilege* (Durham, N.C.: Carolina Academic Press, 2004), 247–48.

27. Ibid., 246–47.

28. Anthony Clark Arend, "Gerald Ford and the Helsinki Accord," http://explore.georgetown.edu/blogs/?id=21610 (accessed February 15, 2007; original emphasis).

29. See, for example, "Moscow Helsinki Group's 30th Anniversary," http://www.state.gov/r/pa/prs/ps/2006/66134.htm (accessed February 15, 2007).

30. National Security Decision Memorandum 280, November 28, 1974, http://www.ford.utexas.edu/library/DOCUMENT/NSDMNSSM/nsdm280a.htm (accessed February 15, 2007).

31. National Security Decision Memorandum 286, February 7, 1975, http://www.ford.utexas.edu/library/DOCUMENT/NSDMNSSM/nsdm286a.htm (accessed February 15, 2007); National Security Decision Memorandum 305, September 15, 1975, http://www.ford.utexas.edu/library/DOCUMENT/NSDMNSSM/nsdm305a.htm (accessed February 15, 2007).

32. National Security Decision Memorandum 345, January 18, 1977, http://www.ford.utexas.edu/library/DOCUMENT/NSDMNSSM/nsdm345a.htm (accessed February 15, 2007).

33. Ford, *A Time to Heal,* 283.

34. This incident is discussed at length in Werth, *31 Days,* esp. 335–36.

35. Quoted in Don Richardson, ed., *Conversations with Carter* (Boulder, Colo.: Lynne Rienner Publishers, 1998), 11, 16.

36. Jimmy Carter, "Veto of the Department of Defense Appropriation Authorization Bill Message to the House of Representatives Returning H.R. 10929 without Approval, August 17, 1978," http://www.presidency.ucsb.edu/ws/print.php?pid=31195 (accessed February 17, 2007).

37. Jimmy Carter, "Veto of Public Debt Extension Bill Message to the House of

Representatives Returning H.R. 7428 without Approval, June 5th, 1980," http://www.presidency.ucsb.edu/ws/print.php?pid=45222 (accessed February 17, 2007).

38. Jimmy Carter, "Proclamation 4483—Presidential Proclamation of Pardon, January 21, 1977," http://www.presidency.ucsb.edu/ws/print.php?pid=7255 (accessed February 17, 2007).

39. Jimmy Carter, "Commutation of G. Gordon Liddy's Prison Sentence Announcement, with the Text of the Order, April 12th, 1977," http://www.presidency.ucsb.edu/ws/print.php?pid=7345 (accessed February 17, 2007).

40. Interview with Patty Hearst, *Larry King Live,* CNN, January 22, 2002, http://transcripts.cnn.com/TRANSCRIPTS/0201/22/lk1.00.html (accessed March 2, 2007).

41. Jimmy Carter, "Presidential War Powers Bill Statement on Signing H.R. 7738 into Law, December 28th, 1977," http://www.presidency.ucsb.edu/ws/print.php?/pid=7071 (accessed February 17, 2007).

42. Jimmy Carter, "Amtrak Improvement Act of 1978 Statement on Signing S. 3040 into Law, October 5th, 1978," http://www.presidency.ucsb.edu/ws/print.php?pid=29935 (accessed February 17, 2007).

43. Jimmy Carter, "Proclamation 4702—Oil Imports from Iran, November 12th, 1979," http://www.presidency.ucsb.edu/ws/print.php?pid=31675 (accessed February 17, 2007).

44. Mark J. Rozell, *Executive Privilege: The Dilemma of Secrecy and Democratic Accountability* (Baltimore: Johns Hopkins University Press, 1994), 102.

45. Ibid., 103–104.

46. Ibid., 106.

47. Quoted in ibid., 105–106.

48. Jimmy Carter, "United States–Australia Agreement on Nuclear Energy Message to the Congress Transmitting the Agreement, July 27th, 1979," http://www.presidency.ucsb.edu/ws/print.php?pid=32655 (accessed March 4, 2007).

49. Jimmy Carter, "United States–European Economic Community International Fishery Agreement Message to the Congress Transmitting the Agreement, February 21st, 1977," http://www.presidency.ucsb.edu/ws/print.php?pid=6743 (accessed March 3, 2007).

50. Jimmy Carter, "United States–Canada Transit Pipeline Agreement Message to the Senate Transmitting the Agreement, March 30th, 1977," http://www.presidency.ucsb.edu/ws/print.php?pid=7257 (accessed March 4, 2007).

51. Presidential Directive 59, July 25, 1980, http://www.jimmycarterlibrary.org/documents/pddirectives/pd59.pdf (accessed February 7, 2007).

52. Presidential Directive 63, January 15, 1981, http://www.jimmycarterlibrary.org/documents/pddirectives/pd63.pdf (accessed February 7, 2007).

53. Lyn Ragsdale, *Vital Statistics on the Presidency* (Washington, D.C.: Congres-

sional Quarterly, 1996), 311; Jimmy Carter, *Keeping Faith: Memoirs of a President* (Toronto: Bantam, 1982), 222.

54. Carter, *Keeping Faith,* 518.

55. *Goldwater v. Carter* 444 U.S. 996 (1979).

56. See Ryan J. Barilleaux, "Executive Non-Agreements, Arms Control, and the Invitation to Struggle in Foreign Affairs," *World Affairs* 148 (fall 1986): 217–27.

57. See Barilleaux, "Venture Constitutionalism and the Enlargement of the Presidency," 37.

58. Thomas Franck and Edward Weisband, *Foreign Policy by Congress* (New York: Oxford University Press, 1979).

59. Barilleaux, *The Post-Modern Presidency,* 55.

60. Terence Smith, "The President Said Nyet," *New York Times,* January 20, 1980, http://www.nytimes.com/packages/html/sports/year_in_sports/01.20.html (accessed December 3, 2008).

The Unitary Executive and Review of Agency Rulemaking

MELANIE MARLOWE

A feeble executive implies a feeble execution of the government. A feeble execution is but another phrase for a bad execution; and a government ill executed, whatever it may be in theory, must be, in practice, a bad government.
—ALEXANDER HAMILTON, "FEDERALIST NO. 70"

Beginning with the first administration under the Constitution of 1789, American presidents have sought to control policy formation and the actions of subordinates in the departments and agencies of the federal government. This search for control has largely been accomplished through the issuance of executive orders and presidential proclamations to individuals serving in the executive branch. The first executive order, signed by George Washington, required officials in the new government who had been in office under the Articles of Confederation to submit a report that would give him "a full, precise, and distinct general idea of the affairs of the United States" in their domain.[1] The Proclamation of Neutrality, issued by Washington in 1793, instructed government officials to prosecute individuals who violated the terms of the proclamation.[2] In the twentieth century, presidents attempted, through various means, to gain control over a growing bureaucratic government. Theodore Roosevelt sought to limit communication between government officers and members of Congress. He issued Executive Order 163, prohibiting employees of executive departments from attempting to influence legislation "before Congress or its committees."[3] Franklin Roosevelt, president during two of the greatest crises in the history of the United States, established new agencies designed to exercise some measure of control over the American economy.[4] He also signed an executive order moving the Bureau of Budget from the Department of Treasury to the Executive Office of the President.[5] Lyndon Johnson issued Executive Order 11,246, requiring executive agency and department heads to "establish and maintain a program of equal employment opportunity."[6]

With the rise of the administrative state, and particularly with the rapid growth of federal regulatory activity since 1970, presidents have made a special effort to gain some control of the agency rulemaking process in order to develop a unified, coordinated regulatory program that is consistent with, or at least not subversive of, their policy priorities. Attempts to exercise this control have been met with varying reactions from Congress, which creates federal agencies, federal courts, and, increasingly in recent years, public interest groups. Challenges to presidential control over the federal bureaucracy have been based on assertions that such control is both unconstitutional and bad policy.[7]

This chapter describes the development of presidential review of regulatory policy and focuses on President Nixon and his successors. It explains the programs these presidents implemented and some of the criticisms and institutional obstacles they confronted, and it concludes with a consideration of what greater executive oversight of regulatory activity might hold for the future. While presidents have been able to exert more control over some aspects of agency rulemaking, there remain questions about the constitutional foundations of and practical purposes served by the exercise of presidential regulatory review. Constitutionally and practically, oversight of regulatory review properly belongs with the president.

The Unitary Executive

The text of the Constitution is clear: Article II vests "the executive Power in a President of the United States." Unlike the authority granted to Congress in Article I and to the federal judiciary in Article III, Article II includes no qualifying provision in the vesting clause that would diminish the grant of authority or indicate that either of the other branches of government has the executive power.[8]

At the Constitutional Convention, the framers rejected proposals for a plural executive or an executive council in favor of one president who would hold office with the possibility of being reelected indirectly by the people.[9] Hamilton argued that the unitary nature of the executive could be "destroyed in two ways: either by vesting the power in two or more magistrates of equal dignity and authority, or by vesting it ostensibly in one man, subject in whole or in part to the control and cooperation of others, in the capacity of counselors to him."[10]

Article I, section 8, provides Congress with the authority to create executive departments and officers necessary to assist the president in the execution of the responsibilities of office. Congress, however, may not create officers entirely isolated from presidential control; such a move would impede the ability of the president to execute those responsibilities as the Constitution requires.[11]

The president must "take Care that the laws be faithfully executed," making the chief executive also the nation's chief law enforcement officer. The "Executive" must "execute."[12] The president must administer the laws Congress makes and may announce the implementation of laws through orders and proclamations. Unless Congress has made an explicit requirement to the contrary, the president may exercise broad discretion in determining which laws may apply in a particular situation and how these laws will be enforced. Presidents may also have to rely on their independent constitutional judgment in determining what the law means and how prosecutions for violations will proceed.[13]

The "opinion" clause of the Constitution is essential for understanding presidential oversight of executive agency activity. That clause states that "the President . . . may require the Opinion in writing, of the principal Officer in each of the executive Departments, upon any subject relating to the duties of their respective Offices."[14] Hamilton thought this idea so obvious that, when writing "Federalist No. 74," he somewhat disparaged its inclusion in the Constitution: "This I consider as a mere redundancy in the plan, as the right for which it provides would result of itself from the office."[15] Presidents may rely upon their subordinates for advice, but they may respond to this advice, and it is clear that presidents are to make the final judgment. Were they unable to do so, their control over the executive branch may equate to simply making sure salaries are paid and lunch breaks extended to no more than one hour.

Because presidents have the executive power, they may choose to execute federal laws personally. Most often, however, presidents will enlist others to serve at their direction. Presidents would be able to appoint individuals, with the exception of "inferior" officers, to assist in their responsibilities.[16] The power to appoint gives presidents the ability to select individuals based on criteria they believe is important for the execution of their offices and with the understanding that the president exercises influence over these individuals.

The framers understood that the multiplication of executive power within and outside the executive branch would have "a direct tendency to conceal faults, and destroy responsibility," which would "leave people in suspense" as to whom they should blame when a particular course of action led to bad results.[17] But because the nature of the executive office requires assistance, and the ultimate constitutional responsibility for the execution of laws lies with the president, subordinates in the executive branch must understand that failure to obey the commands of the president may result in dismissal. It is a logical extension of this power that if presidents may dismiss an agency head, they may overrule that officer's discretionary judgment.[18]

Executive Orders

An executive order is one of several unilateral tools presidents may use to carry out their policy objectives. Executive orders direct executive branch officers to "take an action, stop a certain type of activity, alter policy, change management practices, or accept a delegation of authority under which they will henceforth be responsible for the implementation of law."[19] Presidents have come to favor the use of executive orders because they provide speed and flexibility and bypass the complicated legislative process, particularly when it appears Congress may be hostile to a president's goals. In *Wilcox v. Jackson* the Supreme Court affirmed that presidents may issue orders through department heads.[20] These orders will have the same legal effect as if the president had issued them personally.[21]

The preamble of a typical modern executive order explains the constitutional and statutory authority of the president to issue the order, and the body of the order explains the actions to be taken or policy changes to be made. Most of the significant developments in presidential regulatory review have been initiated by executive orders. (Unless otherwise specified, none of the regulatory review orders discussed in this chapter was based on anything besides the authority vested by the Constitution in the president and a general reference to statutes of the United States.[22])

President Nixon

In 1970, as part of a larger executive branch reorganization plan and with hopes of gaining some control over rapidly increasing regulatory activity, President Nixon transformed the Bureau of the Budget into the Office of Management and Budget (OMB).[23] It was not to be a change in name only. In his message to Congress accompanying the plan, Nixon noted that it would be a "change in concept and emphasis, reflecting the broader management needs of the Office of the President. . . . The new Office of Management and Budget will place much greater emphasis . . . on assessing the extent to which programs are actually achieving their intended results." Agencies would continue to gauge program effectiveness, but OMB would support the president's efforts to coordinate policy and evaluate consistency across agency lines.[24] At a time when the regulatory burden on the economy was an issue of increasing significance, Nixon expected the changes to save government, businesses, and citizens money through "improved efficiency" and by "curtailing the waste that results when programs simply fail to achieve their objectives."[25]

At first OMB exercised oversight only of regulations proposed by the newly created Environmental Protection Agency (EPA). The growing number and expense of its staff and programs were of particular concern and became a frequent target for administrative action.[26] OMB review was later extended to cover other executive agencies concerned with public health and safety and consumer protection under what became known as the "quality of life" (QOL) review.[27] The QOL review directed agencies to provide OMB with draft regulations at least thirty days before initial publication in the *Federal Register.* An analysis of the regulation's goals and anticipated costs and benefits would supplement the drafts. Proposed rules would be subject to public comment and review by sister agencies, and any interagency disputes over rule substance or effects would be settled with OMB guidance before regulation publication.[28] Final rules followed a similar, abbreviated process.

Several criticisms were leveled at the QOL process, including the charge that on paper QOL was applied to several executive agencies but in practice was applied only to the EPA.[29] QOL, it was said, was simply a way for administration officials to interfere with and delay for extended periods (up to two years) the implementation of environmental rules that might have adverse effects on favored industries, which were heavily represented among various Cabinet department officials.[30] Opponents of

QOL also claimed that manipulation of "procedural techniques, such as interagency review," would give challengers an opportunity to step in.[31] Furthermore, interagency comments were not included in the public record, thus limiting substantive discussion and giving rise to questions about how decisions were made.[32]

The goals of the Nixon process were met with mixed success. Although OMB did not have the authority to directly overrule an agency's final decision, the office did have an impact on EPA regulations, as the agency relaxed regulations in order to avoid regulatory review, fulfilling to some extent the wishes of the administration.[33] The EPA also developed an internal clearance process to carefully review proposed regulations.[34] However, the growth of regulatory activity continued apace in the last few years of the Nixon administration as several prominent regulatory agencies were established and the *Federal Register* more than doubled in size.[35]

President Ford

President Ford retained the Nixon administration's QOL review program, but he made his own mark on the regulatory review process. On November 27, 1974, he issued Executive Order 11,821, which gave the newly organized Council on Wage and Price Stability (CWPS) the authority to evaluate proposed agency regulations.[36] "Major legislative proposals, regulations, and rules" were to be submitted to the CWPS for an economic analysis according to standards created by OMB. Drafted rules would be accompanied by an "inflation impact statement" demonstrating that any proposal's effect on competition and productivity had been carefully considered in relation to the public benefits it might provide. CWPS provided written reviews that were included in the public record. In contrast to the Nixon review process, under Ford the EPA was not a target of regulatory reform.[37] It should be noted that although CWPS was empowered to review agency proposals, it did not have the authority to demand that agency officials make changes. In the end, if an agency rule's costs outweighed its benefits, it was up to the agency head to make a final determination on implementation.[38]

Executive Order 11,821 was challenged in federal district court in *Independent Meat Packers Association v. Butz.*[39] Plaintiffs argued that because the secretary of agriculture had not complied with the inflationary impact evaluation established in the order, regulations promulgated by his department were not binding. The district court ruled that the department's evaluation was "arbitrary, capricious," and "an abuse of discretion," and it issued a preliminary injunction to stop implementation of the regulations.[40] The Eighth Circuit Court of Appeals reversed the district court's decision, holding that the order was promulgated "primarily as a managerial tool for implementing the President's *personal economic policies* [emphasis added] and not as a legal framework enforceable by private action." Therefore, judicial review was not available in this matter.[41]

Because the procedures introduced by the Ford program encouraged but did not require agencies to participate in the review process, the program had limited practical effect.[42] However, reports by the American Bar Association and the House Committee on Energy and Commerce found that the review process forced agencies to improve their methods of economic analysis and opened a way for more assertive presidential control of agency administration.[43]

President Carter

In 1975, David Johnson and future White House counsel Lloyd Cutler published an article in the *Yale Law Journal* advocating greater presidential control of agencies.[44] Johnson and Cutler noted that the scope of agency regulatory activity, particularly in economic policymaking, had greatly increased. They argued that while much of this activity was accepted by the public, serious concerns about political accountability remained. There was growing recognition that the work of agencies was not always value free. Much of the rulemaking in which administrative bureaucracies engaged involved making "choices between competing social and economic values and competing alternatives for government action."[45] Particularly in a time of economic insecurity and limited resources, more participation by "politically accountable decisionmakers" was required in a democratic regulatory process.[46]

Immediately upon taking office, Carter administration officials began developing plans for enlarging executive oversight of agency activity, but in a way that promoted public participation and political responsibility.[47] A draft executive order regarding regulatory review was finally published in the *Federal Register* on November 18, 1977.[48] It was accompanied by a memo from Wayne Granquist, associate director for management and regulatory Policy, seeking public comment on the order and asking whether the order should apply to independent regulatory agencies.[49] President Carter believed it should, the public in general supported that view, and the Justice Department opined that applying some provisions would be legally permissible.[50] However, hoping to steer clear of a "confrontation with Congress" that "would only detract from the important reform steps being taken," Carter's final order did not apply to independent agencies, although he did request that these agencies voluntarily comply with its provisions.[51]

Executive Order 12,044, "Improving Government Regulations," was issued on March 23, 1978, and immediately went into effect. In his statement accompanying the order, President Carter commented that the "Federal Government has become like a foreign country, complete with its own interests and its own language." This order, he promised, would make "Federal regulations clearer, less burdensome, and more cost-effective."[52] These goals were addressed in the first section of the order.[53]

The second section of the order required agendas of proposed significant rules to be published semiannually, mandated review of these regulations by agency heads, and called for a public participation and comment period in order to encourage a "meaningful" regulatory process.[54]

Section three of Executive Order 12,044 directed agencies to prepare regulatory impact analyses (RIAs) for proposed regulations that would have an effect of at least $100 million per year or would have "major economic consequences" for the general economy or particular industries, regions of the country, or levels of government.[55] The analysis was to demonstrate that alternative regulations had been considered and that the most cost-effective regulation had been selected for implementation.

Carter established two new executive oversight organizations: the Regulatory Analysis Review Group (RARG) and the Regulatory Council. The RARG, with members from OMB, the Council of Economic Advisers, and other executive branch agencies, was charged with reviewing important regulations, coordinating the regulatory review process, and monitoring agency compliance.[56] The Regulatory Council, which had members from all executive departments and agencies as well as from several independent regulatory commissions, had the responsibility of ensuring the semiannual publication of pending and proposed rules. The Regulatory Council was also charged with previewing regulations to coordinate consistent rulemaking among agencies with overlapping subject areas.[57]

Carter's regulatory review program met a challenge in *Sierra Club v. Costle*, which was decided during the Reagan administration.[58] This case involved a White House meeting between President Carter and EPA administrator Douglas Costle during which they discussed pending new source performance standards for coal-fired power plants before the final rules were published. The meeting was not reported in the EPA's rulemaking record, spurring environmental groups to charge that the ex parte communications were a violation of due process.[59] In her opinion, Judge Patricia Wald recognized a constructive role for the president in the rulemaking process: "The authority of the President to control and supervise executive policymaking is derived from the Constitution; the desirability of such control is demonstrable from the practical realities of administrative rulemaking. Regulations such as those involved here demand a careful weighing of cost, environmental, and energy considerations. They also have broad implications for national economic policy. Our form of government simply could not function effectively or rationally if key executive policymakers were isolated from each other and from the Chief Executive."[60] In the last few months of the Carter administration, Congress passed the Regulatory Flexibility Act of 1980, which required federal agencies to write regulations in a way that would reduce the costs of small business compliance.[61] The law was to take effect January 1, 1981, and therefore did not have any effect on regulations issued during the Carter administration.

In December 1980, just weeks before he left office, President Carter signed the Paperwork Reduction Act (PRA), which took effect when Reagan came into office.[62] This legislation established the Office of Information and Regulatory Affairs (OIRA) in the OMB. OIRA would monitor agencies' compliance with PRA's goal of reducing federal reporting requirements, and it came to play a significant role in regulatory review in succeeding administrations.

Like the Nixon and Ford programs, Carter's did not impose sanctions for noncompliance, and the final determination on economic analysis remained with agency heads. Even though President Carter's review program did not have the teeth that succeeding programs would have, he did have some success in formalizing a stronger role for the president in regulatory policymaking.[63]

President Reagan

In his speech accepting the Republican nomination for president in 1980, candidate Ronald Reagan promised "a government that will not only work well, but wisely." He refused to "accept the excuse that the federal government has grown so big and powerful that it is beyond the control of any president, any administration, or Congress."[64]

Reagan wasted no time in acting on his promise. On January 22, 1981, his second full day in office, President Reagan announced the creation of the Presidential Task Force on Regulatory Relief (TFRR), to be chaired by Vice President Bush and composed of the secretaries of commerce, labor, and treasury, as well as the chair of the Council of Economic Advisers, the attorney general, the OMB director, and a presidential assistant. The purpose of the Cabinet-level TFRR was to "coordinate an interagency effort to end excessive regulation."[65] TFRR would evaluate pending regulations on the bases of compelling need, the burden on the economy, and benefits to society. Executive Order 12,288, which terminated CWPS, was issued on January 29.[66] In his opening statement at a news conference on that day, the president accused the CWPS of imposing "unnecessary burdens on labor and business." He also announced the imposition of a sixty-day freeze on pending federal regulations in order to prevent more than one hundred rules issued in the last month of the Carter administration from going into effect.[67]

On February 18, 1981, President Reagan addressed a joint session of Congress and outlined his plan to revitalize the dismal national economy. In this message he introduced a plan to cut taxes, proposed cuts in government spending, and announced that on February 17 he had signed an executive order that would reduce the regulatory burden felt by taxpayers, workers, and business owners across the country.[68] Noting the recent enormous growth in agencies' budgets and the numbers of regulations these agencies produced, he promised that the Office of Management and Budget would work to alleviate the situation.

The issuance of Executive Order 12,291 surprised not only members of Congress but also members of the president's Cabinet.[69] The preamble explains the goals of the order: to "reduce the burdens of existing and future regulations, increase agency accountability for regulatory actions, provide for presidential oversight of the regulatory process, minimize duplication and conflict of regulations, and insure well-reasoned regulations."[70] The order's provisions, designed to fulfill these goals, are the tools of a president making an aggressive attempt to rein in what he considered to be an expensive, unrestrained bureaucracy.

Whereas President Carter's order 12,044 examined regulations and encouraged cutting costs, Executive Order 12,291 considered a regulation's costs and justified those against its benefits. Each federal agency was required to provide the director of OMB with a regulatory impact analysis for proposed or final rules. "Major rules" were those that might have an economic impact of at least $100 million annually or those that could impose significant costs on "consumers, individual industries," or local, state, or national governments by adversely affecting "competition, employment, investment, productivity, innovation," or the ability of American businesses to compete with foreign companies.[71]

Section 2 prohibited agencies from implementing regulations where the RIAs demonstrated that the costs outweighed the benefits.[72] Agencies were required to choose the alternative that imposed the "least net cost to society."[73] OMB, not each agency, was given the substantive authority to establish the definitions and standards used in agency analysis.[74]

Section 3 dictated that after an agency submitted an RIA, the OMB director could either clear it or notify the agency of further OMB or interagency review. The RIA or proposed regulation could not be published until OMB had completed its review.[75] The director's decisions could be reviewed by the vice president's task force.[76] Finally, OMB was authorized to commence review of existing regulations and supervise agency compliance with Executive Order 12,291.[77]

Executive Order 12,291 was challenged on both constitutional and policy grounds. The most serious constitutional charge was that the president did not have the authority to issue the order based on the vesting clause and a reference to broad statutory powers.[78] This challenge also included the argument that by issuing the order, the president usurped the legislative prerogatives of Congress.[79]

Critics also claimed that the rulemaking requirements of the Administrative Procedures Act, particularly those regarding public comment and recordkeeping, took precedence over any order the president might give.[80] The order, however, purported to apply only "to the extent allowed by law," professing to recognize the agencies' statutory responsibilities and thus limiting the order as a basis for legal challenges. There was concern, especially in the early years of the Reagan administration, that OIRA communications were insufficiently maintained in the public record.[81]

Opponents further argued that the substantive criteria set out in Executive Order 12,291 would effectively give the administration, via OIRA, the ability to indefinitely stall regulation publication or even displace agency discretion.[82] There was particular concern, at the time of the order's issuance and in the years after, that environmental regulations would be a favorite target of the regulatory review process and that this would frustrate the will of Congress in an entire policy field.[83] Other criticisms included the inability (for technical and political reasons) of OMB to properly measure regulatory impact and benefits and the suggestion that OMB was simply biased against regulation.[84]

Pressure by organized interests, especially environmental groups, led Congress to reject reauthorization of the Paperwork Reduction Action, in 1983, and thus the OIRA, which received its statutory authority from that act. Congress's action did not matter, however; "Reagan countered by instructing OIRA to do what it had always done," and the office continued functioning, funded, but without act authorization, in 1984 and 1985. A deal with congressional leaders was finally struck in 1986 whereby the Paperwork Reduction Act was reauthorized with OIRA funding, but agency heads would now be subject to Senate confirmation and OIRA would have more public disclosure requirements.[85]

On January 4, 1985, just prior to his second inauguration, President Reagan issued Executive Order 12,498, "Regulatory Planning Process."[86] As with Executive Order 12,291, this order was based on his constitutional authority as president of the United States and gave the director of the OMB the authority to monitor agencies' compliance with the order. Regulatory oversight would extend to the planning process to coordinate a prospective regulatory program that was coherent and in accord with the broader policy goals of the administration.

The order required agencies covered by Executive Order 12,291 to provide OMB, at the beginning of each year, with a "draft regulatory program" that explained all possible regulatory actions for the calendar year.[87] The director of OMB would then assess agency compliance with 12,291 and overall policy consistency among agencies and could recommend regulatory or deregulatory actions to the agencies.[88] This kind of review benefited the administration by giving it an idea of what regulations might be forthcoming *prior* to actual drafting, at the time when it is easiest to shape the content of the regulations.

Together, the Reagan orders constituted a major shift in the way executive regulatory oversight was conducted. The orders drew fire because they were the most sweeping claims of regulatory oversight power a president had asserted to that time. However, succeeding administrations essentially established their regulatory review programs on the principles of these orders.

President George H. W. Bush

President Bush continued to rely on the Reagan executive orders as the basis for his regulatory program, but he created a new interagency organization in order to solidify executive oversight of the process. The Council on Competitiveness was established in March 1989 with Vice President Dan Quayle as its chair and with permanent council membership that included the director of OMB, the secretaries of commerce and the treasury, the attorney general, the White House chief of staff, and the chair of the president's Council of Economic Advisers.[89] The purposes of the council were to review regulations, eliminate those that had an adverse effect on American competitiveness, and resolve disagreements between agencies and OIRA.

The industry-friendly makeup of the council provided a basis for environmentalists' concerns that EPA regulations would continue to fall victim to regulatory review. The council's first major determination stopped a provision in a proposed rule that would have required municipalities to recycle (instead of incinerate) a quarter of incoming solid waste.[90] Environmentalists were particularly infuriated that OMB had previously cleared this regulation but then acquiesced to the will of the council. When the decision to delete the provision was challenged in *New York v. Reilly*, the Court of Appeals for the District of Columbia held that EPA "supported its new view of the materials separation policy with adequate evidence" and that the process was "neither arbitrary nor capricious."[91] Even though the EPA had been encouraged to reevaluate its rules at the suggestion of the council, the court found sufficient support in the rulemaking record to provide a foundation for the agency's change of position.

Throughout the Bush administration, Congress's hostility to his system of regulatory review was evident. The Senate refused to confirm the president's nominee for OIRA administrator, a position that remained vacant for the duration of the administration.[92] Reacting to what it considered the council's unwarranted secrecy, conflicts of interest, and excessive power to control agency discretion, various subcommittees of the House Government Operations Committee held investigative hearings. Finally, OIRA was not reauthorized by the 102nd Congress.[93]

President Bush was clearly not opposed to all regulatory measures. He signed the Clean Air Act of 1990 and the Americans with Disabilities Act and supported regulations in areas such as banking, tax policy, and airplane noise. In fact, the numbers of regulations under review and of people writing them increased significantly in the first three years of the Bush administration when compared with the entire eight years of the Reagan administration.[94] But because of the difficult state of the economy and the need to shore up his business base before the election in November, on January 28, 1992, President Bush issued a memorandum to certain agency and department heads asking them to place a ninety-day moratorium on regulation issuance and to focus instead on evaluating current rules and hastening "action on initiatives that will eliminate any unnecessary regulatory burden or otherwise promote economic growth."[95] The moratorium, which was extended for another four months, affected regulations in drug testing, workplace safety, and endangered species.[96]

Those who hoped the antiregulatory leanings of the Reagan years would continue were disappointed by the enthusiasm President Bush displayed as he signed legislation that created regulatory gold mines. However, Bush did demonstrate a willingness to confront Congress over OIRA and to restrict regulatory activity when the economy (and his personal interests) called for it, and the Council on Competitiveness did manage to delay the promulgation of some rules the administration opposed.

President Clinton

President Clinton wasted no time in seizing control of the administrative tools of government. On his first full day in office, January 21, 1993, he eliminated the Council on Competitiveness, and incoming OMB director Leon Panetta canceled all as-yet unpublished rules proposed by the Bush administration.[97] Vice President Al Gore would be given a large role in the administration's regulatory program.

In September 1993 President Clinton issued Executive Order 12,866, which revoked Executive Orders 12,291 and 12,498 and detailed the young administration's regulatory review process.[98] The preamble to the order emphasized the need to "reaffirm the primacy of Federal agencies in the regulatory decisionmaking process." Several parts of the Clinton program resembled the regulatory review legacy left by Reagan. In both instances, the vice president was given important authority in the review process, and OIRA was the reviewing and coordinating agency. Rules having an economic impact of at least $100 million, which were likely to disturb other agency activity and which raised new legal and policy issues, were of particular concern and would be subject to cost-benefit analysis.[99]

Other features of the order included a regulatory working group involving the heads of important domestic agencies and the vice president.[100]

The OIRA administrator was to be the chair, and the group was to meet at least four times a year. The purpose of the group was to "assist agencies in identifying and analyzing important regulatory issues." The group had the authority to commission informational reports by any agency, and the vice president could designate existing regulations as needing review. OIRA review was to take no more than 90 calendar days, thus avoiding charges of purposeful delay that previous administrations had heard.[101] The process was to be more public than were reviews from previous administrations, and there was a requirement that proposed regulations returned to an agency by OIRA for reconsideration must be accompanied by "a written explanation for such return."[102]

In some respects, the Clinton order implemented a review process that provided for more executive oversight than the Reagan administration had implemented. For example, for the first time, independent agencies would now be subject to participation in the regulatory plan. They would also be required to reconsider proposed rules that might conflict with the "President's priorities" or other agency activity.[103]

A stronger presidential presence is also seen in section 7, which addresses disagreements among agency heads or between OMB and an agency. In instances where the OIRA administrator is unable to satisfactorily reconcile differences, the order states, the president or vice president will step in to resolve disputes, and "the President or Vice President acting at the request of the President . . . shall notify the affected agency . . . of the President's decision with respect to the matter."[104] Elena Kagan, deputy director of the Domestic Policy Council in the Clinton administration, boldly notes that this provision indicates "something significant about the relationship between the agencies and the President—to say that they were *his* and so too were their decisions."[105]

Following the Republicans' winning a majority of congressional seats in the 1994 midterm elections, the Clinton policymaking strategy focused on avoiding the obstacle of a hostile Congress and thus became solidly administrative.[106] To this end, the number of memoranda to agency heads skyrocketed from fifteen issued in his first three years in office to ninety-two in his last five years.[107] President Clinton understood these memoranda, which were designed to initiate administrative activity, as a means of commencing and directing his policy preferences on such topics as hate crimes, environmental concerns, and food safety. Executive orders were issued requiring agency compliance with the administration's land, environmental, and labor policy preferences.[108]

Congress did pass the Congressional Review Act, which required agencies to send major regulations to the General Accounting Office, where they are assessed for compliance with existing laws.[109] If Congress is not satisfied with the proposed regulation, it may enact a joint resolution of disapproval.

President Clinton did have one significant setback to his administrative strategy. It originated in his issuance of Executive Order 12,954 on March 8, 1995.[110] This order established the administration policy that "contracting agencies shall not contract with employers that permanently replace lawfully striking employees." In the order, the president cited the problems that "prolonged labor disputes" have on the "economy, efficiency, and cost of operations" of the federal government and noted that when contractors hire permanent replacement workers, a "broader, more contentious struggle" is likely to ensue, thus "exacerbating the problems that initially led to the strike." As sources for his authority to issue the order, President Clinton cited "the Constitution and the laws of the United States of America, including 40 U.S.C. 486(a) and 3 U.S.C. 301" (the Federal Property and Administrative Services Act, or FPASA).[111]

The Chamber of Commerce of the United States led a coalition of business organizations in federal court to challenge the order. The federal district court concluded that the FPASA was a sufficient statutory basis for the order. Relying on *AFL-CIO v. Kahn,* the court determined that the executive order was reasonably related to economic matters and that there was a plausible nexus between the FPASA's goals of "economy and efficiency" and removing federal contractors who hire replacements from the government contract pool.[112]

On appeal, the appellants argued that the National Labor Relations Act permitted employers doing business with the federal government to hire replacement workers and that that statute preempted Executive Order 12,954.[113]

Judge Laurence H. Silberman of the appeals court relied on *NLRB v. MacKay Radio and Telegraph Co.,* which acknowledged the right of employees to strike but also upheld the right of an employer to hire permanent replacement workers during an economic strike.[114] The appeals court also chided the administration for its claim that the executive order was narrowly tailored to meet the demands of the FPASA. Judge Silberman noted that the order was not simply designed to affect the administration of the executive branch but that it was an obvious attempt to directly affect the employment conditions of millions of workers.[115] In the end, the court ruled that the order was "regulatory in nature" and thus an improper use of the president's authority to issue executive orders.[116] The case was not appealed to the Supreme Court.

The Clinton regulatory review program was broad in jurisdiction and deep in scope, even profoundly affecting private rights traditionally considered outside the field of normal presidential interference, such as child labor, land, and nondiscrimination policies.[117] This breadth of coverage was especially helpful for a president who came into office with just 43 percent of the popular vote and who needed a mechanism for effecting his policies. The more open nature of the program, compared to those of the two previous administrations, was a relief to supporters and perhaps drew attention away from what may have been more controversial components of the order, such as requirements imposed on the independent agencies and the possibility of direct intervention by the president.[118] Executive Order 12,866 firmly established a role for oversight of a pro-regulatory program.

President George W. Bush

The election of George W. Bush brought hope to those who believed that the regulatory review process had been misused during the Clinton administration. Early signals from the White House were encouraging to that group, the first sign being the distribution of a memo by OIRA administrator John Graham on September 20, 2001.[119] The memo, which was issued to officials at more than twenty departments and agencies, announced that Executive Order 12,866 would continue in effect "until a modified or new Executive order is issued" and reaffirmed the place of OIRA in the regulatory review process. The memo also reasserted the importance of RIAs and the administration's requirement that these be attached to all rules that may have an "economically significant" impact as determined by OIRA, "regardless of the extent to which an agency is permitted by law to consider risks, costs, or benefits in issuing a regulation." OIRA could return a rule to an agency for reconsideration if OIRA found a problem with the agency's analysis or if the resulting rule was not consistent "with the President's policies and priorities" or "other Executive orders or statutes." "Reconsideration" was a feature of the Clinton regulatory review process, but it was rarely used.[120]

One of the more striking features of Graham's memo is the introduction of the "prompt letter," which OIRA could issue to agencies at the request of OMB to "suggest an issue that OMB believes is worthy of agency priority."[121] OIRA would expect a response to the prompt letter within thirty days.

President Bush did make some noteworthy changes to the Clinton regulatory review process. Executive Order 13,258, issued in February

2002, transferred the vice president's authority in the review process, established under Executive Order 12,866, to the White House chief of staff or the director of OMB.[122]

On January 18, 2007, Executive Order 13,422 was issued, making other significant changes to Executive Order 12,866.[123] While Executive Order 12,866 called for identification of the problem to be solved, Executive Order 13,422 required each covered agency to "identify in writing the specific market failure . . . or other specific problem" that any rule might be intended to fix. The new order did not specify where the identification would be published or to whom it had to be made available (e.g., the public). In the order, "market failure" was clearly defined and appeared to be a—if not the—primary concern of the administration.[124]

Executive Order 13,422 also required each agency head to "designate one of the agency's Presidential Appointees to be its Regulatory Policy Officer," without whose approval "no rulemaking shall commence nor be included" in the annual regulatory plan.[125] This is a more active role than that of the regulatory policy officer under Executive Order 12,866, who would "be involved in each stage of the regulatory process" and was to ensure agency compliance with presidential priorities.[126] The agency head under order 12,866 was not restricted to selecting regulatory policy officers from among presidential appointees.[127]

A third important modification of Executive Order 12,866 was the requirement that significant guidance documents, which are used to explain laws and regulations, had to be reviewed by OIRA. The Bush administration had concerns that these documents were quasi-regulatory in themselves, as they outlined what kind of behavior would be compliant with regulations. The regulatory policy officer was required to "ensure the agency's compliance" with this provision.[128]

Reaction to the order by consumer and environmental interests was strongly critical, while representatives of business groups praised the president's action.[129] Sally Katzen, OIRA administrator in the Clinton administration, told a House committee that problems "caused by market failures are in a favored class and possibly the only class warranting new regulations."[130] The new regulatory policy officer provisions caused concern that the presidential-agency relationship would become so politicized that the agencies would not be able to carry out their missions. Finally, as with other review programs, doubts about the transparency of the process remained.

Congress was also displeased with the antiregulatory possibilities of the order. On June 28, 2007, in an amendment to an appropriations bill, the House of Representatives voted to deny OMB funding for the implementation of Executive Order 13,422.[131] The Senate did not take action on the bill.

As required by the Clean Air Act, the EPA administrator was required to establish primary (public health) and secondary (public welfare) national ambient air quality standards (NAAQS) for pollutants, including ozone. On February 22, 2008, EPA submitted to OIRA its final regulation setting ozone standards. EPA proposed tightening the primary standard to 75 parts per billion and the secondary standard to 70 parts per billion, the first time that the two standards would be set at different levels. Two weeks later, on March 6, OIRA administrator Susan E. Dudley issued a memo to EPA administrator Steve Johnson requesting further analysis of the benefits to be achieved by setting the public welfare standard tighter than the public health standard and asking for clarification of this in the record.[132]

Marcus Peacock, EPA regulatory policy officer, promptly responded to the memo. He defended his agency's position, telling Dudley that "EPA appreciates the concerns raised but believes they have been addressed in the existing proposal."[133] Administrator Steve Johnson planned to introduce the new regulation at a press conference set for 1:00 P.M. on March 12, the statutorily imposed deadline.[134]

On March 12, Dudley reported to Johnson that the "President has concluded that, consistent with Administration policy, added protection should be afforded to public welfare by strengthening the secondary ozone standard and setting it to be identical to the new primary standard," both at 75 parts per billion.[135] Johnson postponed the press conference until 6:00 P.M., at which time he announced the standards formulated by the president.

The president's personal intervention in the dispute between EPA and OMB was criticized by John Walke, clean-air director of the National Resources Defense Council, as an "unprecedented and an unlawful act of political interference."[136] Business interests and local government concerned with compliance costs were relieved.

President Bush largely relied on the strong Clinton order for most of his presidency. It was when he was faced with a hostile Congress after the 2006 midterm elections that he developed a more aggressive oversight program. Columbia law professor Peter Strauss speculated that President Bush was perhaps following the post-1994 strategy of President Clinton:

"Having lost control of Congress, the president is doing what he can to increase his control of the executive branch."[137]

Bush's Executive Order 13,422 regularized the articulation of particular problems to be addressed, forcing agencies that might be more sympathetic to a Democratic Congress to further clarify just what it was they were seeking to accomplish. The president knew he had a loyal ally in each agency in the form of the regulatory policy officer. This individual could be a valuable source of information for the president and was able to influence agency officials to pursue the president's plans. However, as was demonstrated in the example of the ozone standards, even the regulatory policy officer could have policy disagreements with the president.

Conclusion

It is clear that whatever one thinks of the legal or political questions surrounding presidential review of regulatory activity, such review has become an established power that the president holds and will not give up any time soon. The framers created an executive who was to be accountable for the execution of the laws, and thus the president should exert significant control over how agency discretion is exercised. If Congress wants to retain control over regulatory activity, it should clearly spell out its intentions in legislation. When Congress fails to do so, presidents have the ability to weigh competing claims and make determinations in the rulemaking process. They have a constitutional responsibility to "take Care that the Laws be faithfully executed" and, in so doing, must use their best judgment. In addition, the other institutions of government are reluctant or unable to discourage presidential review of agency activity. In fact, as we have seen from the Clinton and George W. Bush examples, it may be when Congress is most hostile that the president may make the most aggressive moves to oversee agency activity.

When Congress has moved to restrict or disrupt the president's regulatory review authority, the president has defended his program. President Reagan continued OIRA in the absence of the authorization of the Paperwork Reduction Act. President George H. W. Bush refused to nominate an OIRA administrator who would be a tool of the Congress and instead gave the Council on Competitiveness more responsibility. Although presidents have made some concessions that are disappointing to defenders of the unitary executive (such as Reagan agreeing to submit the OIRA head to Senate confirmation), presidents have made these concessions with a view toward the political circumstances at the time, not because they believed they were lacking constitutional authority to control the executive branch.[138]

Federal courts have exercised some review of the processes of agency rulemaking, but when there is general evidence in the rulemaking record for the agency's determination, a president's influence is usually supported and sometimes welcomed. Courts, however, should be wary of intervening in disputes that might restrict the ability of executive branch officials to communicate or otherwise carry out the constitutional responsibility to execute the laws. As we saw in the Clinton example, his executive order was overturned when he directly attempted to alter statutory law and a judicial ruling.

Finally, presidents and their advisers will continue to devise new methods of putting the federal agencies more closely under their watch. Presidents have regularized procedures such as cost-benefit analysis and the positioning of regulatory policy officers in order to maximize their information and limit agency discretion. Of course, how these methods are received by the other institutions of government and the public varies, but it matters to presidents as they seek to bind the agencies more closely to them and to legitimize and gain public support for their policies.

The Reagan orders were controversial. Those who opposed centralized presidential regulatory review generally argued that Congress had created federal agencies to be essentially independent of presidential control. There were also concerns that Reagan administration officials with antiregulatory inclinations would use the new procedures to dismantle social benefit programs through the use of cost-benefit analysis and reporting requirements. Those who supported the orders argued that, constitutionally, only the president has "the executive power." Presidents must "take Care that the Laws be faithfully executed," but this requires the assistance of others—others in the executive branch who are responsible to the president.

By the time President Clinton's Executive Order 12,866 was issued, there was little questioning of his legal authority. Most observers either supported or acquiesced in the view that the president could assert his priorities on regulatory agencies, especially as they realized that executive oversight did not have to mean deregulation.[139] The foremost issue may not be so much whether or not the president will engage in this kind of activity but whether it is done for regulatory or antiregulatory purposes.

The assertion of executive authority over agency rulemaking has been a wise development from a policy perspective. Centralized regulatory review helps presidents shape broad rulemaking agendas and determine agency priorities, and it forces them to hold themselves and their subordinates responsible for the execution of good government.[140] Most importantly, however, the practice is authorized by the Constitution, giving the president the ability to *lawfully* execute the laws.

Notes

1. Harold C. Relyea, "Presidential Directives: Background and Overview," *CRS Report for Congress*, April 23, 2007, 5, http://www.fas.org/irp/crs/98–611.pdf (accessed July 5, 2007).

2. George Washington, Proclamation of Neutrality, April 22, 1793, http://www.yale.edu/lawweb/avalon/neutra93.htm (accessed May 14, 2006).

3. Kenneth R. Mayer, *With the Stroke of a Pen: Executive Orders and Presidential Power* (Princeton: Princeton University Press, 2001), 115.

4. Frank B. Cross, "Executive Orders 12,291 and 12,498: A Test Case in Presidential Control of Executive Agencies," *Journal of Law and Politics* 4 (1988): 491.

5. Executive Order 8,248, Code of Federal Regulations, title 3, 217 (1939 Supp.).

6. Executive Order 11,246, Code of Federal Regulations, title 3, 339 (1964–1965 Comp.).

7. Morton Rosenberg, "Beyond the Limits of Executive Power: Presidential Control of Agency Rulemaking under Executive Order 12,291," *Michigan Law Review* 55 (December 1981): 193–247; Morton Rosenberg, "Presidential Control of Agency Rulemaking: An Analysis of Constitutional Issues That May Be Raised by Executive Order 12,291," *Arizona Law Review* 23, no. 4 (1981): 1205–20; Leon Rodriguez, "Constitutional and Statutory Limits for Cost-Benefit Analysis Pursuant to Executive Orders 12,291 and 12,498," *Boston College Environmental Affairs Law Review* 15 (1988): 505–46.

8. In Article I, Congress's powers are limited to those "herein granted." The power of the federal judiciary "shall extend to" particular instances of jurisdiction. The construction of the executive vesting clause and a comparison with those of the other branches also indicate that the president's enumerated powers are not the full extent of presidential power but are instead specified for emphasis.

9. Charles C. Thach, *The Creation of the Presidency, 1775–1789: A Study in Constitutional History* (Baltimore: Johns Hopkins University Press, 1969), 25–54.

10. Alexander Hamilton, "Federalist No. 70," *The Federalist Papers*, ed. Charles Kesler (New York: Penguin Books, 2003), 423.

11. *Bowsher v. Synar,* 474 U.S. at 478 (1986).

12. In his opinion in *In re Neagle*, Justice Samuel Freeman Miller wrote that the president's constitutional responsibility to "take care that the laws be faithfully

executed" includes not just "enforcement of acts of Congress or of treaties according to their express forms" but also "the rights, duties, and obligations growing out of the Constitution itself . . . and all the protection implied by the nature of the government under this Constitution." 135 U.S. 1 at 64 (1890).

13. "By the Constitution of the United States the President is invested with certain important political powers, in the exercise of which he is to use his own discretion, and is accountable only to his country in his political character, and to his own conscience." Chief Justice John Marshall's opinion in *Marbury v. Madison* 1 Cranch 137, 166 (U.S. 1803).

14. Article II, sec. 2, cl. 1.

15. Hamilton, "Federalist No. 74," http://thomas.loc.gov/home/histdox/fed_74.html (accessed June 2, 2009).

16. "The persons, therefore, to whose immediate management these different matters ["the administration of government"] are committed ought to be considered as the assistant or deputies of the chief Magistrate, and on this account they ought to derive their offices from his appointment, at least from his nomination, and ought to be subject to his superintendence." Hamilton, "Federalist No. 72," 434. This point is confirmed in *Williams v. United States:* "The President's duty in general requires his superintendence of the administration; yet this duty cannot require of him to become the administrative officer of every department and bureau, or to perform in person the numerous details incident to services which, nevertheless, he is, in a correct sense, by the Constitution and laws required and expected to perform." 42 U.S. 290 at 296 (1843).

17. Hamilton, "Federalist No. 70," 426.

18. Congress, for reasons that may include fear of political outcomes, disagreements within its branch, or a judgment that "experts" might evaluate rules more capably, frequently grants agency heads the authority to establish rulemaking standards. A president could not prevent an officer from performing a statutorily compelled ministerial act. *Kendall v. United States,* 37 U.S. at 524, 611 (1838).

19. Phillip J. Cooper, *By Order of the President: The Use and Abuse of Executive Direct Action* (Lawrence: University Press of Kansas, 2002), 16. Cooper also covers presidential memoranda, proclamations, national security directives, and signing statements in his study.

20. 38 U.S. 498 at 499 (Pet.) (1839).

21. "[T]he acts of the heads of departments, within the scope of their powers, are in law the acts of the President. . . . [A]n order sent out from the appropriate executive department in the regular course of business is the legal equivalent of the President's own order to the same effect." *Wolsey v. Chapman,* 101 U.S. 755, at 769–70 (1879).

22. Harold H. Bruff, "Presidential Power and Administrative Rulemaking," *Yale Law Journal* 88, no. 3 (January 1979): 465.

23. Executive Order 11,541, *Code of Federal Regulations,* title 3, 939 (1966–1970).

24. *Weekly Compilation of Presidential Documents* 6 (March 16, 1970), 355.

25. Ibid., 356.

26. George C. Eads and Michael Fix, *Relief or Reform? Reagan's Regulatory Dilemma* (Washington, D.C.: Urban Institute Press, 1984), 47.

27. House Committee on Energy and Commerce, *Presidential Control of Agency Rulemaking: An Analysis of Constitutional Issues That May Be Raised by Executive Order 12,291,* 97th Cong., 1st sess., June 15, 1981, Committee Print 97–0, 10 (hereafter, 1981 House Report).

28. Ibid.; Bruff, "Presidential Power and Administrative Rulemaking," 464–65.

29. Robert V. Percival, "Checks without Balance: Executive Office Oversight of the Environmental Protection Agency," *Law and Contemporary Problems* 54, no. 4 (1991): 135; Barry D. Friedman, *Regulation in the Reagan-Bush Era: The Eruption of Presidential Influence* (Pittsburgh: University of Pittsburgh Press, 1995), 28.

30. 1981 House Report, 10–11. For example, the Department of Commerce frequently opposed EPA rules. Bruff, "Presidential Power and Administrative Rulemaking," 464.

31. Bruff, "Presidential Power and Administrative Rulemaking," 464.

32. Ibid.; 1981 House Report, 10.

33. Leon Rodriguez, "Constitutional and Statutory Limits," *Boston College Environmental Affairs Law Review* 15 (1988): 513.

34. Eads and Fix, *Relief or Reform?* 50.

35. Percival, "Checks without Balance," 139.

36. 39 *Federal Register* 41501 (November 29, 1974). This order was amended by Executive Order 11,949 on December 31, 1976, and expired on December 31, 1977.

37. Percival, "Checks without Balance," 140.

38. 1981 House Report, 11; Robert V. Percival, "Presidential Management of the Administrative State: The Not-So-Unitary Executive," *Duke Law Journal* 51 (2001): 987.

39. 395 F. Supp. 923, 932 (D. Neb. 1975).

40. Ibid., 933.

41. *Independent Meat Packers Association v. Butz,* 526 F.2d 228, 235, 236 (8th Cir., 1975), cert. denied, 424 U.S. 966 (1976). In order to clearly distinguish inflation impact statements from the environmental impact statements used as a basis for litigation under the National Environmental Protection Act, President Ford issued Executive Order 11,949 in December of 1976, which changed the name of the inflation impact statement to "economic impact analysis." 42 *Federal Register* 1017 (1977).

42. Percival, "Checks without Balance," 140.

43. 1981 House Report, 11; American Bar Association Commission on Law and the Economy, *Federal Regulation: Roads to Reform* (Washington, D.C.: American Bar Association, 1979), 85 (hereafter ABA Report).

44. Lloyd N. Cutler and David R. Johnson, "Regulation and the Political Process," *Yale Law Review* 84, no. 7 (June 1975): 1395–1418.

45. Ibid., 1399, 1402.

46. Ibid., 1399.

47. Eads and Fix, *Relief or Reform?* 55; Edward P. Fuchs, *Presidents, Management, and Regulation* (Englewood Cliffs, NJ: Prentice-Hall, 1988), 51.

48. 42 *Federal Register* 59742 (November 18, 1977).

49. Ibid., 59741; "A majority of the [ABA Law and Economy] Commission regrets this omission. Many of the independent agencies have been entrusted with primary missions that may conflict with other statutory goals, and they ought to be subjected to the same balancing discipline as other regulatory agencies." ABA Report, 85.

50. Fuchs, *Presidents, Management, and Regulation,* 52; Bruff, "Presidential Power and Administrative Rulemaking," 499.

51. 43 *Federal Register* 12670 (March 23, 1978). A confrontation would have been forthcoming, as the Democratic chairs and ranking Republicans of several important Senate committees, as well as various House members, were prepared for just that. James E. Anderson, "The Carter Administration and Regulatory Reform: Searching for the Right Way," *Congress and the Presidency* 18, no. 2 (autumn 1991): 9; President Jimmy Carter, letter to the heads of independent regulatory agencies, *Public Papers of the Presidents of the United States* (March 23, 1978), 563.

52. Statement on Executive Order 12,044, *Public Papers of the Presidents of the United States* (March 23, 1978), 561.

53. Executive Order 12,044, *Code of Federal Regulations,* title 3, 152 (1979).

54. Ibid., sec. 2(a), at 153, sec. 2(b), at 153, sec. 2(c) and (d), at 153–54.

55. Ibid., sec. 3(a)(1), at 154.

56. 1981 House Report, 11.

57. Paul R. Verkuil, "Jawboning Administrative Agencies: Ex Parte Contacts by the White House," *Columbia Law Review* 80 (1980): 948–49.

58. *Sierra Club v. Costle,* 657 F.2d 298 (D.C. Cir. 1981).

59. Ibid., 404.

60. Ibid., 406. Judge Wald did leave the door open for the federal courts to review future claims of excessive executive interference in the rulemaking process. Ibid., 408.

61. Public Law 96–354, *U.S. Statutes at Large* 94 (1980): 1164.

62. Public Law 96–511, *U.S. Statutes at Large* 94 (1980): 2812.

63. Verkuil, "Jawboning Administrative Agencies," 949; Cross, "Executive Orders 12,291 and 12,498," 495.

64. Reagan acceptance speech, July 17, 1980, http://www.millercenter.virginia.edu/scripps/digitalarchive/speeches/spe_1980_0717_reagan (accessed November 14, 2007).

65. Ronald Reagan, "Remarks Announcing the Presidential Task Force on Regulatory Relief," *Public Papers of the President of the United States* (January 22, 1981), 33–34.

66. Executive Order 12,288, "Termination of the Wage and Price Regulatory Program," *Code of Federal Regulations,* title 3, 424 (1979 Comp.).

67. Ronald Reagan, "The President's News Conference of January 29, 1981," *Public Papers of the President of the United States* (January 29, 1981), 64–65.

68. Executive Order 12,291, *Code of Federal Regulations,* title 3, 127 (1981); Ronald Reagan, "Program for Economic Recovery: Address before Joint Session of Congress," 17 *Weekly Compilation of Presidential Documents* 17 (February 18, 1981): 130.

69. James F. Blumenstein, "Regulatory Review by the Executive Office of the President: An Overview and Policy Analysis of Current Issues," *Duke Law Journal* 51, no. 3 (December 2001): 859–60.

70. Executive Order 12,291, *Code of Federal Regulations,* title 3, 127 (1981).

71. Executive Order 12,291, 3(c)(2), at 129, 1(b)(3), at 128.

72. Ibid., 2(b), at 128.

73. Ibid., 2(d), at 128. The order recognized that not all costs can be "quantified in monetary terms." Ibid., 3(d)(1)–(4), at 129.

74. Ibid., 6(a)(2), at 131.

75. Ibid., 3(e)(1), at 129.

76. The task force was disbanded in August 1983.

77. Ibid., 6(a)(5)–(8), at 131.

78. Rosenberg, "Beyond the Limits of Executive Power," esp. 195–220.

79. Presidents Carter and Reagan in particular wanted to issue orders to preempt legislation Congress was considering but that they opposed. Rosenberg, "Beyond the Limits of Executive Power." The Department of Justice issued a legal memorandum just days prior to the signing of 12,291, stating that precedent in *Myers v. United States* and the dissent in *Youngstown Sheet and Tube Co. v. Sawyer* provided ample authority for the president's general supervisory role. U.S. Department of Justice, Memorandum, "Proposed Executive Order Entitled 'Federal Regulation,'" *Opinions of the Office of Legal Counsel* 5 (February 13, 1981): 60. The OLC opinion also cited the "opinion" clause of the Constitution as providing the president with a

"constitutional right to consult with officials in the Executive Branch." Ibid., 62. This memo also claimed that the president had the authority to constitutionally apply at least some provisions of the order to independent agencies, but in the end this was not done. Seven independent agencies ultimately voluntarily complied. Friedman, *Regulation in the Reagan-Bush Era,* 78.

80. Erik D. Olson, "The Quiet Shift of Power: Office of Management and Budget Supervision of Environmental Protection Agency Rulemaking under Executive Order 12,291," *Virginia Journal of Natural Resources* 2 (1984): 1–80b; Andrew Jack, "Usurpation of Legislative Power or Blueprint for Legislative Reform?" *George Washington University Law Review* 54, no. 4 (May 1986): 530–31.

81. Executive Order 12,291, sec. 2, at 128 (quote); Percival, "Presidential Management of the Administrative State," 991.

82. Percival, "Presidential Management of the Administrative State," 991; Rosenberg, "Beyond the Limits of Executive Power," 214–15.

83. See *Environmental Defense Fund v. Thomas,* 627 F. Supp. 566, 570 (D.D.C. 1986). In this case, OMB prevented the EPA from issuing a rule after a statutory deadline for its completion had passed. The court found that OMB could not use it review procedures to indefinitely delay rulemaking requirements beyond statutory deadlines. The court did note that some "deference must be given to the authority of the President to control and supervise executive policy making." Ibid.

84. Alan B. Morrison, "OMB Interference with Agency Rulemaking: The Wrong Way to Write a Regulation," *Harvard Law Review* 99, no. 5 (March 1986): 1066; Olson, "The Quiet Shift of Power," 40–43.

85. Terry Moe and Scott Wilson, "Presidents and the Politics of Structure," *Law and Contemporary Problems* 57, no. 2 (spring 1994): 40.

86. Executive Order 12,498, *Code of Federal Regulations,* title 3, 323 (1985).

87. Ibid., 2(a), at 324.

88. Ibid., 3(a)(i) and (ii), at 324.

89. Percival, "Checks without Balance," 155; Friedman, *Regulation in the Reagan-Bush Era,* 165.

90. Percival, "Checks without Balance," 155; Percival, "Presidential Management of the Administrative State," 994; "EPA Drops Plans to Require Waste Incinerators to Recycle," *New York Times,* December 21, 1990.

91. *New York v. Reilly,* 969 F.2d 1147, 1152–53 (D.C. Cir. 1992). "The fact that EPA reevaluated its conclusions in light of the Council's advice, however, does not mean that EPA failed to exercise its own expertise in promulgating the final rules." Ibid., at 1153.

92. James Blumstein, "Regulatory Review by the Executive Office of the President: An Overview and Policy Analysis of Current Issues," *Duke Law Journal* 51, no. 3

(December 2001): 857. Blumstein, the nominee, notes that because President Bush refused to put forward another nominee, more power was placed in the Office of the Vice President and, therefore, the Competitiveness Council. Ibid., 857.

93. Friedman, *Regulation in the Reagan-Bush Era,* 172. OIRA continued to operate, as an earlier reauthorization permitted funding to continue in case of a lapse.

94. David E. Rosenbaum and Keith Schneider, "Bush Is Extending Regulation Freeze as a Great Success," *New York Times,* April 29, 1992.

95. Memorandum on Reducing the Burden of Government Regulation, *Public Papers of the President of the United States,* 167 (January 28, 1992).

96. Rosenbaum and Schneider, "Bush Is Extending Regulation Freeze."

97. Martin Tolchin, "Rewriting the Rules: Last-Minute Bush Proposals Rescinded," *New York Times,* January 23, 1993. More than one hundred regulations were rescinded.

98. Executive Order 12,866, "Regulatory Planning and Review," *Code of Federal Regulations,* title 3, 638 (1993).

99. Ibid., 3(f), at 641–42.

100. Ibid., 4(c)(F)(7), at 643.

101. Ibid., 5(c), at 644, 6(b)(2), at 647.

102. Ibid., 6(b)(3), at 647.

103. Ibid., 4(c), at 642, 4(c)(5)–(6), at 643.

104. Ibid., 648.

105. Elena Kagan, "Presidential Administration," *Harvard Law Review* 114, no. 8 (2001): 2290.

106. "Clinton came to view administration as perhaps the single most critical—in part because [it was] the single most available—vehicle to achieve his domestic policy goals." Kagan, "Presidential Administration," 2281–82.

107. This number of directives far exceeds the total issued by Ronald Reagan (nine) and George H. W. Bush (four). Kagan, "Presidential Administration," 2294–95.

108. Kagan, "Presidential Administration," 2295. Reagan did not issue any directives ordering agency heads to initiate or complete rulemaking activity. Ibid., 2294.

109. Congressional Review Act of 1996, codified at *U.S. Code* 5 801(a)(2)(A)–802.

110. Executive Order 12,954, *Code of Federal Regulations,* title 3, 329 (1995).

111. Ibid., sec. 1, at 329.

112. *AFL-CIO v. Kahn,* 618 F.2d 784 (D.C. Cir.) (en banc), cert. denied, 443 U.S. 915 (1979); *Chamber of Commerce v. Reich,* 57 F.3d 1099 (D.C. Cir. 1995).

113. *Chamber of Commerce of the United States et al. v. Reich,* 74 F.3d 1322 at 3 (D.C. Cir. 1996).

114. *NLRB v. MacKay Radio and Telegraph Co.,* 304 U.S. 333 (1938).

115. "[T]he impact of the Executive Order is quite far reaching. It applies to all contracts over $100,000, and federal government purchase[s] totaled $437 billion in 1994, constituting approximately 6.5% of the gross domestic product. . . . Federal contractors and subcontractors employ 26 million workers, 22% of the labor force." *Chamber of Commerce v. Reich,* 74 F.3d 1322 at 52–53 (D.C. Cir. 1996).

116. *Chamber of Commerce v. Reich,* 74 F.3d 1322 at 55 (D.C. Cir. 1996).

117. Kagan, "Presidential Administration," 2292.

118. Kagan notes that most reviewers of the order were satisfied with its rhetoric, which seemed to play down "controversial aspects of the Regan oversight system." Kagan, "Presidential Administration," 2286.

119. John D. Graham, "Memorandum for the President's Management Council," September 20, 2001, www.whitehouse.gov/omb/inforeg/oira_review-process.html (accessed February 14, 2008).

120. Susan E. Dudley, "Bush's Rejuvenated OIRA," *Regulation,* winter 2001, 6.

121. http://www.reginfo.gov/public/jsp/EO/promptLetters.jsp (accessed February 12, 2008). The Bush administration issued two prompt letters in the days prior to the distribution of Graham's memo.

122. Executive Order 13,258, *Federal Register* 67 (February 28, 2002): 9386.

123. Executive Order 13,422, "Further Amendment to Executive Order 12,866 on Regulatory Planning and Review," *Federal Register* 72 (January 18, 2007): 2763.

124. The order explains "market failure" as "externalities, market power," and "lack of information." Executive Order 13,422, 1(a)(1), at 2763.

125. Executive Order 13,422, 5(b), at 2764, 4(b), at 2764.

126. Executive Order 12,866, 6(a)(2), at 645.

127. During the Clinton administration, the regulatory policy officer was usually the agency's general counsel, who was appointed by the president and confirmed by the Senate. Curtis W. Copeland, "Changes to the OMB Regulatory Review Process by Executive Order 13,422," *CRS Report for Congress,* February 5, 2007.

128. Executive Order 13,422, 7, at 2764.

129. Robert Pear, "Bush Directive Increases Sway on Regulation," *New York Times,* January 30, 2007.

130. Katzen testimony before House Committee on Science and Technology, Subcommittee on Investigation & Oversight, February 13, 2007. Reprinted as "Amending Executive Order 12,866: Good Governance or Regulatory Usurpation?" (AEI-Brookings Joint Center for Regulatory Studies, Washington, D.C.), 8, http://aei-brookings.org/admin/authorpdfs/redirect-safely.php?fname=../pdffiles/Testimony07–01_topost.pdf. There was also some concern that "market failure" would displace statutorily imposed standards, such as "best available technology" or "public health."

131. http://thomas.loc.gov/cgi-bin/bdquery/z?d110:HZ00461; http://www.ombwatch.org/article/articleview/3896/1/132?TopicID=1 (accessed March 20, 2008); Jim Abrams, "House Balks at Bush Order for New Powers," *Washington Post,* July 3, 2007.

132. Susan E. Dudley, Memorandum for Administrator Steve Johnson, March 6, 2008, http://www.reginfo.gov/public/postreview/Steve_Johnson_Letter_on_NAAQs_final_3–13–08_2.pdf (accessed March 27, 2008).

133. Marcus Peacock, Memorandum for Susan Dudley, March 7, 2008, http://www.reginfo.gov/public/postreview/Steve_Johnson_Letter_on_NAAQs_final_3–13–08_2.pdf (accessed March 27, 2008).

134. Juliet Eilperin, "Ozone Rules Weakened at Bush's Behest," *Washington Post,* March 14, 2008.

135. Susan Dudley, OIRA administrator, Memorandum to Stephen Johnson, EPA administrator, March 12, 2008, http://www.reginfo.gov/public/postreview/Steve_Johnson_Letter_on_NAAQs_final_3–13–08_2.pdf (accessed March 27, 2008).

136. Eilperin, "Ozone Rules Weakened at Bush's Behest."

137. Quoted in ibid.

138. "Should they go too far or too fast, or move into the wrong areas at the wrong time, they would find that there are heavy political costs to be paid. . . . It is a matter of strategy. . . . They have to pick their spots." Terry Moe and William Howell, "The Presidential Power of Unilateral Action," *Journal of Law, Economics, and Organization* 15 (1999): 138.

139. Some have implied that the "consensus" on presidential authority regarding regulatory review occurred because of sympathy for President Clinton's policies that favored regulation. Blumstein, "Regulatory Review by the EOP," 871; Kagan, "Presidential Administration," 2247–48. Blumstein questions whether those who supported President Clinton's assertion of oversight authority would offer the same support for a president with whom they disagreed on policy issues. Blumstein, "Regulatory Review by the EOP," 899. It is difficult to believe that, had George W. Bush asserted the authority over independent regulatory agencies that Executive Order 12,866 purported to do, he would have met with as little resistance as the Clinton administration did.

140. Thus, a body such as the Clinton administration's regulatory working group, which was able to call for reports and assess information, could assist the president in developing a cross-agency policy platform.

The Unitary Executive and the Clinton Administration

CHRISTOPHER S. KELLEY

The unitary executive and the George W. Bush administration may seem indistinguishable because Bush aggressively defended his actions by pointing to the provisions of the unitary executive. Unfortunately, that defense has led to the public perception that the unitary executive theory is intertwined with the Bush presidency without any consideration of the theory's historical underpinnings. Thus, for most Americans, before the Bush administration there was no unitary executive and after President Bush there is no longer a unitary executive. As this chapter demonstrates, the unitary executive existed in theory and practice before Bush came to power—and in a Democratic administration.

The Clinton administration often gets overlooked in discussions of the push toward the expansion of presidential power. Such discussions tend to begin with the Reagan administration and its dedication to restoring the powers of the presidency taken by an aggressive Congress in the years following Watergate and the resignation of President Nixon (the so-called "imperiled presidency" thesis).[1] The restoration continued through the George H. W. Bush administration, and the George W. Bush administration worked to restore the powers lost when the Clinton administration frittered them away for personal gain. While this is the story that partisans may like to tell, it is, much like all partisan logic, overlooking certain truths. And one truth is that the Clinton administration behaved very much like its Republican predecessors, to the advantage of its successor.

This chapter focuses on two important ways that the Clinton administration exercised and advanced "unitarian" power: by pulling the executive branch agencies closer to the White House in order to advance political goals and by protecting the president's right to exercise so-called "coordinate" constitutional power.

The Theoretical Backdrop of the Unitary Executive

The unitary executive theory began to be articulated inside the Reagan Justice Department and among members of the Federalist Society, a conservative legal organization. Those who advance its tenets often refer to themselves as "unitarians," not to be confused with the religious sect with which it shares its name.

The theory argues that the presidency, as a coordinate branch of government, is the only nationally elected public office (and is thus able to speak for the nation) and is responsible for independently interpreting the Constitution. As the representative of the entire public, the president may be held accountable for bills signed into law and for the way in which the law is administered. The core tenets of the theory give the president the sole authority to remove subordinate executive officers, the power to direct subordinate executive officers in their administration of the law, and the power to veto or nullify the way in which subordinate executive branch officers use discretionary executive power.[2]

The unitary executive is a constitutional theory of presidential power. It argues that presidents draw their power from three clauses in the Constitution. First, the "vesting" clause of Article II, section 1, gives the president *all of the executive power,* meaning the powers explicitly written into Article II and other executive power, or the so-called prerogative power. Second, the "oath" clause of Article II, section 1, acts as a shield, protecting the president from enforcing any law independently determined to be unconstitutional. This responsibility is shared by the president and the attorneys in the Department of Justice, in particular the Office of Legal Counsel (OLC), and with close advisors in the Office of the White House Counsel. And third, the "take care" clause of Article II, section 3, obligates the president, with the advice and assistance of subordinate executive officers, to take care that the laws are faithfully executed. As Michael Herz has argued, the "'Take Care' Clause insures that the president will not only execute the law personally, but also it obligates him to oversee the executive branch agencies to insure that they are faithfully executing the laws," as opposed to executing them without regard for the president's wishes or even executing them to satisfy the wishes of some other body, such as the Congress.[3]

Thus, each president since Reagan has advanced these core tenets of the theory—by using devices such as signing statements or executive orders or through justification via OLC opinions—but most of their actions have been beyond the view of Congress, the press, and the public.

While many believe that, since the theory arose from conservative groups, only Republican presidents have put it in practice, the Clinton administration positioned itself in 1993 to advance the cause of the unitary executive but never used the term *unitary executive* in defense of its actions.

Controlling the Regulatory Process

A key strategy of Republican presidents dating to the Nixon administration has been to neutralize the bureaucracy, which they believed was dominated by liberal Democrats who could frustrate their agenda. Thus, the Reagan administration usually gets the credit for advancing presidential control of the executive branch agencies.

The Reagan administration made the Office of Management and Budget (OMB)—and in particular the Office of Information and Regulatory Affairs (OIRA)—the primary protector of the Reagan vision inside the regulatory agencies. Reagan issued two important executive orders that would move the entire executive branch closer to the White House (and, more importantly, away from the Congress). The first, issued in 1981, was Executive Order 12,291.[4] The executive order allowed President Reagan to impose restraints on any regulation that cost the economy at least $100 million per year. If the agency or department could not justify the cost, it would have to go back and revise the regulation to balance the costs with the benefits. The OMB could force agencies to respond to its criticisms of the regulation, even forcing a withdrawal of those regulations whose costs could not be defended.

The second important order issued by the Reagan administration enhanced the first. In 1985, Reagan issued Executive Order 12,498 to gain even greater control over the regulatory process.[5] This order gave the White House greater control at the front end of the process, before a regulation was finalized—in fact, before it was written—by requiring all agencies to prepare annual reports on all "ongoing or contemplated rulemaking activities and to explain to OMB how such activities are 'consistent with the administration's regulatory principles."[6]

Taken together, these two orders injected the White House into the regulatory process in a way that no previous president could—in effect, installing an early warning alarm system that alerted the White House to potentially problematic rules. A rigorous cost-benefit system at the end ensured that the agency would issue regulations that satisfied important constituencies. As one regulator observed, "You don't spend two years thinking about a regulation without thinking about whether OMB is going to shoot it down."[7]

The George H.W. Bush administration continued this process of regulatory control begun by the Reagan administration. It would not, however, be able to continue using the OIRA as its muscle. In 1989, the Democrats, who controlled the Congress, were frustrated at their inability to assess just how much influence the Reagan administration was exerting over the executive branch agencies. In particular, they were concerned about the actions of the OIRA and were determined not to spend another year watching their influence over the regulatory process diminish. That year, the Democrats placed restrictive language in the Paperwork Reduction Act of 1989 that required the OMB to keep the Congress apprised of all communication it had with the regulatory agencies.[8] This drew a veto threat from the Bush administration, and when a compromise was worked out between the OMB and the Congress, it was scuttled by the White House Counsel's Office. Congress retaliated by refusing to reauthorize funding for OIRA, and it also refused to confirm Bush's appointment to head that office.[9]

Rather than return to the drawing board and work out a compromise with the Congress, the Bush administration simply pushed OIRA activities into the vice president's office, creating a new entity called the President's Council on Competitiveness or simply the Quayle Council. The Quayle Council was far more effective at influencing the regulatory process because it was not prohibited from having conversations with industry and was not influenced by congressional budgetary pressures. As one observer noted, the Quayle Council proved very effective in rewarding key Bush constituencies who were unable to win battles during the legislative process.[10]

When Bill Clinton won the presidency in 1992, he promised to break with the past—to govern differently than his immediate predecessors had. And to some, it appeared that he was sincere. Clinton abolished the Quayle Council but retained the underlying power to influence the regulatory process. As Elena Kagan, a policy advisor inside the Clinton administration, writes, "Clinton built on the legacy Reagan had left him to devise a new and newly efficacious way of setting the policy direction of agencies—of converting administrative activity into an extension of his own policy and political agenda."[11]

Thus, instead of obliterating this process and allowing bureaucrats to make decisions without pressure from the White House, the Clinton administration found the White House regulatory strategy of his predecessors too good to pass up. Kagan argues that the Clinton administration continued to use the OMB to

> manage a regulatory review process, but with certain variations from the Reagan and Bush model. At the front end of the regulatory process, Clinton regularly issued formal directives to the heads of executive agencies to set the terms of administrative action and prevent deviation from his proposed course. At the back end of the process (which could not but affect prior stages as well), Clinton personally appropriated significant regulatory action through communicative strategies that presented regulations and other agency work product, to both the public and other governmental actors, as his own, in a way new to the annals of administrative process.[12]

While the Reagan and Bush administrations both used the OMB as a negative in the regulatory process—to thwart any regulation that presented a cost on business—the Clinton administration used the OMB as a positive, to institute many of the social programs that Clinton was not able to get through the Congress, particularly after the Republicans achieved a majority midway through his first term. Clinton, it is clear, embraced what the unitary executive had to offer and used its powers to manage policy so as to achieve his own goals. And while President Clinton is not brought into the story of the unitary executive, it is clear, as I will describe below, that his actions both nurtured and perpetuated it.

When Clinton came to office in 1993, he quickly moved to exert influence over the regulatory process in a manner similar to how the Reagan and Bush administrations proceeded. He used a number of key unilateral devices—memoranda and executive orders—to obtain some measure of control. For example:

- On his first day in office, Clinton issued a memorandum to OMB and the executive branch agencies terminating the system put in place by the Quayle Council and made all new regulations subject to approval by a political appointee put in place by the Clinton administration.[13]
- Days later, he issued an executive order centralizing and coordinating all economic policy within a council that consisted entirely of Clinton political appointees.[14]

- In September 1993, Clinton issued another memorandum designed to directly connect the heads of agencies and departments with the political apparatus inside the White House in order to "streamline" the regulatory process by keeping these regulators updated on the Clinton agenda. Significantly, this memorandum broadened the circle of regulators to include the independent regulatory agencies and commissions, something that was unthinkable in the previous Republican administrations.[15]

Most significant was Executive Order 12,866, which replaced the two key Reagan orders, 12,291 and 12,498.[16] The word *replace* is actually deceptive because the new Clinton order incorporated the most important provisions of the two previous orders—giving the OMB the power of regulatory review and clearance, as well as requiring the agencies to give the White House the regulatory agenda for the year. One of the more significant changes made by the Clinton order was to extend regulatory planning to the independent agencies and commissions, which were then required, along with the other executive branch agencies, to send to the OMB their planned regulations for the upcoming year. As James Blumstein, an OMB official from the George H. W. Bush administration, observed, "The Clinton administration not only accepted, but also extended the *Unitarian* premises of the Reagan and Bush administrations" (emphasis added).[17]

The administration would come to depend on the regulatory strategy after the Republicans gained control of Congress in 1994, much to the consternation of the Congress. In an attempt to blunt Clinton's maneuvers, the Congress passed the Congressional Review Act of 1996, which was part of the Republican "Contract with America." The Congressional Review Act was folded into a larger bill that dealt with regulatory relief for small businesses.[18] The bill required all agencies to provide Congress and the General Accounting Office with a final rule.[19] If the rule was considered a "major" rule—costing the economy $100 million or more—then the Congress could prevent it from going into effect, assuming both chambers passed a resolution of disapproval and it was signed by the president. In all, the Congress was successful only once in overturning a rule—one that dealt with ergonomics in the workplace—after Clinton left office in 2001.[20]

President Clinton would use other unilateral methods to achieve political ends when he was unable to get the Congress to work with him. For instance, Clinton

- tapped a special Treasury fund to bail out Mexico in 1995;
- barred federal agencies from signing contracts with companies that permanently replaced striking workers;
- made 18 percent of executive position appointments temporary to skirt the Senate confirmation process;
- designated millions of acres of land as a national monument using a law passed during the Theodore Roosevelt administration;
- deployed military troops, despite enormous congressional opposition, justifying the action based on NATO and UN treaty obligations; and
- refused to discharge any military personnel who were HIV-positive despite a law requiring him to do so.[21]

Coordinate Construction

As I discussed at the beginning of the chapter, one of the major tenets of the unitary executive theory deals with the oath the president takes upon inauguration to "protect and defend" the Constitution of the United States. This oath means presidents are obligated—as a coordinate branch of government—to refuse enforcement of any law that they *independently* determine to be unconstitutional. While many suggest that the veto is the only tool the president may rely upon when faced with a law that is unconstitutional, historic practice has demonstrated that there are times when presidents face bills that cannot be vetoed, thus creating a dilemma. Do presidents in this situation veto a bill that is vital or do they sign it into law despite a part that would involve violating the oath of office? This question seemed to be on the minds of President Clinton and the legal team he assembled in the White House Counsels' Office and in the Office of Legal Counsel (OLC) inside the Department of Justice from the moment they took office.

In 1994, White House counsel Abner Mikva posed this very question to the OLC and received his answer from Walter Dellinger, head of the OLC. Dellinger's answer, in the form of an OLC memorandum, was titled "Presidential Authority to Decline to Execute Unconstitutional Statutes," and it was very much to the point. The president has, Dellinger wrote, "enhanced responsibility to resist unconstitutional provisions that encroach upon the constitutional powers of the Presidency. Where the President believes that an enactment unconstitutionally limits his powers, he has the authority to defend his office and decline to abide by it, unless he is convinced that the Court would disagree with his assessment. [However], if a resolution in the courts is unlikely and the President cannot look to a judicial determination, he must shoulder the responsibility of protecting the constitutional role of the presidency."[22] One of the mechanisms by which the president can best protect the office from enforcing unconstitutional provisions is the signing statement, something that received a great deal of attention during the George W. Bush administration.

The presidential bill signing statement is commentary the president makes when signing a bill into law. The history of the signing statement reaches back to the James Monroe administration, but its contemporary use as a weapon to protect the prerogatives of the presidency or to advance the president's preferences is credited to the Reagan administration. It was the Reagan administration that added the signing statement to the legislative history of bills signed into law, ostensibly to give it equal weight with congressional interpretations over the meaning of law.[23] The strategic use of the signing statement to challenge the constitutionality of law—to either refuse defense or refuse enforcement—was something that continued from Reagan's terms into the Clinton administration. And Clinton wanted the legal basis to use it right from the beginning of his first term in office and before he was faced with an opposition Congress.

In 1993, Walter Dellinger wrote a memo to Bernard Nussbaum, counsel to the president, titled "The Legal Significance of Presidential Signing Statements." In it, Dellinger argued that the president may use the signing statement to "declare that legislation (or relevant provisions) would be unconstitutional in certain applications; statements that purport to construe the legislation in a manner that would 'save' it from unconstitutionality; and statements that state flatly that the legislation is unconstitutional on its face." For Dellinger, when the president determines that a provision of a law is unconstitutional, it is the same as when the Supreme Court declares a law unconstitutional. Dellinger argued, "If the President may properly decline to enforce a law, at least when it unconstitutionally encroaches on his powers, then it arguably follows that he may properly announce to Congress and to the public that he will not enforce a provision of an enactment he is signing. If so, then a signing statement that challenges what the President determines to be an unconstitutional encroachment on his power, or that announces the President's unwillingness to enforce (or willingness to litigate) such a provision, can be a valid and reasonable exercise of Presidential authority."[24]

The Department of Energy Controversy

Late in President Clinton's second term in office, he butted heads with the Congress over an added layer of bureaucracy, with semi-independence, in the Department of Energy. This controversy illustrates how Clinton used the power of coordinate construction to refuse enforcement, as is, of what he perceived to be an unconstitutional intrusion into the prerogatives of the presidency.

The controversy began as a result of some security breaches at the nation's nuclear laboratories, where it was believed that employees of the laboratories had passed some nuclear secrets to representatives of the Chinese government. In 1999, the *New York Times* reported that employees at the Los Alamos National Laboratory in New Mexico had provided the Chinese government with classified information.[25] As a result of this appearance of the story in the news media, and the scandal that it caused, President Clinton requested that the Presidential Foreign Intelligence Advisory Board (PFIAB) "undertake a review of security threats at the Department of Energy's (DOE) weapons labs and [assess] the adequacy of measures that have been taken to address it."[26] The PFIAB report, known as the "Rudman Report," found that a substantial part of the problem with the nation's laboratories was a lack of accountability in and oversight from a dysfunctional bureaucracy that was in desperate need of reorganization. The report recommended that the responsibility for the nation's weapons program be given to the leader of a new group inside the DOE, the Agency for Nuclear Stewardship, who would be solely responsible for monitoring the weapons program and would report directly to the secretary of energy.[27]

In the Congress, there were five different bills that attempted to put the PFIAB recommendations into law.[28] The bill that finally emerged to enact the recommended changes was the National Defense Authorization Act for FY 2000.[29] The Clinton administration had objected to the provision of the bill that would place a new administrator in the DOE who would be somewhat outside White House control.[30] This new administrator would report directly to the secretary of energy. This arrangement proved to be a sticking point, and in negotiations, the Congress agreed to drop the provision for this semi-autonomous administrator and the Clinton administration agreed to sign the bill into law. However, when the bill reached the conference committee, the congressional Republicans slipped their new agency, the National Nuclear Security Administration

(NNSA), back into the bill, which eventually was sent to the president for his signature.[31]

In President Clinton's signing statement, he noted his displeasure at the last-minute switch, given how the disputed provision had earlier elicited a veto threat. He argued that the new agency limited "the Secretary's ability to employ his authorities to direct—both personally and through subordinates of his own choosing—the activities and personnel of the NNSA. Unaddressed, these deficiencies of the Act would impair effective health and safety oversight and program direction of the Department's nuclear defense complex."[32] Clinton refused to appoint someone to become the national nuclear security administrator and instructed the secretary of defense to take over the duties of the new administrator (a practice called "dual-hatting") in order to "mitigate the risks to clear chain of command presented by the Act's establishment of the new, semi-autonomous agency."[33]

When word got to the Congress that President Clinton would not enforce the law as it was written, members expressed outrage and ordered Secretary of Energy Bill Richardson to appear before a joint hearing of the Senate Energy and Natural Resources and Government Affairs committees to explain what had happened. The Senate Energy and Natural Resources Committee chair, Frank Murkowski (R-Alaska), summarized the action of the Clinton administration and Clinton's defiance of the law in his signing statement and concluded that the hearing "brings us to the question of the administration's implementation of the law that Congress passed. Although he signed the legislation into law, the president seems to have directed the secretary of Energy to ignore the intent of that law. The president appears to have directed the secretary to disregard the law's clear mandate to create a semiautonomous agency inside the DOE. Well, frankly I find that astonishing. . . . Mr. Secretary, do you plan on implementing the laws as Congress intended, or do you plan on ignoring the law as the president directed?" Senator Fred Thompson (R-Tenn.), chair of the Senate Government Affairs Committee, argued that Clinton could have taken one of two actions when presented with the bill: he could have vetoed the bill with his objections contained in the signing statement or he could have signed it, which he did, and "faithfully" execute the law. Faithfully executing the law would require appointing someone with an extensive background "in national organizational management in appropriate technical fields, and . . . well qualified to manage the nuclear weapons non-proliferation and materials disposition programs of the newly-created [NNSA]." Thompson argued that instead of choosing one of the two methods mandated by the Constitution, Clinton took a third way—"he signed the bill, but immediately directed the secretary of Energy to perform the duties of the overall bill but denying effect to certain provisions. That approach is unconstitutional."[34]

The rest of the committee members were given an opportunity to make statements, with the Republicans aghast at President Clinton's open defiance of the law and the Democrats siding with the administration and the need for "accountability." After they were finished, Secretary Richardson was allowed to respond, and he addressed Senator Thompson's specific points. Richardson made the case that the president had made clear his intent to veto the bill if it contained the NNSA as a semi-autonomous agency but negotiated in good faith a bipartisan compromise with the Congress to both create the NNSA and preserve accountability to the president. In fact, Richardson's line of reasoning parallels nicely with unitary executive theory, which stipulates that the president is the only nationally elected officer with responsibility to the public for any and all actions. Thus, inferior *independent* executive officers violate that accountability and must be excised whenever and wherever possible.

This line of reasoning takes Richardson to his next point: since the Republicans in the House switched the language in conference without any input from the president, the deal was void. Richardson argued that "a very different bill emerged from behind closed doors in the House-Senate conference. What surfaced was a bill that offered much needed pay raises to the military, among other laudable language. But the bill also abandoned key provisions in the Senate-passed reorganization plan. Mr. Chairman, that wasn't what we agreed to. And while the president did sign this act to get the raises for our men and women in uniform, among other worthy goals, he believes there are still fundamental problems with much of the language."

Richardson then detailed how the final conference report differed from the agreement the administration had made prior to conference: the "direct management authority . . . is limited to one person, the secretary is stripped of his prior authority to direct and delegate authority to all personnel of the department, and . . . highly sensitive special access programs have been removed from the secretary's jurisdiction and control and placed with a new undersecretary."[35]

The law was not set to take effect until March 2000, and Richardson suggested to the members of the committee that perhaps they could work with the administration to revise the current language so that the differences could be worked out in a way that would not cause a constitutional confrontation between the two branches. The offer was not received warmly by the Republicans on the committee.

The Clinton administration appointed an interim administrator to the NNSA while it worked out the problems with the position, which only led to additional problems. In the revised legislation, the Congress clearly indicated the lines of responsibility for the new director, giving the Clinton administration more control over the position but making the removal of the director next to impossible. Section 313(b) of the law read, "The exclusive reasons for removal from office as Under Secretary for Nuclear Security . . . shall be inefficiency, neglect of duty, or malfeasance in office."[36]

The administration understood what the Congress was attempting to do. Congress sent the president a bill he had to sign, since they had worked with the administration to make the changes the administration wanted. But on the backside they wrote in an administrator who would be extremely difficult to fire. Instead, the president turned to the signing statement. President Clinton outlined his objections to the actions of the Congress and then defined "neglect of duty" to mean "among other things, a failure to comply with the lawful directives of policies of the President."[37] While seeking to retain the upper hand, the Congress quickly added to another bill headed for the president's desk the same criteria they had used for removal of the NNSA administrator. Congress made this move just three days after the president signed the previous bill.

Once again President Clinton used his signing statement to interpret "neglect of duty" as "failure to comply with the lawful directives or policies of the President."[38] And it appears that Clinton's interpretation triumphed as the "removal" language in both laws is not part of 50 USC 2402 of the *U.S. Code*, which deals with the qualifications for the administrator for nuclear security.

Conclusion

Curtis Bradley and Eric Posner argue that if you look at the language of the Clinton administration's signing statements and the things they challenged or interpreted, then you have to conclude that it embraced the core tenets of the unitary executive theory.[39] Furthermore, there are the comments of James Blumstein, a member of the first Bush administration, who argued that the Clinton administration was every bit as comfortable with the unitary executive theory as his Republican predecessors were.[40] And then there is testimony from individuals inside the Clinton administration who embraced the theory. In the Justice Department, there is former assistant attorney general Walter Dellinger, whose 1994 memo openly embraced the obligation of the president to protect and defend the Constitution by refusing to enforce unconstitutional laws. And Clinton's domestic policy advisor Elena Kagan argued that the Clinton administration exercised unfettered influence within the regulatory agencies both prior to the establishment of a regulatory agenda and at the end of the regulatory process by forcing the agencies to issue final rules with the president's interpretation in mind.[41]

President Clinton, despite campaigning in 1992 for a break from Republican unilateralism and defiance of the law, openly embraced those very practices upon taking office in 1993. While many argue that the shift took place following the Republican victories in the 1994 midterm elections, there is evidence that supports his embracing of the theory from the moment he took office. His two OLC opinions defending the use of the signing statement and coordinate construction were issued in 1993 and 1994, respectively, and his important executive orders and memoranda taking hold of the regulatory agencies all occurred within his first year in office. While the point is moot, had the Democrats not lost control of the Congress in his first term, President Clinton may have behaved in a manner very similar to that of his Republican successor simply because his ambitions and desire to be reelected encouraged unilateralism as opposed to the state of virtual gridlock that defines the legislative process in the United States.

President Barack Obama took office nearly thirty years after President Reagan was first inaugurated. This means that the unitary executive has at least two decades of institutionalization throughout the executive branch, and President Obama will have a difficult time resisting the pressures that encourage unitarian behavior. When he faces intense public pressure or declining poll numbers and a Congress that is unwilling to cooperate or is openly threatening presidential prerogatives, it is highly likely that he will become a unitarian, despite any campaign pledges to the contrary.

Notes

1. On this larger point, see Andrew Rudalevige, *The New Imperial Presidency: Renewing Presidential Power after Watergate* (Ann Arbor: University of Michigan Press, 2005).

2. Christopher S. Yoo, Steven G. Calabresi, and Anthony Colangelo, "The Unitary Executive in the Modern Era, 1945–2001," *Iowa Law Review* 601 (2005): 7.

3. Michael Herz, "Imposing Unified Executive Branch Statutory Interpretation," *Cardozo Law Review* 15, nos. 1–2 (October 1993): 252–53.

4. Executive Order 13,193, February 17, 1981.

5. 50 *Code of Federal Regulations* 1036, January 4, 1985.

6. Joseph Cooper and William F. West, "Presidential Power and Republican Government: The Theory and Practice of OMB Review of Agency Rules," *Journal of Politics* 50, no. 4 (November 1988): 874.

7. Quoted in ibid., 873–74.

8. *Paperwork Reduction Act of 1980,* Public Law 96–511, 44 *U.S. Code* 3501; Peter Shane, "Political Accountability in a System of Checks and Balances: The Case of Presidential Review of Rulemaking," *Arkansas Law Review* 48 (1995): 168.

9. Shane, "Political Accountability in a System of Checks and Balances," 168.

10. Charles Tiefer, *The Semi-Sovereign Presidency: The Bush Administration's Strategy for Governing without Congress* (Boulder, CO: Westview Press. 1994), 72.

11. Elena Kagan, "Presidential Administration," *Harvard Law Review* 118 (June 2001): 2282.

12. Ibid., 2249.

13. William J. Clinton, "Memorandum on Review of Regulations," *Weekly Compilation of Presidential Documents* 29, no. 4 (January 21, 1993): 93.

14. William J. Clinton, "Executive Order 12,835—Establishment of the National Economic Council," *Federal Register* 58, no. 26 (January 27, 1993): 6189–90.

15. William J. Clinton, "Memorandum on Streamlining the Bureaucracy," *Weekly Compilation of Presidential Documents* 29, no. 37 (September 11, 1993): 1738–39.

16. William J. Clinton, "Executive Order 12,866—Regulatory Planning and Review," *Federal Register* 58, no. 190 (October 4, 1993): 51735–44.

17. James F. Blumstein, "Regulatory Review by the Executive Office of the President: An Overview and Policy Analysis of Current Issues," *Duke Law Journal* 51, no. 851 (December 2001): 874.

18. *The Small Business Regulatory Enforcement Fairness Act* (SBREFA), Public Law 104–121.

19. The General Accounting Office was later renamed the Government Accountability Office.

20. See this analysis at http://www.tpub.com/content/cg2001/d01852t/d01852t0017.htm (accessed February 5, 2008).

21. Robert Pear, "The Presidential Pen Is Still Mighty," *New York Times,* June 28, 1998, sec. 4, p. 3.

22. Dellinger memorandum, Office of Legal Council, November 2, 1994, http://www.usdoj.gov/olc/nonexcut.htm (accessed February 7, 2008).

23. For a different interpretation of the Reagan strategy, see Christopher S. Kelley, "A Matter of Direction: The Reagan Administration, the Signing Statement, and the 1986 Westlaw Decision," *William and Mary Bill of Rights Journal* 16, no. 1 (December 2007).

24. Dellinger memorandum to Nussbaum, November 3, 1993, http://www.usdoj.gov/olc/signing.htm (accessed February 7, 2007).

25. James Risen and Jeff Gerth, "Breach at Los Alamos: A Special Report," *New York Times,* March 6, 1999, A1.

26. William J. Clinton, "Statement by the President," Office of the Press Secretary, June 15, 1999, http://www.fas.org/irp/news/1999/06/990615-prc-wh1.htm (accessed April 15, 2003).

27. Warren Rudman, "Science at Its Best, Security at Its Worst: A Report on the Security Problems at the U.S. Department of Energy," President's Foreign Intelligence Advisory Board, June 15, 1999, http://www.fas.org/sgp/library/pfiab/ (accessed April 15, 2003).

28. Those five bills were S. 896, "The Department of Energy Abolishment Act"; H.R. 1649, "The Department of Energy Abolishment Act"; S. 1059, "The National Defense Authorization Act for FY 2000"; H.R. 2032, "A Bill to Amend the DOE Organization Act to Establish a Nuclear Security Administration and an Office of Under Secretary for National Security in DOE"; and S. 1009, "The Intelligence Authorization Act for FY 2000."

29. H.R. 1401, 106th Cong., 1st sess., May 24, 1999.

30. Floyd D. Spence, "Statement of Chairman Floyd Spence, Full Committee Hearing on National Nuclear Security Administration," March 2, 2000, http://www.house.gov/hasc/openingstatementsandpressreleases/106thcongress/00–03–02spence.pdf (accessed April 15, 2003).

31. House of Representatives, *National Defense Authorization Act for Fiscal Year 2000: Conference Report to S. 1059,* 106th Cong., 1st sess., August 6, 1999, Public Law 106–301.

32. William J. Clinton, "Statement on Signing the National Defense Authorization Act for Fiscal Year 2000," *Weekly Compilation of Presidential Documents* 35, no. 40 (October 5, 1999): 1928.

33. Ibid., 1928–29.

34. Senate Energy and Natural Resources Committee and the Senate Governmental Affairs Committee, "Joint Hearing on Creation of the National Nuclear Security Administration," 106th Cong., 1st sess., *Federal News Service,* October 19, 1999.

35. Ibid.

36. *Making Appropriations for the Departments of Veterans Affairs and Housing and Urban Development, and for Sundry Independent Agencies, Board, Commissions, Corporations, and Office for the Fiscal Year Ending September 30, 2001 and for Other Purposes,* Public Law 106–377, 106th Cong., 1st sess. (October 27, 2000).

37. William J. Clinton, "Statement on Signing the Fiscal Year 2001 Appropriations Legislation—H.R. 4635," *Weekly Compilation of Presidential Documents* 36, no. 44 (November 6, 2000): 2660.

38. William J. Clinton, "Statement on Signing the *Floyd D. Spence National Defense Authorization Act for Fiscal Year 2001—H.R. 4205,*" *Weekly Compilation of Presidential Documents* 36, no. 44 (October 30, 2000): 2651–2760.

39. Curtis A. Bradley and Eric A. Posner, "Presidential Signing Statements and Executive Power," *Constitutional Commentary* 23 (2006): 329.

40. Blumstein, "Regulatory Review by the Executive Office of the President," 874.

41. Kagan, "Presidential Administration," 2282.

PART II

The Unitary Executive and the George W. Bush Presidency

Foundations of the Unitary Executive of George W. Bush

MICHAEL A. GENOVESE

The greatest dangers to liberty lurk in insidious encroachments by men of zeal, well-meaning but without understanding.

—JUSTICE LOUIS BRANDEIS

Politics makes strange bedfellows. Who could have imagined that the same conservatives who decried the powerful central authority of the federal government in the post–World War II era would, haltingly in the 1980s but more robustly in the post–September 11, 2001, world, become the staunchest defenders of federal and executive power? Yet such is the case as the United States confronts an age of terrorism and a new set of threats to security.

The road to what is called the "unitary executive" is littered with the carcasses of Whig and conservative suspicions of central executive power, as today, the Right embraces a version of presidential power that is imperial in scope and anything but conservative in philosophy or operation. How did this come about?

The Road to the Unitary Executive

"War," James Madison reminds us, "is in fact the true nurse of executive aggrandizement." And in 1942 Justice Robert Jackson, in *Hirabayashi v. United States*, wrote that the war power is "the Achilles Heel of our Constitutional system."[1] If, as the Bush administration asserted, the war against terrorism may well be a war without end, it is imperative that we come to grips with the potential internal threats the war powers pose to the constitutional republic. If the war power is used too hesitantly or unwisely, the security and future of the nation are put at risk. If it is used too aggressively or too expansively, the security of the constitutional republic is endangered. The United States now confronts its Achilles heel. How well or how poorly we resolve this paradox will determine what type of polity we will have and what type of people we will be for the coming decades.

The scope and limits of a president's executive and war powers are somewhat ill defined. Historically, the president has been granted wide authority to react to crisis and wars, yet such authority is never absolute. And while, as Supreme Court Justice Frank Murphy wrote in the *Hirabayashi v. United States* decision, war gives the president "authority to exercise measures of control over persons and property which would not in all cases be permissible in normal times," such powers are not without limits. For as the Supreme Court reminded us in *United States v. Robel* (1967), "[E]ven the war power does not remove constitutional limitations safeguarding essential liberties." And nearly forty years later, Justice Sandra Day O'Connor wrote in *Hamdi v. Rumsfeld* (2004) that "a state of war is not a blank check for the president" and that the commander in chief powers do not give the president authority to "turn our system of checks and balances on its head."[2]

The academic cachet for the unitary executive comes primarily from several law journal articles touting an originalist construction of this robust version of presidential power.[3] These law review articles have given a brand of academic legitimacy if not acceptability to the unity executive view. Yet even many conservatives are skeptical of this newly discovered originalist construction of presidential power. Dissecting this new originalist view, columnist George F. Will refers to "this monarchical doctrine," writing that "it is that whenever the nation is at war, the other two branches of government have a radically diminished pertinence to governance and the president determines what the pertinence shall be."[4]

The post-9/11 presidency of George W. Bush was a muscle-flexing, assertive, and, in many ways, a unilateral presidency. The opportunity to exercise power afforded the administration in the aftermath of the September 11, 2001, attacks went, at first, virtually unchallenged. The "rally 'round the flag" effect of the attacks opened a wide door to power, and the Bush administration was anything but shy about using that power to impose its will both at home and abroad.

But as the results of the administration's actions in Iraq and elsewhere came home to roost and wore out their welcome with the public, allies, and political opponents, the Bush presidency was compelled to move beyond its bold power assertions and present a political and intellectual defense of its unilateral actions. The result was the development of what is called the "unitary executive." While the roots of the unitary executive reach back to the administration of Ronald Reagan, it was not until the Bush administration that this theory became more fully developed and implemented.[5]

The Crisis Presidency of George W Bush

On September 10, 2001, President George W. Bush was the object of more derision than respect. The president's folksy style, twangy Texas accent, and penchant for inventing words such as "strategery" made him an irresistible target for ridicule from late-night television comedians. Media portrayals of the president's bumbling, fumbling syntax and bland rhetoric thus made him seem more like a national joke than an admired world leader.

Twenty-four hours can be a lifetime in politics. The 9/11 attacks so dramatically changed political circumstances and public expectations of presidential leadership that the political ground on which George W. Bush stood shifted dramatically. The tectonic plates of this political geography shifted, producing a crisis presidency, and power shifted to the White House and into the hands of George W. Bush.

After 9/11 the Democratic opposition in Congress fell nearly silent, the public rallied around the president, and once the United States launched a military assault on Afghanistan, the president's popularity soared. Bush benefited not by a sudden infusion of skill or will but as a result of the changed conditions created by the 9/11 attacks.

But what was the president to do in these changed circumstances? Not all presidents exercise, wisdom, or courage in the face of crisis. In the nineteenth century as the United States edged closer to civil war, as the southern states pulled out of the Union, President James Buchanan had an opportunity to exercise bold leadership. But Buchanan, rather than being energized by the challenge, became paralyzed by it. He shrank when he needed to rise. By the time Abraham Lincoln took office, the crisis had deepened. Unlike his predecessor, Lincoln rose to meet the crisis and exercised wisdom and good judgment in the face of enormous pressure.

Some officeholders have a more limited repertoire of political skills or will or can do but one or two things well. Some apply the same style of leadership to virtually every circumstance. But different circumstances demand different styles of leadership. In war, one may need authority, good judgment, and decisiveness. In peacetime, a more collaborative style might be useful. In times of great confusion or challenge, a president with vision might be necessary. In times of grief, the president might need to be a national healer. In short, good leaders are astute enough to see what is needed, skilled enough to apply wisdom to the problem, and flexible enough to make appropriate alterations in style as circumstances and demands change.

Lincoln had this instinct of good leadership; Buchanan did not. Franklin D. Roosevelt, known to many as "the juggler," also had it. Winston Churchill did not. In war, Churchill was an accomplished leader. But in times of peace, he often floundered. Why? Because Churchill's style and skill were well suited to the demands of war but ill suited to times of peace. And Churchill could not or would not "style-flex"—adjust his style to different circumstances.

Thus, truly effective leadership is a function of *context*, which grants a president wide or narrow opportunity to lead; of *wisdom*, or the ability to see clearly and understand what must be done; of *skill*, applied to circumstances, which helps determine the level of power available to a leader; of *vision*, by which a president is able to recognize the possibility of a good and just outcome. Within this framework, we can ask how well or how poorly President George W. Bush applied wisdom and skill to the circumstances of 9/11.

In response to 9/11, the Bush administration argued that a new approach to foreign policy was required in order to address the new dangers. The cold war was over and the international war against terrorism had begun. The president declared an international war against terrorism; the USA PATRIOT Act was passed, the Department of Homeland Security was established, a doctrine of "first strike" or preventive/preemptive war was adopted, a war against the Taliban government in Afghanistan took place, the al-Qaida terrorist network was pursued, and a war against Saddam Hussein in Iraq was launched.

With his popularity hovering at the mid–80 percent range, the president felt emboldened by a clear mission, and he possessed political capital that was unrivaled. But his popularity did not last. As the war in Iraq soured, as examples of the U.S. torture of prisoners came to light, as memos defending torture and extralegal authority for the president were leaked to the press, as news of "extraordinary renditions" hit the media, as details about the U.S. detention center at Guantánamo Bay surfaced, as the president's plans for military tribunals and denial of rights laid out in the Geneva Conventions became known, the administration was forced into a defensive posture. Could all of these acts emanate solely from the executive? Did the president truly have that much unchecked unilateral authority?

Critics charged that the president's actions threatened the separation of powers, checks and balances, and even the rule of law. And while Bush was not the first president to move beyond the law, his bold assertion that the rule of law did not bind a president in time of war marked a new approach and was a grave challenge to the Constitution and the separation of powers.

Efforts to Defend the President's Prerogative

At first, the Bush administration's efforts to justify the apparent power grab were restricted to the president repeating the administration's mantra: "I'm a war president." That mantra, along with notable efforts by key administration officials (including Attorney General John Ashcroft) to paint critics as unpatriotic or even as traitors, all but silenced early criticisms.[6]

In effect, 9/11 created conditions in which a public defense of the imperial presidency proved unnecessary. Bush was handed a "blank check," and no one—certainly not the Congress—was required to endorse power over to the executive. But over time, the oft-used "fear card" began to diminish in value, and as the glow from "victory" in Afghanistan gave way to the ongoing crisis in Iraq, the president was forced to defend not only his programs but also the intellectual and constitutional basis for his power.

The administration, it must be admitted, initially did a terrible job of justifying its power grab. At first, it did not feel it had to justify its actions at all. However, the repetitious "I'm a war president" response to critics began to wear thin, and as the public demanded a more credible defense of the imperial presidency, the administration was caught with its intellectual pants down.

When the "I'm a war president" defense grew stale, the administration began to employ a "best defense is a good offense" strategy and viciously attacked its critics. When that approach also lost its impact, the administration was compelled to cobble together a more robust intellectual justification. But the intellectual defense came too late. Prior to employing the cloak of an intellectual patina, the administration bumbled, and fumbled, and appeared arrogant and politically tone deaf. They had to scramble for a justification of their power.

President Bush was comfortable exercising a swaggering style of leadership, which I have previously dubbed the "Un-Hidden Hand" style. There was nothing subtle about this ostentatious approach; it was leadership by sledgehammer. At first it worked. Over time, however, boldness proved insufficient. But what the basis of this boldness?[7] It was a theory of power known as the unitary executive.

Origins of the Unitary Executive

James Madison wrote in "Federalist No. 47" that "the accumulation of all powers, legislative, executive, and judiciary, in the same hands, whether of one, a few, or many, and whether hereditary, self-appointed, or elective, may justly be pronounced the very definition of tyranny."[8] In essence, the intellectual pedigree for the Bush administration's expansive view of executive power can be seen in what is called the unitary executive (some members of the Bush administration referred to it as the New Paradigm). While the administration rarely provided a comprehensive defense of its actions, we can nonetheless make the arguments the administration should have been making in defense of its aggressive use of executive power.

The unitary executive is a constitutional model of presidential power positing that "all" executive powers belong exclusively to the president.[9] In its most expansive form, the unitary executive is disembodied from the separation of powers and checks and balances and thus seems in contradiction or contradistinction to the original model of constitutionalism as envisioned by the framers.

The unitary executive consists of seven parts:

1. executive prerogative, based on John Locke's *Second Treatise;*
2. "energy" in the executive, grounded in Alexander Hamilton's defense of presidential authority;
3. the "coordinate constitution" view of the Constitution, whereby the "executive power" is fused with the "commander in chief" clause;
4. the doctrine of "necessity," as practiced by Abraham Lincoln during the Civil War;
5. supportive court decisions;
6. the "constitutional dictatorship," as described by Clinton Rossiter; and
7. precedent, or the past practices of U.S. presidents.

JOHN LOCKE'S "EXECUTIVE PREROGATIVE"

Is a president ever justified in violating the Constitution? While the word emergency does not appear in the Constitution, some scholars suggest that the founders did envision the possibility of a president exercising "supraconstitutional powers" in a time of national emergency.[10]

Historically, during a crisis the president has assumed extraconstitutional powers.[11] The separate branches—which, under normal circumstances, are designed to check and balance one another—will usually defer to the president in times of national crisis or emergency. The president's institutional position offers a vantage point from which to more easily exert crisis leadership, and the Congress, the courts, and the public usually will accept the president's judgments and extraordinary use of power.

The idea that the United States has one set of legal and constitutional standards for normal conditions and another for crisis or emergency conditions raises unsettling questions regarding democratic governments and constitutional systems.[12] Can democratic regimes function in any but peaceful circumstances? Or must the United States constantly rely upon the strength of a despotic ruler to save it from disaster? Are constitutional governments incapable of meeting the demands of crisis? Can democracy work in the twenty-first century, or is it a relic of quieter times? Democratic theory is rather weak in addressing itself to the problem of crisis government and democratic objectives. In most instances, democratic political theorists have seen a need to revert to authoritarian leadership in times of crisis. John Locke called this the "executive prerogative," and to Rousseau, it was an application of the "general will." In cases of emergency, when extraordinary pressures are placed on democratic regimes, many theorists suggest that these democratic systems—in order to save themselves from destruction—must embrace the ways of totalitarian regimes.

Laws decided upon by democratic means may be ignored or violated under this concept. As Locke wrote, in emergency situations the Crown retains the prerogative or "power to act according to discretion for the public good, without the prescription of the law and sometimes even against it."[13] While this prerogative could properly be exercised only for the "public good," one cannot escape the conclusion that for democratic governments this is shaky ground on which to stand. And what if an executive acts wrongly? Here Locke is forced to abandon secular concerns, and he wrote that "the people have no other remedy in this, as in all other cases where they have no judge on earth, but to appeal to Heaven."[14]

ALEXANDER HAMILTON'S "ENERGY"

While most scholars of the presidency and the Constitution conclude that the framers invented an executive with limited authority grounded in a separation and sharing of power under the rule of law some executive power advocates choose to "cherry pick" their evidence from the literature and ignore the bulk of it.[15] In other words, they choose to highlight only those bits and pieces that support their strong executive preference and disregard the voluminous arguments and evidence against their preferred view.[16] Executive power proponents dismiss their critics without facing them, creating a convenient constitutional shroud for presidential power (without doing the hard work of truly making the case for the robust presidency they so desire) and making the separation of powers sing with a distinctly, almost exclusively presidential voice. Who, among the framers, is their guiding light? Not James Madison, the father of the Constitution, but Alexander Hamilton. And while most scholars do not associate Hamilton with a unitary executive, advocates of the Bush position nonetheless claim Hamilton as an intellectual father.

Elements of Hamilton's case for an energetic presidency can be found in Federalist Paper No. 70. It reads in part:

> There is an idea, which is not without its advocates, that a vigorous Executive is inconsistent with the genius of republican government. . . .
>
> Energy in the Executive is a leading character in the definition of good government. It is essential to the protection of the community against foreign attacks; it is not less essential to the steady administration of the laws; to the protection of property against those irregular and high-handed combinations which sometimes interrupt the ordinary course of justice; to the security of liberty against the enterprises and assaults of ambition, of faction and of anarchy. . . .
>
> A feeble Executive implies a feeble execution of the government. A feeble execution is but another phrase for a bad execution; And a government ill executed, whatever it may be in theory, must be, in practice, a bad government.
>
> Taking it for granted, therefore, that all men of sense will agree in the necessity of an energetic Executive, it will only remain to inquire, what are the ingredients which constitute this energy? . . .

> The ingredients which constitute energy in the executive are, first, unity; secondly, duration; thirdly, an adequate provision for its support; fourthly, competent powers.[17]

But, it must be noted, an energetic presidency is not an imperial presidency, or at least it should not be. And Hamilton's energetic executive is but a part of the framers' story. Even Hamilton did not advocate so robust a presidency as the unitary executive advocates suggest. Taken in its totality, the evidence that emerges from a thorough examination of the writings, speeches, and constitutional handiwork of the framers reveals a more circumscribed presidency than the Bush advocates chose to acknowledge.

COORDINATE CONSTRUCTION OF THE CONSTITUTION

In combining two constitutional provisions—the "executive power" clause and the "commander in chief" clause (both in Article II)—advocates of the unitary executive theory see a geometric expansion of executive authority in which the parts, when added together, are considerably greater than the whole. Conveniently forgotten is the fact that presidents take an oath of office to "preserve, protect, and defend the Constitution of the United States." They must therefore "take Care that the Laws be faithfully executed," even the laws with which they may personally disagree.

Some Bush administration officials viewed presidential authority in times of war as creating an executive of virtually unchecked power. A memo the Office of Legal Counsel issued on September 25, 2001, argued that "these decisions [in wartime] under our Constitution are for the President alone to make."[18] Other memos suggested that the president may transform things that are unlawful into lawful actions and that neither the Congress nor the courts have the authority to review presidential acts in a time of war.

But such an expansive reading violates both the spirit and the letter of the law. The Supreme Court, in cases such as *Hamdi v. Rumsfeld* (2004) and *Rasul v. Bush* (2004), and the Congress, in efforts such as their ban on the use of torture (a bill President Bush signed but argued in his signing statement that he did not consider himself bound by the law he had just signed), have attempted to reclaim some of the power that was lost, delegated, ceded, or stolen.

THE DOCTRINE OF NECESSITY

Perhaps no other claim by the Bush administration resonated as powerfully as the "necessity" argument. The old Roman adage *inter arma silent leges* (in wartime, the laws are silent), while not constitutionally valid, still holds persuasive power.[19] Abraham Lincoln relied on the doctrine of necessity during the Civil War, arguing to a special session of Congress on July 4, 1861, that

> the attention of the country has been called to the proposition that one who is sworn to "take care that the laws be faithfully executed," should not himself violate them. Of course some consideration was given to the questions of power, and propriety, before this matter was acted upon. The whole of the laws which were required to be faithfully executed, were being resisted, and failing of execution, in nearly one-third of the States. Must they be allowed to finally fail of execution, even had it been perfectly clear, that by the use of the tenderness of the citizen's liberty, that practically, it relieves more of the guilty, than of the innocent, should, to very limited extent, be violated? To state the question more directly, are all the laws, but one, to go unexecuted, and the government itself to go to pieces, lest that one be violated? Even in such a case, would not the official oath be broken, if the government should be overthrown, when it was believed that disregarding the single law, would tend to preserve it?[20]

Lincoln believed that it was a union (nation) that above all else had to be preserved, because without that union, the Constitution and the rule of law would be meaningless.[21] In a letter to Albert Hodges, editor of the Frankfort, Kentucky, *Commonwealth*, in 1864, Lincoln gives his rationale for the exercise of extraordinary presidential power:

> I am naturally anti-slavery. If slavery is not wrong, nothing is wrong. . . . And yet I have never understood that the Presidency conferred upon me an unrestricted right to act officially upon this judgment and feeling. It was in the oath I took that I would, to the best of my ability, preserve, protect, and defend the Constitution of the United States. I could not take the office without taking the oath. Nor was it my view that I might take an oath to get power, and break the oath in using the power. I understood, too, that in ordinary civil administration this oath even forbade me to practically indulge my primary abstract judgment on the moral question of slavery. . . . I did understand however, that my

> oath to preserve the constitution to the best of my ability imposed upon me the duty of preserving, by ever indispensable means, that government—that nation—of which that constitution was the organic law. Was it possible to lose the nation, and yet preserve the constitution? By general law life and limb must be protected; yet often a limb must be amputated to save a life; but a life is never wisely given to save a limb. I felt that measures, otherwise unconstitutional, might become lawful, by becoming indispensable to the preservation of the constitution, through the preservation of the nation. Right or wrong, I assumed this ground, and now avow it. I could not feel that, to the best of my ability, I had even tried to preserve the constitution, if, to save slavery, or any minor matter, I should permit the wreck of government, country, and Constitution all together.[22]

Even the "small government" advocate Thomas Jefferson resorted to a "necessity" argument in his constitutionally questionable purchase of the Louisiana Territory. Jefferson wrote, "A strict observance of the written law is doubtless one of the high duties of a good citizen, but it is not the highest. The laws of necessity, of self-preservation, of saving our country when in danger, are of the higher obligation. To lose our country by scrupulous adherence to the written law, would be to lose the law itself, with life, liberty, property and all those who are enjoying them with us; thus absurdly sacrificing the end to the means."[23] If the Bush administration had relied on the necessity argument, it would have been on powerful (if unconstitutional) ground. But the administration went further, claiming not only that it was necessary (for national security reasons) to go beyond the law but also that, in such cases, violating the law was not really violating the law. To wit, the president was above the law; the president was the law in times of war.

Lincoln never made such audacious claims. Even as he went beyond the letter of the law, he never claimed an inherent authority to breach the law, and he always recognized that Congress had the authority to reject his claims of power. If Lincoln momentarily went beyond the law—out of necessity—it was still the law and not his will that was supreme.

During the crisis of Civil War, Lincoln exercised extraordinary (some say extraconstitutional) powers. On what basis did he act? The president recognized a clear emergency situation; there was widespread agreement that there was indeed a crisis and that the president should act; Lincoln placed his actions before the Congress, hoping for (and receiving) their approval (after the fact, of course). He never claimed to be above the law or above the Constitution. The doctrine of necessity guided Lincoln.

Only if particular actions are truly necessary to preserve the nation can a president act in ways beyond the scope of the Constitution. Lincoln was a servant of the law and the Constitution, even as he acted beyond their literal scope; he never claimed an inherent power to go beyond the law. Lincoln believed that the authority of the government was, during a crisis, the authority to act in defense of the nation. He feared he was venturing into congressional territory and skating on thin constitutional ice. He never claimed that all authority was his but only that, in a crisis, the doctrine of necessity embodied authority in the government, authority that the president brought to life. He suggested that acts "whether strictly legal or not, were ventured upon, under what appeared to be a popular demand, and a public necessity. It is believed that nothing has been done beyond the constitutional competency of Congress." Thus, in a legitimate emergency, the people demand that the president act, and the president's actions are constitutionally permissible if the Congress maintains its authority to ultimately control and limit the actions of a president. "Must," he asked, "a government, of necessity, be too strong for the liberties of its own people or too weak to maintain its own existence?" He also said that "actions which otherwise would be unconstitutional could become lawful if undertaken for the purpose of preserving the Constitution and the Nation."[24]

In similar fashion, President Franklin D. Roosevelt, responding to the crisis of the Great Depression, confronted the task ahead by admitting that some of his actions might go beyond expectations. In his first inaugural address, on March 4, 1933, Roosevelt sounded the call for expanded power:

> It is to be hoped that the normal balance of Executive and legislative authority may be wholly adequate to meet the unprecedented task before us. But it may be that an unprecedented demand and need for undelayed action may call for temporary departure from that normal balance of public procedure. I am prepared under my constitutional duty to recommend the measures that a stricken Nation in the midst of a stricken world may require. These measures, or such other measures as the Congress may build out of its experience and wisdom, I shall seek, within my constitutional authority, to bring to speedy adoption.
>
> But in the event that Congress shall fail to take one of these

> two courses, and in the event that the national emergency is still critical, I shall not evade the clear course of duty that will then confront me. I shall ask the Congress for the one remaining instrument to meet the crisis—broad Executive power to wage a war against the emergency, as great as the power that would be given to me if we were in fact invaded by a foreign foe.[25]

Contemporary defenders of the rule of law and constitutionalism are rightly concerned with such visions of expansive power. But adherents to the doctrine of necessity do not see the Constitution as a suicide pact and instead see the Constitution as "bendable" in times of crisis.[26] But, as Justice David Davis wrote in *Ex parte Milligan,*:

> The Constitution of the United States is a law for rulers and people, equally in war and in peace, and covers with the shield of its protection all classes of men, at all times, and under all circumstances. No doctrine involving more pernicious consequences was ever invented by the wit of man than that any of its provisions can be suspended during any of the great exigencies of government. Such a doctrine leads directly to anarchy or despotism, but the theory of necessity on which it is based is false; for the government, with the Constitution, has all the powers granted to it, which are necessary to preserve its existence.[27]

Likewise, Justice Robert Jackson's concurring opinion in the Youngstown case also rebuts the necessity doctrine. Jackson wrote that the framers "knew what emergencies were, knew the pressures they engender for authoritative action, knew, too, how they afford a ready pretext for usurpation. We may also suspect that they suspected that emergency powers would tend to kindle emergencies."[28]

SUPPORTIVE COURT DECISIONS

Overall, the courts have not served as a very effective check on presidential power.[29] While there have been times when the courts were willing to stand up to the president (e.g., some of the Civil War cases, early in the New Deal era, late in the Watergate period, and after the initial period of the war against terrorism), in general, the courts have tended to shy away from direct confrontations with the presidency and were often willing to defer to or add to the powers of the presidency.

Defenders of the powerful presidency gravitate toward one court case in particular, *United States v. Curtiss-Wright Export Corp.* (1936). In that case, Justice George Sutherland, drawing on a speech in the House of Representatives by John Marshall, referred to the president as the "sole organ" of American foreign policy. While Sutherland's "sole organ" remark was a judicial aside (dicta), it has become the unofficial executive branch mantra for the president's bold assertion of a broad and unregulated power over foreign affairs. But scholars have found little in *Curtiss-Wright* to rely on in the defense of the robust presidency, and other than what defenders of presidential power perceive in it, this case is generally not seen as significant in granting presidents expansive powers.[30] The case may be of comfort, but only small comfort, to defenders of presidential power and exclusivity in foreign policy.

THE CONSTITUTIONAL DICTATORSHIP

In his book of the same name, Clinton Rossiter invoked the notion of constitutional dictatorship as a modern version of the same problem that democratic theorists had attempted, with little success, to solve.[31] The constitutional dictatorship is an admission of the weakness of democratic theory and of its failure to cover the full range of governing requirements. To save democracy, we must escape from it. To protect democracy, we must reject it. In cases of emergency, we must reject democracy for the more expedient ways of the dictator. In this manner, democratic theory opens the door to a strong power-aggrandizing executive.

Of course, nowhere in the Constitution is it specified that the president should have additional powers in times of crisis. But history has shown us that in times of crisis or emergency, the powers of the president have greatly expanded. And while Abe Fortas has written that "under the Constitution the President has no implied powers which enable him to make or disregard laws," under the microscope of political reality we can see that this is precisely what American presidents have done and gotten away with.[32]

The result of this view of an enlarged reservoir of presidential power in emergencies has been characterized by Edward S. Corwin as "constitutional relativity."[33] Corwin's view considers the Constitution to be broad and flexible enough to meet the needs of an emergency situation. By this approach, the Constitution can be adapted to meet the needs of demanding times. If the times call for quasi-dictatorial action by the executive, the Supreme Court might well find such action acceptable.

The dilemma of emergency situations in democratic systems cannot be easily solved. If the power of the state is issued too little or too late, the democratic state faces the possibility of destruction. But if used arbitrarily and capriciously, this power could lead the system to accept a form of permanent dictatorship. In a contemporary sense, the constant reliance on the executive to solve the many "emergencies" (often self-defined by the executive) facing America could well lead to the acceptance of the overly powerful executive and make the meaning of the term "emergency" shallow and susceptible to executive branch manipulation. With each new "emergency" in American history, the public and our political system may become more accustomed to accepting a broader definition of presidential power to meet each new crisis.

But the Court under Rossiter's theory of constitutional dictatorship generally recognizes the need for government to have inflated powers with which to deal with the crisis, and it will allow for a "flexible" interpretation of constitutional powers of the president, who is expected to deal with the emergency. Rossiter comes to this conclusion: "In the last resort, it is always the executive branch in the government which possesses and wields the extraordinary powers of self-preservation of any democratic, constitutional state."[34] The Court, under Rossiter's theory, recognizes the emergency and allows the president to acquire additional powers. But to be legitimate, constitutional dictators must recognize the limits of their responsibilities. In 1942 Franklin D. Roosevelt, after requesting that Congress grant him an usually large amount of power, assured the legislative body that "when the war is won, the powers under which I act automatically revert to the people—to whom they belong."[35] Presidents, in short, are to return to their rightful place the extraordinary powers granted during times of crisis. But serious questions remain as to (1) whether presidents have in fact returned such powers and (2) whether, even if the president desires it, a complete return to normality is possible after dictatorial or quasi-dictatorial power is placed in the hands of one leader.

PRECEDENT

Advocates of President Bush's position argued that there was sufficient precedent to justify his activities. Lincoln during the Civil War, Woodrow Wilson in World War I, Franklin D. Roosevelt in the Great Depression and World War II, and others paved the path that Bush followed. But so too did Richard Nixon, and while his acts were and are condemned, his motto that "when the president does it that means it is not illegal" lived on in the Bush administration.[36]

Precedent is an uncertain guide in the war against terrorism. After all, this is war without end. Even if one is tempted to give the president some leverage in this context, a permanent imperial presidency would do such constitutional violence to the American system as to force the abandonment of constitutional government in favor of something more closely resembling one-man rule. It would be full circle from a revolution against the executive tyranny of the king of England to the embrace of imperial rule in the modern era.

Presidents Abraham Lincoln, Woodrow Wilson, and Franklin D. Roosevelt were said to have exercised legitimate emergency powers in the midst of crises. But other presidents, such as Nixon and Reagan, also attempted to grab extra constitutional power and were rebuffed and condemned. What made Lincoln and FDR heroes but Nixon and Reagan usurpers? The predicate is, first, a legitimate and widely recognized crisis. Only when there is a genuine emergency can a president attempt to exercise extraconstitutional power. Second, the other branches of government and the public must be willing to cede to the president these extra constitutional powers. Third, the president must remain willing to bow to the will of Congress if it chooses to set policy or limits the president's exercise of power. And the president cannot use secrecy and distortion to hide from congressional scrutiny. In general, Lincoln and FDR followed these guidelines; Nixon and Reagan did not. And what of the case of George W. Bush in the post-9/11 era? Bush may have had the predicate, but he was reluctant to place himself within the rule of law, bowing only when his popularity plummeted to the 30 percent range, the courts chided him, and the Congress belatedly asserted some authority. Until then, he exercised extraconstitutional power and claimed that his acts were not reviewable by Congress or the courts, often cloaking his actions in secrecy and duplicity. Such a bold and illegitimate interpretation of the president's powers is unsupportable in law or history.

The Bush administration took the unitary executive further than any predecessor, claiming that "in wartime, it is for the President alone to decide what methods to use to best prevail against the enemy."[37] Thus, the Bush administration asserted a crisis presidency, one that it considered above the law, above the Constitution, and unrestricted by separation of powers, the rule of law, and checks and balances. In this, the Bush defense added a seventh leg to the unitary executive: no other branch may question our actions. And if the Bush administration's view becomes accepted, who is to say that the emperor has no clothes?

Extreme times may sometimes lead to extreme measures. The terrorist attacks of September 11, 2001, became the predicate allowing an obscure and intellectually threadbare theory of presidential unilateralism to assume center stage and attack the patina of legitimacy to what otherwise would be dismissed out of hand as an extreme and indefensible proposition.

After all, the framers rejected Locke's prerogative in favor of checks and balances. They also rejected Hamilton's expansive executive for Madisonian equilibrium; and while "necessity" is a powerful argument, it is not a constitutional argument. They did, in Article II, give the president executive power, but it was not absolute, and they did make the president commander in chief, but subject to the Congress, so the coordinate construction doctrine cannot be seen in isolation but can only be understood along with Article I. The constitutional dictatorship may well describe our political response to crisis, but that by no means confers constitutional legitimacy. Precedent clearly establishes that over time the powers of the president have evolved and grown, but so too has history shown us times when the Congress has chosen to tame the prince and limit executive authority. And while *Curtiss-Wright* may be canonical to executivists, a thorough examination of court cases dealing with executive power reveals a much more nuanced and complex portrait of a high court that may shrink from confrontations with the executive but may also stand up to and limit power grabs by the president (as *Hamdi, Rasul,* and *Hamdan* all suggest).

If the unitary executive today has appeal to the Right, such a flirtation may well end with a liberal Democrat in the White House. After all, do conservative Republicans really want a unitary executive when put into the cause of the Left? The integrity test for conservatives will come when the unitary executive is in the hands of their political adversaries.

Conclusion

In an age of terrorism, is the unitary executive or the imperial presidency a permanent fixture of our political system? Or can we strike the right balance between the needs of presidential power and the demands of the rule of law? We need a presidency both powerful and accountable, robust, yet under the rule of law. But how do we achieve such ends? The answers to these questions will shape the nation for the coming generation and determine whether the experiment in self-government was a fool's game or the solution to our problems.

Notes

1. James Madison, "Political Observations," April 20, 1795, *Letters and Other Writings of James Madison* (Philadelphia: J. B. Lippincott, 1867), 4:491; *Hirabayashi v. United States,* 320 U.S. 81 (1943).

2. *Hirabayashi v. United States,* 320 U.S. 81 (1943); *United States v. Robel,* 389 U.S. 258 (1967); *Hamdi v. Rumsfeld,* 542 U.S. 507 (2004).

3. Michael Stokes Paulsen, "The Constitution of Necessity," *Notre Dame Law Review* 79 (July 2004): 1257. See also Steven G. Calabresi and Kevin H. Rhodes, "The Structural Constitution: Unitary Executive, Plural Judiciary," *Harvard Law Review* 105 (1992): 1153.

4. George F. Will, "No Checks, Many Imbalances," *Washington Post,* February 16, 2006, A27.

5. Louis Fisher, "'The Unitary Executive': Ideology versus the Constitution," paper presented at the annual meeting of the American Political Science Association, Philadelphia, August 31–September 3, 2006.

6. See Nancy V. Baker, *General Ashcroft: Attorney* at War (Lawrence: University Press of Kansas, 2006).

7. See Betty Glad and Chris J. Dolan, eds., *Striking First* (New York: Palgrave Macmillan, 2005).

8. James Madison, "Federalist No. 47," http://thomas.loc.gov/home/histdox/fed_47.html (accessed June 12, 2009).

9. Christopher S. Yoo, Steven G. Calabresi, and Anthony J. Colangelo, "The Unitary Executive in the Modern Era, 1945–2004," *Iowa Law Review* 90 (2004): 601; Christopher S. Yoo, Steven G. Calabresi, and Laurence D. Nee, "The Unitary Executive during the Third Half-Century, 1889–1945," *Notre Dame Law Review* 80 (2004): 1; Steven G. Calabresi and Christopher Yoo, "The Unitary Executive during the Second Half-Century," *Harvard Journal of Law and Public Policy* 26 (2003): 668; Steven G. Calabresi and Christopher S. Yoo, "The Unitary Executive during the First Half-Century," *Case Western Reserve Law Review* 47 (1997): 1451; Steven G. Calabresi and Saikrishna B. Prakash, "The President's Power to Execute the Laws," *Yale Law Journal* 104 (1994): 541.

10. Daniel P. Franklin, *Extraordinary Measures: The Exercise of Prerogative Powers in the United States* (Pittsburgh: University of Pittsburgh Press, 1991).

11. Michael A. Genovese, "Presidential Leadership and Crisis Management," *Presidential Studies Quarterly* 16 (spring 1986): 300–309; Genovese, "Presidents and Crisis: Developing a Crisis Management System in the Executive Branch," *International Journal on World Peace* 4, no. 1 (spring 1987): 108–17.

12. Michael A. Genovese, "Democratic Theory and the Emergency Powers of the President," *Presidential Studies Quarterly* 9 (summer 1979): 283–89.

13. John Locke, *Treatise of Civil Government and a Letter Concerning Toleration* (1689–1690; New York: Appleton-Century, 1937), 109.

14. Ibid., 113.

15. For a discussion of how most scholars view the framers' intent, see Michael A. Genovese, *The Power of the American Presidency, 1789–2000* (New York: Oxford University Press, 2001).

16. One example of "cherry picking" is Terry Eastland, *Energy in the Executive: The Case for the Strong Presidency* (New York: Free Press, 1992).

17. Alexander Hamilton, "Federalist No. 70," http://thomas.loc.gov/home/histdox/fed_70–2.html (accessed June 12, 2009).

18. Quoted in Jane Mayer, "The Hidden Power," *New Yorker,* July 3, 2006, 51.

19. See Niccolò Machiavelli, *The Discourse in Livy,* chap. 34, on the Roman use of temporary dictatorship in times of crisis.

20. Abraham Lincoln, "Special Session Message," July 4, 1861, http://www.presidency.ucsb.edu/ws/?pid=69802 (accessed May 27, 2009).

21. Daniel Farber, *Lincoln's Constitution* (Chicago: University of Chicago Press, 2003).

22. Abraham Lincoln, President of the United States, to Albert G. Hodges, April 4, 1864, in Farber, *Lincoln's Constitution,* 585.

23. Thomas Jefferson to John B. Colvin, September 20, 1810, in *Basic Writings of Thomas Jefferson,* ed. Phillip S. Foner (New York: Willey Book Company, 1944), 682.

24. Lincoln, "Special Session Message," July 4, 1861.

25. Franklin D. Roosevelt, "Inaugural Address," March 4, 1933, http://www.presidency.ucsb.edu/ws/?pid=14473 (accessed May 27, 2009).

26. Richard A. Posner, *Not a Suicide Pact* (New York: Oxford University Press, 2006).

27. *Ex parte Milligan,* 71 U.S. 2 (1866).

28. *Youngstown Sheet & Tube Co. v. Sawyer,* 343 U.S. 579 (1952).

29. See Glendon A. Schubert, *The Presidency and the Courts* (Minneapolis: University of Minnesota Press, 1957); Michael A. Genovese, *The Supreme Court, the Constitution, and Presidential Power* (Washington, D.C.: University Press of America; 1980); and Louis Fisher, "Judicial Review of the War Power," *Presidential Studies Quarterly* 35 (September 2005): 466–95.

30. David Gray Adler, *United States v. Curtiss-Wright* (Lawrence: University Press of Kansas, forthcoming).

31. Clinton Rossiter, *Constitutional Dictatorship: Crisis Government in the Modern Democracy* (Princeton: Princeton University Press, 1948).

32. Abe Fortas, "The Constitution and the Presidency." *Washington Law Review* 49 (August 1974): 100.

33. Edward S. Corwin, *Total War and the Constitution* (New York: Knopf, 1947), 80.

34. Rossiter, *Constitutional Dictatorship*, 12.

35. "President Speaks," *New York Times*, September 8, 1942, 1 (text of speech is on p. 17).

36. See Genovese, *The Power of the American Presidency.*

37. Defense Department memo, 2003 (often referred to as the "torture memo"), http://www.aclu.org/pdfs/safefree/you_army_torture_memo.pdf (accessed May 27, 2009).

The Unitary Executive and Secrecy in the Bush Presidency

The Case of the Energy Task Force Controversy

MITCHEL A. SOLLENBERGER AND MARK J. ROZELL

The George W. Bush administration was especially aggressive in its efforts to defend and expand what it considered constitutionally based presidential prerogatives. The terrorist attacks of September 11, 2001, certainly provided a powerful context in which an administration might seek to expand executive power. But Bush's efforts to establish executive dominance in Washington preceded the terrorist attacks. Indeed, Vice President Richard Cheney had said early in Bush's first term that the administration was committed to reversing a perceived trend of legislative encroachments on executive powers combined with weak presidential responses to those encroachments.[1] Whether Cheney was correct in his estimation that the modern presidency has suffered at the hands of assertive Congresses is not the point of our analysis. Rather, it is important to present this framework of understanding at the outset in order to assess the administration's efforts to protect its powers in the controversy over internal discussions regarding energy policy development.

On January 29, 2001, President George W. Bush announced the creation of the National Energy Policy Development Group (NEPDG), better known as the energy task force.[2] The group's purpose was to develop "a national energy policy designed to help the private sector, and government at all levels, promote dependable, affordable, and environmentally sound production and distribution of energy for the future."[3] President Bush appointed various federal officials to the task force with Vice President Cheney as chair.[4] The task force held a total of ten sessions between January and May 2001, with group members and staff conducting numerous supplemental meetings "to collect individual views" for future energy policy decisionmaking.[5] These meetings included "nonfederal energy stakeholders, principally petroleum, coal, nuclear, natural gas, and electricity industry representatives and lobbyists" and, to "a more limited degree[,] . . . academic experts, policy organizations, environmental advocacy groups, and private citizens."[6] The task force issued its final report on May 16, 2001, and the group formally disbanded on September 30, 2001.[7]

The Bush administration resisted efforts by members of Congress and outside interest groups to make it reveal information about the task force meetings. This struggle developed into a full-blown legal controversy and ultimately a Supreme Court decision that addressed broader issues pertaining to presidential secrecy, the protection of internal deliberations in an administration, and separation of powers. In this chapter we describe the controversy over the energy task force meetings and how this controversy developed into a major legal battle, and we then analyze the outcome of these events and its relevance to the administration's theory of a unitary executive.

Congress and the Energy Task Force

Challenges to the secrecy of the task force began with a letter from Democratic representatives John Dingell and Henry Waxman on April 19, 2001. They wrote the task force's executive director, Andrew Lundquist, and requested that he answer "a series of questions relating to the participants, the purpose, the outcome, and the role of federal employees at these meetings" and that he send "copies of all documents and records produced or received by the task force" under the Federal Advisory Committee Act (FACA).[8] This act, originally passed in 1972, mandates that executive branch advisory committees adhere to various openness requirements, such as making available to the public their minutes, records, reports, and other documents.[9] That same day, Dingell and Waxman wrote the General Accounting Office and encouraged Comptroller General David Walker to investigate the operations of the energy task force.[10] These congressional requests were due in large part to press reports that the task force had been meeting in secret with representatives of various groups that had a direct interest in the development of the nation's energy policy.

After two weeks, the vice president's legal counsel, David Addington, responded to the April 19 letter. However, he refused to divulge significant information germane to the request and noted that "the FACA does not apply to" the task force because section 3(2) of the act exempts "any committee that is composed wholly of" federal employees.[11] Addington's letter sparked an angry reply from Dingell and Waxman. Again, the congressmen stated that the energy task force was in violation of FACA—not only in failing to fully answer their questions but also by refusing to hand over all relevant documents.[12] Meanwhile, the GAO, as a result of Dingell and Waxman's April 19 letter, requested detailed information, including copies of documents and telephone logs concerning the task force. On May 16, Addington replied that the GAO needed to state where the agency's power to investigate originated because it might very well "intend to intrude into the heart of Executive deliberations," which "the law protects to ensure the candor in Executive deliberations necessary to effective government."[13]

On May 22, Representatives Dingell and Waxman wrote another strongly worded letter to Addington, stating, "We are dismayed by your lack of full cooperation with GAO." Turning to the assertion that "the law protects" the task force from congressional oversight, the congressmen asserted that they were "not aware of any . . . law [of executive protection] which is applicable to Congressional investigations." Furthermore, they questioned the idea of invoking executive privilege, stating that only "the President himself" could claim such a right and if he had done such, to send a note of clarification on the subject.[14] Three days later, Addington replied with an admonishment for the congressmen: "The letter of May 22, 2001 [,] confirms that it is the GAO, and not the House of Representatives, whose power is intended to be exercised by the conduct of the proposed inquiry, and thus it appears that the letter of May 16th to the General Counsel of the GAO *was addressed to the proper party.*"[15]

As requested, GAO's general counsel, Anthony Gamboa, answered Addington's May 16 letter with the assertion that the agency did have the authority to investigate the energy task force. "Under 31 U.S.C. § 717," Gamboa declared, the "GAO is required to evaluate a program or activity when requested by a congressional committee of jurisdiction." That request came from Representatives Dingell and Waxman with their April 19 letter. In addition, Gamboa said that 31 U.S.C. § 712 and 31 U.S.C. § 716(a), respectively, gave the GAO the power to review matters involving "public money" and the "broad statutory right of access to" all energy task force records.[16]

In a rejoinder, Addington raised the concern that § 717 did not truly apply to the task force. That section only gave the GAO the power over "a program or activity," not "the Vice President and the other officers of the United States." Addington asserted that the GAO had no authority over constitutional officers in the executive branch. Without a doubt, the GAO's power should be "narrowly circumscribed," and it has "limited" ability to investigate. Furthermore, as ranking minority members, Dingell and Waxman "do not constitute a 'request' from 'a committee of Congress with jurisdiction over the program or activity.'" Only a majority of a committee of Congress can issue such a request, which was something that had not yet been done. However, Addington did state that the GAO had the narrow authority to investigate the use of public money. Therefore, he assured Gamboa that the vice president would send copies of all documents related to the costs incurred by the task force.[17]

The GAO's response was to send two letters. The first asserted the agency's right to investigate all matters related to the task force, and the second demanded a detailed list of documents concerning organizational makeup and energy policy deliberations.[18] On August 2 these letters compelled Vice President Cheney to inform Congress that the comptroller general had "exceed[ed] his lawful authority" under § 716.[19] Cheney further claimed that the GAO lacked the authority to seek access to task force information regarding policy development because the organization only has the power to review the results of programs. In turn, the GAO issued a statement in which it refuted Cheney's interpretations of the scope of its authority and continued to request information relating to the task force.[20]

Dingell and Waxman, taking into consideration Addington's June 7 remarks concerning the GAO's power to investigate only when requested by a congressional committee, sent a general letter of Congress to Cheney in which they expressed their dismay at his refusal to cooperate with the GAO.[21] The last substantial action before the September 11 terrorist attacks came from a GAO statement that professed the need for more candid information from the vice president's office. As Comptroller General Walker stated, "This is a very serious matter with significant implications for GAO, the Congress, and the American people." Walker's remarks ended with a warning of "possible litigation."[22] However, shortly after September 11 the GAO curtailed its threat to sue: "[G]iven our current national focus on combating terrorism and enhancing homeland security, this matter is not a current priority. We will determine whether and when we should proceed to court on this matter in due course."[23]

By early December, Waxman again had requested information about the task force. "In light of Enron's financial collapse," he ordered that

Cheney's office "release information about secret contacts . . . with [the] Enron Corporation." Waxman now had an issue that could galvanize the public. Indeed, he warned the Bush administration that its actions created "an appearance of impropriety."[24] Waxman had tied the task force to the Enron collapse and thus made the claims of secrecy and cover-up much more convincing.

On January 3, 2002, Addington announced that although the energy task force met with Enron representatives on numerous occasions, these officials "did not communicate information about its financial position in any of the meetings with the Vice President or with the National Energy Policy Development Group's support staff." Addington's letter listed the number and dates of these meetings.[25] However, in a January 8 reply Waxman again asserted his dissatisfaction with the information given. Although he commended Cheney "for revealing the information disclosed," he stated that Addington's letter of January 3 failed to provide any of the "important details about these meetings." Waxman listed a number of needed facts: (1) "the subjects discussed at the meetings," (2) "any requests for changes in federal policies made by Enron executives at the meetings," (3) "copies of any documents presented or discussed at the meetings," and (4) "the names of persons attending the meetings."[26] Cheney's office did not respond. Waxman then sent two additional letters, on January 16 and 25, concerning disclosure of matters relating to Enron.[27]

In the meantime, Comptroller General Walker announced that he would decide within a month "whether to file suit regarding GAO's access to NEPDG records."[28] Despite this statement, various members of both the Senate and the House began to pressure the GAO to move forward with its lawsuit. On January 22, Senators Joseph Lieberman, Ernest Hollings, Carl Levin, and Byron Dorgan sent a letter of support to the GAO in its investigation of the task force.[29] Two days later, Dingell and Waxman requested that the GAO legally challenge the task force's refusals to hand over all energy policy information.[30] In response to all of these maneuverings, Vice President Cheney declared on January 27 that the administration was steadfast in its refusal to provide even some of the most basic information about the meetings because of an important principle involved: doing so would contribute to a further withering of traditional presidential prerogatives. In a news interview, Cheney made the following extraordinary statement: "In 34 years [in Washington], I have repeatedly seen an erosion of the powers and the ability of the president of the United States to do his job. We saw it in the War Powers Act. We saw it in the Budget Anti-Impoundment Act. We've seen it in cases like this before, where it's demanded that presidents cough up and compromise on important principles."[31]

On January 30, the GAO had finalized its decision to "take the steps necessary to file suit in United States District Court." Walker defended the GAO's statutory authority to access the energy task force's records and refuted Cheney's defense for withholding information. Furthermore, Walker stated that if the Bush administration wanted to stop the GAO it could at any time through the president's power "under GAO's statutory access authority . . . to preclude judicial enforcement of GAO's access rights" or an assertion of executive privilege. Yet the administration did neither. Walker therefore stated that the GAO would bring the matter to the courts "to enforce our access rights against a federal official."[32]

On February 22 Walker filed suit against the vice president, stating that GAO's "repeated attempts to reach a reasonable accommodation on this matter have not been successful."[33] In U.S. district court, Judge John Bates ruled against Walker, dismissed the suit, and rejected the organization's standing claims.[34] The GAO decided not to attempt an appeal because doing so would require significant time and resources and because other private litigants were already pursuing the same information through other lawsuits.[35] In its final report, the agency stated that the vice president's "unwillingness to provide NEPDG records and other related information precluded us from fully achieving our objectives in accordance with generally accepted government auditing standards and substantially limited our ability to answer" Congress.[36]

The efforts of Congress and the GAO to gain access to various energy task force documents were thus unsuccessful. The Bush administration used three primary justifications to prevent disclosure. First, FACA did not apply to the task force because it consisted only of federal employees and thus was exempt from disclosure requirements. Second, the GAO had no authority to investigate the executive branch other than when dealing with public money. Finally, Democratic members of Congress could not hold the White House accountable because, as minority members of Congress, they lacked the power to make a committee request for information.

Judicial Watch and the Sierra Club Join Forces

The only recourse then was for private litigants to pursue the disclosure of information against the administration. Judicial Watch Inc. and the Sierra

Club soon filed separate suits, later consolidated, against the energy task force.[37] The two groups alleged that the task force gave significant roles to private individuals, which was a FACA violation.[38] They sought the release of documents relating to task force meetings to determine the extent of the allegedly illegal nature of the group. In July 2002, D.C. district court judge Emmet G. Sullivan granted the groups' request for discovery.[39] In so doing, he held that the terms of FACA created "substantive requirements to which the government must adhere." Continuing, the court reasoned that if the facts of the complaints were true, the government then would be in violation of "the public access provisions of [FACA]." Sullivan did not address the administration's separation of powers argument, which asserted that the application of FACA in this circumstance "interferes with the President's constitutionally protected ability to receive confidential advice from his advisors, even when those advisors include private individuals." The court merely noted that a resolution to this question was "premature."[40]

The administration immediately requested a motion for a stay of the proceedings and argued "that requiring [the White House] to review documents responsive to plaintiffs' discovery requests, disclose those for which no viable claim of [executive] privilege exists, and assert any applicable privileges with respect to specific documents, impermissibly interferes with 'core Article II' functions and imposes an unconstitutional burden on the Executive Branch."[41] The D.C. district court rejected this argument and held that the White House responds "to discovery requests on a regular basis, asserting executive privilege with respect to specific requests for particular items when necessary." The court determined that the administration was seeking a new constitutional right of immunity against disclosures under FACA. The result would be "to relieve" the president of his "responsibility" of even asserting executive privilege. The stay was therefore denied.[42]

Rather than comply with the discovery order, Cheney filed an interlocutory appeal in which he asked for review of the complex and serious constitutional issues raised. The D.C. district court dismissed the appeal and held that it did not disregard the "defendants' constitutional challenges"; rather, "it is out of concern for the seriousness of this issue that" it decided discovery was appropriate.[43] The administration then asked the D.C. circuit court of appeals to issue a writ of mandamus to require the district court to stop the discovery process and argued that the broad inquiry would violate the principle of separation of powers.[44] The appeals court declined and determined that "so long as the separation of powers conflict that petitioners anticipate remains hypothetical, we have no authority to exercise the extraordinary remedy of mandamus." Any alleged harm, the court concluded, would be mitigated through a "narrow, carefully focused discovery" process.[45]

The Supreme Court Takes Up the Case

On December 15, 2003, the Supreme Court granted certiorari to decide whether the discovery was constitutional and if the appeals court had the power to stop it.[46] In the Bush administration's brief to the Court, the central component of its argument was a separation of powers claim that hinged on the president's "specific constitutional authority under both the Opinion and Recommendations Clauses to request the opinions of department heads and to propose such legislation as the President may deem necessary."[47] Turning to the issue of executive privilege, the White House argued that such a claim was limited and would not protect the president from all discovery requests. The fact was that "the President's constitutional interests in being able to obtain confidential advice regarding his constitutionally assigned responsibilities is not coextensive with, nor fully protected by the possibility of invoking, Executive privilege."[48]

The administration next asserted that "Congress does not have the power to inhibit, confine, or control the process through which the President formulates the legislative measures he proposes or the administration actions he orders." FACA thus violates separation of powers concerns because Congress cannot "validly regulate the process by which the President gathers advice and information to formulate his policies and recommendations, and it has no greater legislative authority to empower private individuals to intrude into that process." The end result was that a separation of powers claim, not just the use of executive privilege, prevents both Congress and private citizens from intruding upon executive branch deliberations.[49]

During oral argument Solicitor General Theodore Olson specifically addressed the concern of why the president had not made an executive privilege claim: "The act of forcing the President to invoke executive privilege every time someone files a lawsuit . . . means that FACA would be used in every case to file a lawsuit to challenge the President and the Vice President's ability to . . . obtain opinions."[50] Olson also remarked that executive privilege might not cover "every scrap of paper" whereas an assertion of a separation of powers violation would guarantee protection from disclosure. Finally, Olson argued that using executive privilege would place too big of an administrative burden on the White House by requiring "the President and the Vice President to spend time with documents" searching for what is and is not privileged.[51] What the administration sought was blanket protection from any discovery request, which was something executive privilege could not provide.

In its opinion the Supreme Court vacated the judgment of the D.C. appeals court, and remanded the case for rehearing.[52] Speaking for the Court, Justice Anthony Kennedy sided with the administration's argument that separation of powers considerations were of paramount concern. Citing *U.S. v. Nixon,* he declared that the lower courts must "give recognition to the paramount necessity of protecting the Executive Branch from vexatious litigation that might distract it from the energetic performance of its constitutional duties." These concerns are even greater when considering civil litigation, the Court held. Rejecting the appeals court's claim that *Nixon* stood as an absolute barrier against discovery protection, Kennedy asserted that the need for information in civil cases "does not share the urgency or significance of" a criminal subpoena request.[53] The failure to disclose information in a civil case, he reasoned, "does not hamper another branch's ability to perform its 'essential functions' in quite the same way."[54] Addressing the application of FACA to the White House, Kennedy argued that even if the Court declared that the act "embodies important congressional objectives, the only consequence from respondents' inability to obtain the discovery they seek is that it would be more difficult for private complainants to vindicate Congress policy objectives under FACA."[55]

After it declared that the "Executive Branch, at its highest level" needs judicial help "to protect its constitutional prerogatives," the Court turned to the issue of executive privilege. Here, Kennedy held that, "given the breadth of the discovery requests in this case compared to the narrow subpoena orders in *United States* v *Nixon,* our precedent provides no support for the proposition that the Executive Branch 'shall bear the burden' of invoking executive privilege with sufficient specificity and of making particularized objections."[56] Contrary to what the lower courts determined, "*Nixon* does not leave them the sole option of inviting the Executive Branch to invoke executive privilege while remaining otherwise powerless to modify a party's overly broad discovery requests." Using executive privilege, Kennedy declared, "is an extraordinary assertion of power 'not to be lightly invoked.'"[57] Once invoked, the judicial branch "is forced into the difficult task of balancing the need for information in a judicial proceeding and the Executive's Article II prerogatives. This inquiry places courts in the awkward position of evaluating the Executive's claims of confidentiality and autonomy, and pushes to the fore difficult questions of separation of powers and checks and balances." Kennedy therefore ordered the appeals court to give due consideration to "the weighty separation-of-powers objections" when reconsidering the appeal and addressing the discovery issue.[58]

The Significance of the Supreme Court's Action

As one commentator said of *Cheney,* even "a dense reader could not possibly miss the Court's point."[59] Not only had many of the lower courts' arguments been refuted but the high court had handed to the administration a significant victory in the unitary executive debate. The Supreme Court appears to have bought into the administration's assertion that forcing disclosure would have a negative impact on presidents' ability to carry out their responsibilities under Article II of the Constitution. The decision thus established a rather high standard of judicial deference to executive authority.

Acting on the Supreme Court's clarifications the D.C. appeals court had no other choice but to rule for Cheney and issue a writ of mandamus ordering the district court to dismiss Judicial Watch's and the Sierra Club's complaints.[60] Circuit Judge A. Raymond Randolph wrote that FACA must be interpreted "strictly" in light of the "severe" separation of powers concerns. He therefore reasoned that Congress could not have intended FACA coverage to include presidential advisory committees (which are normally exempt from FACA if composed of federal employees) when private citizens merely participate in "meetings or activities." "The outsider," Raymond stated, "might make an important presentation, he might be persuasive, the information he provides might affect the committee's judgment. But having neither a vote nor a veto over the advice the committee renders to the President, he is no more a member of the committee than the aides who accompany Congressmen or cabinet officers to committee meetings." Raymond concluded that "[s]eparation-of-powers concerns strongly support this interpretation of FACA." Therefore, in "making decisions on personnel and policy, and in formulating legislative proposals, the President must be free to seek confidential information from many sources, both inside the government and outside."[61]

Summary and Analysis

The appeals court's decision largely bypassed the constitutional concerns when it focused on the statutory issue of whether FACA even applied to the energy task force. However, in so doing the court greatly enhanced the administration's ability to block the disclosure of information. Narrowing the committee membership standard to only those who have a vote or veto allows for the executive branch to involve any number of private citizens or groups without worrying about openness or accountability as long as they are not given ultimate decisionmaking authority. This understanding, as Michael J. Mongan reports in his review of the act, is misguided. In fact, Mongan notes that "the legislative history—not to mention the text—of FACA reveals no congressional intent to cabin the definition of 'member' so narrowly."[62] In effect the intent of Congress was violated.

The Supreme Court's opinion strengthened the White House's argument that it had the right to withhold from the public and Congress information dealing with public policy discussions that included private parties. No doubt the Court is correct that one should be mindful of the vexing constitutional issues at stake. However, there are also important trade-offs between transparency and secrecy that must be considered and resolved. The disclosure of information has long been held as one of the primary ways to combat fraud and abuse in government. As Supreme Court justice Louis Brandeis once stated, "Publicity is justly commended as a remedy for social and industrial diseases. Sunlight is said to be the best of disinfectants; electric light the most efficient policeman."[63] On the other hand, there needs to be some level of confidentiality at the executive level by which a president may discuss public policy matters in confidence. Such conflicts thus involve a balancing test to determine which branch's interests are more compelling under the circumstances.

The problem with the judiciary's answer to this controversy is that it provided far too much protection to the executive branch at the cost of openness and accountability. The solution, in essence, offset the balance of power between the president and Congress. What the courts ended up endorsing was an immunity from disclosure for the White House, which precludes any type of nuanced approach that could recognize trade-offs and political accommodations that seek to balance the interests of the two branches. These decisions merely give a license for presidents so disposed to maintain a shroud of secrecy at the expense of the accountability that is so essential to our republican form of government.

Nonetheless, some leading thinkers on executive power differ and, like Cheney, perceive the Bush administration's efforts as a corrective against the modern trend of supposedly weak presidential responses to legislative encroachments. They see the judicial resolution as, in essence, restoring the balance. For example, scholar and unitary executive advocate John Yoo maintains that the Bush administration indeed has been "energetic" in its efforts to protect and expand executive powers. He maintains that the president "has re-classified national security information made public in earlier administrations and declined, citing executive privilege, to disclose information to Congress or the courts about its energy policy task force. The White House has [also] declared that the Constitution allows the president to sidestep laws that invade his executive authority. That is why Mr. Bush has issued hundreds of signing statements—more than any previous president—reserving his right not to enforce unconstitutional laws."[64] According to Yoo, these actions are not only perfectly justifiable on administrative and policymaking grounds, but they are constitutionally mandated as well. As for the energy task force controversy, he says that the White House was correct in defending its executive branch prerogatives. In addition, he said the Supreme Court's ruling was the natural conclusion when one looks at the facts of the case. "I would think," Yoo insisted, "that this is the kind of case where you would want the government to get that kind of protection."[65]

In retrospect, could this controversy over access to documents been handled differently? The whole episode was potentially avoidable in the first place. The Bush administration came to office under some suspicion for the president's and vice president's various ties to the oil industry. Thus, as scholar Louis Fisher suggests, it was politically foolish for the administration to so heavily consult industry advocates in the task force meetings without including sufficient countervailing voices from environmental, consumer protection, and labor groups. Had the administration done so, it could have easily replied to any request for information about the task force meetings by revealing that it had invited a balanced group of interested parties and therefore avoided the political fallout from the accusations of a cover-up.[66] Nonetheless, despite the political shortcomings of the administration's actions, it is possible that some in the White House, especially the vice president, actually wanted a constitutional battle because they believed that they could win and that a victory would further the cause of reestablishing presidential prerogatives.

In all likelihood there would have been a resolution more favorable to those seeking access had Congress acted more forcefully and not relied on the GAO or outside groups to file lawsuits. Congress did not exhaust all of its constitutional mechanisms for getting access to the information that it had wanted, and it thus became the architect of its own ultimate defeat at the hands of the judicial branch. But what if Congress instead had held more hearings, issued subpoenas for documents and testimony, and threatened contempt citations against the administration if it failed to cooperate?

During an overlapping period in 2001–2002, the House Government Reform Committee, headed by Representative Dan Burton, a Republican, demanded access to Department of Justice documents for an investigation into a three-decades old Boston organized crime case, despite administration claims of executive privilege.[67] "This is not a monarchy," Burton exclaimed, adding that "[t]he legislative branch has oversight responsibility to make sure there is no corruption in the executive branch."[68] After some contentious hearings and threats of legislative action, the administration struck a deal with the committee to allow it access to key documents needed for the investigation. The committee had held firm and the administration eventually cooperated, as so often happens in these interbranch disputes. The GOP-led committee indeed had challenged the Bush administration in a number of separation of powers disputes, and Burton had made it clear that a part of his job as committee chair was to protect the institutional prerogatives of Congress against what he saw as an administration engaging in frequent power grabs against the legislative body. Yet, in the case of the energy task force controversy, Republican voices against the administration were largely quiet or nonexistent. The administration prevailed ultimately as a consequence of legislative inaction.

The outcome is all the more regrettable because the implicit claim of a form of executive privilege by the administration in this case was not very strong. At the outset, the requests for information about the energy task force were overly broad. The initial GAO request, for example, demanded "records" in the forms of emails, voice mails, drawings, plans, checks and canceled checks, bank statements, ledgers, books, diaries, logs, video recordings, Telexes, notes, invoices, and drafts.

Over time the GAO narrowed its request significantly, to merely factual information, such as the names of persons who attended meetings and the costs of those meetings, but not deliberative information. That was reasonable, although because of the initial broad request Cheney may have dug in because he believed he would ultimately be dragged into a multi-step process of the GAO seeking more and more information over time. He may also have been concerned that releasing the names of those who met with the task force would result in their being called to testify before Congress. Nonetheless, once GAO narrowed its request to fact-based and not deliberative information, the administration's claim to a compelling need for secrecy weakened considerably. It is a bit surprising, therefore, that the Supreme Court gave so much deference to the administration's positions on secrecy and separation of powers.

The lesson for Congress is that it should not rely on outside interests or an arm of the legislative branch (the GAO in this case) to take up a challenge against executive power. Congress has the institutional means to confront the executive branch, although it does not always have the will to do so. There are numerous instances of Congress gaining access to executive branch information by using its constitutionally based powers to challenge administrations. Indeed, when Congress has acted in this fashion, it has prevailed far more often against the executive than it has failed to achieve access. Thus, only Congress is well positioned to protect its own powers and prerogatives.

Notes

1. "The Vice President Appears on ABC's This Week," January 27, 2002, http://www.whitehouse.gov/vicepresident/news-speeches/speeches/vp20020127.html (accessed November 11, 2008).

2. "Remarks Prior to a Meeting with the Energy Policy Development Group and an Exchange with Reporters," *Weekly Compilation of Presidential Documents* 37 (January 29, 2001): 236–37.

3. U.S. General Accounting Office, "Energy Task Force: Process Used to Develop the National Energy Policy," GAO-03–894, August 2003, http://www.gao.gov/new.items/d03894.pdf (accessed November 11, 2008), 1, citing Presidential Memorandum, January 29, 2001; hereafter, GAO report).

4. The following were also NEPDG members: the secretaries of state, treasury, interior, agriculture, commerce, transportation, and energy; the administrator of the Environmental Protection Agency; the director of the Federal Emergency Management Agency; the

director of the Office of Management and Budget; the assistant to the president and deputy chief of staff for policy; the assistant to the president for economic policy; and the deputy assistant to the president for intergovernmental affairs. GAO report, 8.

5. GAO report, 9; David S. Addington to W. J. "Billy" Tauzin, Dan Burton, John Dingell, and Henry Waxman, May 4, 2001, http://oversight.house.gov/Documents/20040831095650–29059.pdf (accessed November 11, 2008).

6. GAO report, 5.

7. Office of the President, Report of the National Energy Policy Development Group, "National Energy Policy," May 2001, http://www.whitehouse.gov/energy/National-Energy-Policy.pdf (accessed November 11, 2008); U.S. Department of Energy, "National Energy Policy Status Report on Implementation of NEP Recommendations," January 2005, 2, http://www.energy.gov/media/NEP_Implementation_Report.pdf (accessed March 24, 2007).

8. John Dingell and Henry Waxman to Andrew Lundquist, April 19, 2001, http://oversight.house.gov/Documents/20040831095838–21952.pdf (accessed November 11, 2008).

9. *Federal Advisory Committee Act,* 5 U.S.C.A. App. 2 (2006).

10. The General Accounting Office was later renamed the Government Accountability Office. "GAO's Name Change and Other Provisions of the GAO Human Capital Reform Act of 2004," http://www.gao.gov/about/namechange.html (accessed November 11, 2008).

11. David S. Addington to W. J. "Billy" Tauzin, Dan Burton, John Dingell, and Henry Waxman, May 4, 2001, http://oversight.house.gov/Documents/20040831095650–29059.pdf (accessed November 11, 2008).

12. John Dingell and Henry Waxman to Andrew Lundquist, May 15, 2001, http://oversight.house.gov/Documents/20040831095447–76303.pdf (accessed November 11, 2008).

13. David S. Addington to Anthony Gamboa, May 16, 2001, http://oversight.house.gov/Documents/20040831095214–51332.pdf (accessed November 11, 2008).

14. John Dingell and Henry Waxman to David S. Addington, May 22, 2001, http://oversight.house.gov/Documents/20040831094829–47374.pdf (accessed November 11, 2008).

15. David S. Addington to Reid Stuntz and Phil Barnett, May 25, 2001 (emphasis added), http://oversight.house.gov/Documents/20040831095041–19071.pdf (accessed November 11, 2008).

16. Anthony Gamboa to David S. Addington, June 1, 2001, http://oversight.house.gov/Documents/20040831095041–19071.pdf (accessed November 11, 2008).

17. David S. Addington to Anthony Gamboa, June 7, 2001, http://oversight.house.gov/Documents/20040831010840–55687.pdf (accessed November 11, 2008).

18. Anthony Gamboa to David S. Addington, June 22, 2001, http://oversight.house.gov/Documents/20040831010638–49718.pdf (accessed November 11, 2008); David Walker to Richard Cheney, June 18, 2001, http://oversight.house.gov/Documents/20040831004316–29355.pdf (accessed November 11, 2008).

19. Richard Cheney to the House of Representatives, August 2, 2001, http://oversight.house.gov/Documents/20040830233716–42929.pdf (accessed November 11, 2008).

20. GAO Statement, August 6, 2001, http://oversight.house.gov/Documents/20040830233320–50377.pdf (accessed November 11, 2008).

21. John Dingell and Henry Waxman to Richard Cheney, August 29, 2001, http://oversight.house.gov/Documents/20040831103738–88498.pdf (accessed November 11, 2008).

22. GAO Statement on the National Energy Policy Development Group, September 7, 2001, http://oversight.house.gov/Documents/20040831103615–65132.pdf (accessed November 11, 2008).

23. Statement of Comptroller General David Walker on the National Energy Policy Development Group, September 28, 2001, http://oversight.house.gov/Documents/20040831103404–31650.pdf (accessed November 11, 2008).

24. Henry Waxman to Richard Cheney, December 4, 2001, http://oversight.house.gov/Documents/20040831103250–77482.pdf (accessed November 11, 2008).

25. David S. Addington to Henry Waxman, January 3, 2002, http://oversight.house.gov/Documents/20040830155258–34566.pdf (accessed November 11, 2008).

26. Henry Waxman to Richard Cheney, January 8, 2002, http://oversight.house.gov/Documents/20040830155227–58704.pdf (accessed November 11, 2008).

27. Henry Waxman to Richard Cheney, January 16, 2002, http://oversight.house.gov/Documents/20040830154908–42327.pdf (accessed November 11, 2008); Henry Waxman to Richard Cheney, January 25, 2002, http://oversight.house.gov/Documents/20040830154529–45198.pdf (accessed November 11, 2008).

28. Statement of Comptroller General David Walker on the National Energy Policy Development Group, January 9, 2002, http://oversight.house.gov/Documents/20040830155126–21933.pdf (accessed November 11, 2008).

29. Joseph Lieberman, Ernest Hollings, Carl Levin, and Byron Dorgan to David Walker, January 22, 2002, http://oversight.house.gov/Documents/20040830154810–75641.pdf (accessed November 11, 2008).

30. John Dingell and Henry Waxman to David Walker, January 24, 2002, http://oversight.house.gov/Documents/20040830154700–91281.pdf (accessed November 11, 2008).

31. "The Vice President Appears on ABC's This Week," January 27, 2002, http://www.whitehouse.gov/vicepresident/news-speeches/speeches/vp20020127.html (accessed November 11, 2008).

32. General Statement of Decision of the Comptroller General Concerning NEPDG Litigation, January 30, 2002, http://oversight.house.gov/Documents/20040830154126–19726.pdf (accessed November 11, 2008).

33. *Walker v. Cheney,* 230 F. Supp. 2d 51 (D.D.C. 2002); GAO Statement Concerning Litigation, February 22, 2002, http://oversight.house.gov/Documents/20040830153549–62303.pdf (accessed November 11, 2008).

34. *Walker v. Cheney,* 230 F. Supp. 2d 51, 75.

35. GAO Press Statement on *Walker v. Cheney,* February. 7, 2003, http://oversight.house.gov/Documents/20040625103334–22539.pdf (accessed November 11, 2008).

36. GAO report, 3.

37. *Judicial Watch, Inc., v. National Energy Policy Dev. Group,* 219 F. Supp. 2d 20, 25–27 (D.D.C. 2002). The National Resources Defense Council also initiated a suit.

38. *Federal Advisory Committee Act,* § 1, 5 U.S.C.A. App. 2 (2006).

39. *Judicial Watch, Inc., v. National Energy Policy Dev. Group,* 219 F. Supp. 2d 20, 56–57.

40. Ibid., 30, 44.

41. *Judicial Watch, Inc., v. National Energy Policy Dev. Group,* 230 F. Supp. 2d 12, 15 (D.D.C. 2002).

42. Ibid., 16.

43. *Judicial Watch, Inc., v. National Energy Policy Dev. Group,* 233 F. Supp. 2d 16, 23 (D.D.C. 2002).

44. *In re Cheney,* 334 F. 3d 1096, 1101 (D.C. Cir. 2003).

45. Ibid., 1105, 1107.

46. *Cheney v. U.S. District Court for District of Columbia,* 540 U.S. 1088 (2003).

47. Brief for the Petitioners, *Cheney v. United States District Court for the District of Columbia* (2004) (No. 03–475), 11. "Those Clauses allow the President a zone of autonomy in obtaining advice, including with respect to formulating proposals for legislation." Ibid., 12. The "opinion" clause states that the president "may require the Opinion, in writing, of the principal Officer in each of the executive Departments, upon any Subject relating to the Duties of their respective Offices." Article II, sec. 2, U.S. Constitution. According to the "recommendations" clause the president "shall from time to time give to the Congress Information of the State of the Union, and recommend to their Consideration such Measures as he shall judge necessary and expedient." Article II, sec. 3, U.S. Constitution.

48. Brief for the Petitioners, *Cheney v. United States District Court for the District of Columbia* (2004) (No. 03–475), 11.

49. Ibid., 12 (first quote), 32, 34 (second quote), 42.

50. *Cheney v. U.S. District Court for District of Columbia,* oral argument transcript, April 27, 2004, 18, http://www.supremecourtus.gov/oral_arguments/argument_transcripts/03–475.pdf (accessed November 11, 2008).

51. Ibid., 21.

52. *Cheney v. U.S. District Court for District of Columbia,* 542 U.S. 367, 378 (2004).

53. Ibid., 382 (first quote), 384 (second quote).

54. Ibid., 384 (citing *United States v. Nixon,* 418 U.S. 683, 707 [1974]).

55. *Cheney v. U.S. District Court for District of Columbia,* 542 U.S. 367, 384–85.

56. Ibid., 385 (first and second quotes), 388 (third quote, citing *In re Cheney,* 334 F. 3d 1096, 1105 [D.C. Cir. 2003]).

57. Ibid., 389 (citing *United States v. Reynolds,* 345 U.S. 1, 7 [1953]).

58. *Cheney v. U.S. District Court for District of Columbia,* 542 U.S. 367, 389, 391.

59. Michael J. Mongan, "Fixing FACA: The Case for Exempting Presidential Advisory Committees from Judicial Review under the Federal Advisory Committee Act," *Stanford Law Review* 58 (December 2005): 917.

60. *In re Cheney,* 406 F.3d 723, 731 (D.C. Cir. 2005).

61. Ibid., 728.

62. Mongan, "Fixing FACA," 918.

63. Louis Brandeis, *Other People's Money and How the Bankers Use It* (1914; New York: St. Martin's Press, 1995), 89.

64. John Yoo, "How the Presidency Regained Its Balance," *New York Times,* September 17, 2006, http://www.nytimes.com/2006/09/17/opinion/17yoo.html?ei=5090&en=2db683b71a2b4606&ex=1316145600&partner=rssuserland&emc=rss&pagewanted=print (accessed November 11, 2008).

65. John Yoo, "Former Deputy Assistant Attorney General John Yoo Talks about Terrorism, the Justice Department, and the Supreme Court," http://www.cfif.org/htdocs/freedomline/current/in_our_opinion/general_john_yoo.htm (accessed November 11, 2008).

66. See Louis Fisher, *The Politics of Executive Privilege* (Durham, N.C.: Carolina Academic Press, 2004).

67. This material on the Boston organized crime controversy draws from Mark J. Rozell, *Executive Privilege: Presidential Power, Secrecy, and Accountability,* 2nd ed. (Lawrence: University Press of Kansas, 2002).

68. Quoted in Ellen Nakashima, "Bush Invokes Executive Privilege on Hill," *Washington Post,* December 14, 2001, A43.

Warrantless Surveillance and the Warrantless Presidency

RICHARD M. PIOUS

On January 17, 2007, Senator Patrick Leahy (D-Vt.), chair of the Judiciary Committee, received a letter from Attorney General Alberto Gonzales informing the senator that a week earlier, a judge on the Foreign Intelligence Surveillance Court had issued an order authorizing "the Government to target for collection international communications in or out of the United States" if there was a reasonable belief that the messages involved members of al-Qaida or associated terrorist organizations. The letter went on to say that the "Terrorist Surveillance Program" run by the National Security Agency (NSA) "will now be conducted subject to the approval of the Foreign Intelligence Surveillance Court."[1] The letter represented a reversal of policy for the Bush administration, which previously had authorized electronic intercepts without obtaining judicial warrants. These intercepts raised a number of constitutional and legal issues: Did warrantless surveillance violate the Fourth Amendment? Did it violate the law? When Congress passed the Authorization for the Use of Military Force (AUMF) Act in the aftermath of the 9/11 terrorist acts, did that constitute congressional authorization to use any means necessary against terrorists—including warrantless surveillance?[2] Or did the president have inherent constitutional prerogatives as commander in chief to authorize the program?

The White House agreement to seek approval for the program from the Foreign Intelligence Surveillance Court (FISC) did not end the controversy, as the incoming chair of the Senate Intelligence Committee, John D. Rockefeller IV (D-W.Va.), announced that he would "move forward with the committee's review of all aspects of this program's legality and effectiveness."[3]

From the president's own party, via Senator Arlen Specter (R-Pa.), came the observation, "It is a little hard to see why it took so long."[4]

At first glance it might appear that the Bush administration, stung by its losses in the midterm congressional elections of 2006, had retreated from one of its contentions about the scope of executive power.[5] A closer look at the controversy demonstrates that the NSA program was part of a set of surveillance efforts that relied primarily or exclusively on executive prerogative rather than statutory authorization. These programs remain part of a system of "parallel governance," in which the executive assumes legislative and judicial powers to create and maintain a "state within a state." Put another way, the warrantless wiretaps were authorized by a warrantless presidency. And far from retreating from presidential prerogatives, it seemed more accurate to characterize the letter from Gonzales to Leahy as a tactical shift, from assertion of "hard" prerogative, in which the president's power is brandished against congressional interference, to "soft" prerogative, in which congressional or judicial authorization is sought and obtained in order to make a claim of "joint concord" that reduces the likelihood of judicial or congressional checks.

Prerogative Power and Parallel Governance

Throughout American history presidents have pushed their prerogatives to the limits, and sometimes beyond. The Bush administration has relied on legal counsel who pushed the theory of the "unitary executive."[6] In brief, the theory consisted of several propositions: there is an "executive branch" that the president controls through "the executive power"; all executive functions are to be exercised by the president and subordinates; Congress may not through its legislation infringe on the "core functions" of the presidency (war, foreign affairs, intelligence, national security); and the president's powers are anterior and superior to those of Congress, which should play a perfecting role in executive initiatives. Under this theory Congress could not, through framework legislation such as the War Powers Act, the Intelligence Oversight Act, or the Foreign Intelligence Surveillance Act, regulate or limit presidential executive power in these areas.

The White House acted opportunistically to exploit James Madison's theory of *partial* rather than complete separation of powers. Madison, who believed that not all legislative powers should be controlled by Congress, lest the entire government fall into the "legislative vortex," claimed that the constitutional system allowed each institution to have partial agency in, and partial control of, the powers of the others.[7] For the Bush White House, this provided an opportunity to use quasi-legislative powers such as military orders and executive orders; to rely on an expansive reading of the commander in chief power to engage in military actions; to sidestep the treaty powers to negotiate executive agreements and reinterpret or abrogate clauses in treaties and international conventions; and to claim judicial powers to establish military tribunals, suspend the privilege of the writ of habeas corpus, and authorize warrantless surveillance.

SURVEILLANCE THROUGH JUDICIAL WARRANT

The Fourth Amendment provides that "the right of the people to be secure in their persons, houses, papers, and effects, against unreasonable searches and seizures, shall not be violated, and no Warrants shall issue, but upon probable cause, supported by Oath or affirmation, and particularly describing the place to be searched, and the persons or things to be seized." In *Katz v. United States* (1967), the Supreme Court held that electronic surveillance that did not require physical intrusion was a search within the meaning of the Fourth Amendment.[8] The following year, in Title III of the Omnibus Crime Control and Safe Streets Act of 1968, Congress acted to prohibit most warrantless surveillance but provided an exception for national security surveillance based on the "constitutional power of the President to take such measures as he deems necessary to protect the Nation against actual or potential attack . . . [and] to obtain foreign intelligence information deemed essential to the security of the United States."[9] For a few years presidents possessed such statutory authority, but the Supreme Court held in 1972 that surveillance within the United States for "domestic security" would require a judicial warrant, presumably eliminating both executive prerogative and statutory dispensation.[10]

WARRANTLESS SURVEILLANCE

Presidents authorized warrantless surveillance prior to the Title III authorization and even after the Supreme Court decision. After World War II, they authorized intelligence agencies to conduct countersurveillance in the United States without warrants. The Signal Security Agency, through Operation Shamrock, monitored overseas cable traffic in the 1950s; Minaret monitored Vietnam protest movements; and COINTELPRO eavesdropped on civil rights organizers and antiwar demonstrators in the 1960s.[11] President Lyndon Johnson authorized army intelligence to spy on the Mississippi Freedom Delegation at the 1964 Democratic national convention.[12] Later, the FBI conducted warrantless surveillance, known as "racial matters," against Dr. Martin Luther King Jr.[13] In the 1970s President Nixon and national security advisor Henry Kissinger authorized FBI use of warrantless taps on National Security Council staffers.[14]

Revelations about the Shamrock program, in which the NSA had monitored the telephone calls of civil rights and antiwar activists, led Congress to pass the Foreign Intelligence Surveillance Act of 1978 (FISA).[15] Congress made clear its intent to prevent warrantless wiretapping. It repealed the Title III provision that the government had relied on in claiming inherent presidential power to tap. It made it a crime for government officials "acting under color of law" to engage in electronic surveillance "other than pursuant to statute." It provided that FISA and other surveillance laws "shall be the exclusive means by which electronic surveillance . . . may be conducted." It established an eleven-member Foreign Intelligence Surveillance Court (FISC) to entertain government petitions for authority to conduct surveillance.[16]

In 1979 President Carter issued an executive order implementing the FISA provisions, which noted that "any monitoring which constitutes electronic surveillance as defined in the *Foreign Intelligence Surveillance Act of 1978* shall be conducted in accordance with that Act as well as this Order."[17] It provided (pursuant to the statute) for authorization without a warrant, provided the attorney general or seven other officials made certifications to Congress. The director of the National Security Agency was not among those officials, though the director of the Central Intelligence Agency (CIA) was included. Officials were required to certify that the electronic surveillance would not target "the contents of any communication in which a United States person is a party." When President Clinton authorized the Echelon program, which involved NSA monitoring of millions of telephone calls, many of which were placed by American citizens, the NSA complied with the FISA procedures and obtained warrants when several thousand American citizens were targeted.[18]

In 1995 Congress amended FISA to provide that no *physical* surveillance could occur without a court order. That same year, Clinton issued an executive order putting physical surveillance under FISA and allowing for the attorney general and other officials to make exceptions, but only under the provisions called for in the statute.[19] These required a certification that the search would not involve "the premises, information, material, or property of a United States person." As of 2000, according to then–NSA director Michael Hayden, the "NSA may only target communications of a U.S. person in the United States if a federal judge finds probable cause to believe that the U.S. person is an agent of a foreign power."[20]

SURVEILLANCE PROGRAMS IN THE BUSH ADMINISTRATION

In the aftermath of the 9/11 attacks, President Bush in 2002 signed a secret executive order authorizing the NSA to target calls made in or out of the United States when one party was abroad and there might be a link to al-Qaida. This program was reauthorized by the president every forty-five days after a review by the attorney general, the White House counsel, the NSA general counsel, and the NSA inspector general. The administration briefed selected congressional leaders more than a dozen times but swore them to secrecy and refused to let them consult with outside counsel on the legality of the program. It also briefed the two presiding judges of the FISA courts, Royce Lamberth in 2002 and Colleen Kotar-Kotelly in 2003.

Under another program begun prior to the 9/11 attacks, Verizon, Bell South, and AT&T cooperated (Qwest did not) with the government in allowing the NSA to conduct surveillance on domestic calls and e-mails without warrants in an effort to detect foreign government attempts to hack into computer networks.[21] Tens of millions of calls were monitored through information provided by the service providers under contract to NSA. This program, on its face, was in violation of section 222 of the Communications Act of 1934, which prohibited telephone companies from giving out information about their customers' calls. (The Federal Communications Commission [FCC] is authorized to levy fines up to $130,000 per day per violation.) In another program, called First Fruits, the NSA spied on the private conversations of its own employees and (CIA) and Defense Intelligence Agency (DIA) employees to prevent leaks to journalists such as James Bamford, James Risen, and Seymour Hersh, who were writing about NSA surveillance programs. Since May 2001 the NSA has passed along the names of ten thousand American citizens to White House officials and those at other federal agencies, who had made up to thirty-five hundred requests; often these were the names of people who were not involved in terrorist activity and were not a threat to national security, but their names had come up in NSA intercepts.[22]

CONGRESSIONAL FRAMEWORK LEGISLATION

None of the "special collection" programs instituted by the Bush administration after 9/11 followed the procedures that Congress had mandated for surveillance when it passed the Foreign Intelligence Surveillance Act of 1978. Under the FISA provisions, the chief justice of the United States chooses the eleven judges of the Foreign Intelligence Surveillance Court (FISC) from judges of the federal courts. All applications for search or surveillance warrants are first reviewed by the Department of Justice's Office of Intelligence Policy and Review, which deals with foreign intelligence matters, and then must be approved by the attorney general, who certifies that the target for surveillance is either a "foreign power" or an "agent of a foreign power," or if a U.S. citizen or resident alien, that the target of a search or surveillance may be involved in a criminal offense against the United States or engages in "international terrorism."

In establishing the FISC, Congress designed what it thought would be a system of accountability for law enforcement agencies and intelligence agencies. It provided that Title III and FISA "shall be the exclusive means by which electronic surveillance . . . and the interception of domestic wire and oral communications may be conducted." It required the concurrence of a federal court to authorize wiretapping and other surveillance. The law made it a criminal offense, punishable by up to five years in prison, to conduct electronic surveillance, except as "authorized by and conducted pursuant to a search warrant or court order."[23] It did not delegate powers to the executive alone, or recognize inherent executive power, or assume under the doctrine of separation of powers that the executive either had sole or concurrent power to act once Congress had passed its framework law.

The law, however, was a compromise between those in the intelligence community who did not believe any Fourth Amendment restrictions should apply and members of Congress who argued for strict adherence to existing standards in obtaining judicial warrants. FISA allowed for a lower standard than "probable cause" in authorizing surveillance and for procedural safeguards that were less rigorous than those used in criminal investigations. Under the pre-9/11 version of the law, the court granted warrants to law enforcement and intelligence agencies, so long as the *primary purpose* was not criminal law enforcement but intelligence gathering linked to foreign espionage. The government had to certify that it could not obtain the information in any other manner. Warrants could be authorized for up to ninety days for U.S. citizens and up to a year for aliens.

FISA procedures took into account that the president might have to act quickly or in emergency conditions. One provision (an amendment in 2001 to an intelligence authorization) allowed surveillance for seventy-two hours before court approval would be required (an expansion from the earlier limit of twenty-four hours). Another provision allowed the president to gather "foreign intelligence information" for up to fifteen days without a court order, "following a declaration of war by the Congress." More than 18,748 FISA applications were made by the Department of Justice between 1979 and 2004, with only 4 being denied in 2003 and 1 in 2004. In 2006, of 2,181 applications, only 1 was denied.[24]

Legitimizing Warrantless Surveillance

President Bush had never acknowledged the existence of warrantless surveillance programs. Instead, during the presidential campaign of 2004 he had gone out of his way to reassure the American people that "when we're talking about chasing down terrorists, we're talking about getting a court order before we do so."[25] In 2005, at his confirmation hearings to be attorney general, Alberto Gonzales, at that time White House counsel, dismissed a question from Senator Russell Feingold (D-Wisc.) about whether, for targeted American citizens, the president would have the power to order wiretaps and surveillance without a court order. At the hearing Gonzales said it was "not the policy or the agenda of this president" to authorize actions that conflicted with existing law.[26] Eventually reporters for the *New York Times* obtained information about the program. President Bush, acting as presidents have before him, called in *Times* publisher Arthur Sulzberger Jr. and executive editor Bill Keller and asked them not to report on a story that they had held for more than a year.[27] The *Times* refused and on December 15, 2005, it published its story and ended the program's secrecy.[28]

THE ADMINISTRATION RESPONDS

The typical response of the executive when accused of lawbreaking or acting beyond the office's constitutional powers is to deny that the events occurred or to minimize them. This response is usually followed by an investigation that focuses on operatives rather than officials in the White House or eventually forces the resignation of some officials on the White House staff. In rare instances the attempt to contain the issue fails and a crisis of governance ensues, which paralyzes the presidency and results in a major shakeup within the administration, leading even to resignation or impeachment.

The surveillance controversy did not follow this pattern. On December 17, 2005, President Bush took full responsibility for authorizing the "highly classified" program in his weekly radio address to the nation and indicated that it would continue. "The authorization I gave the National Security Agency . . . is fully consistent with my constitutional responsibilities and authorities," Bush said, adding, "I'm also using constitutional authority vested in me as commander in chief."[29] He noted that he had renewed authorization for the program thirty times (each for a forty-five-day period) and would continue to do so. In a news conference Bush indicated that the government had to "be able to act fast," and he criticized what he claimed was a slow and cumbersome FISA review process. Even the attorney general's power to bypass the warrant, under existing FISA procedures, required preparation and review that could slow surveillance in the first critical few hours.[30] President Bush in his 2006 State of the Union address claimed that "previous presidents have used the same Constitutional authority" and that "federal courts have approved the use of that authority."[31]

At the White House on December 19, 2005, Alberto Gonzales and Michael Hayden, deputy director for national intelligence, gave reporters a briefing on the legal issues. They indicated that the program was "highly classified" and that they would not discuss operational details but only "legal underpinnings." Gonzales indicated that the program involved instances in which "we . . . have a reasonable basis to conclude that one party to the communication is a member of al Qaeda, affiliated with al Qaeda, or a member of an organization affiliated with al Qaeda or working in support of al Qaeda." They pointed out that the president as commander in chief had inherent authority as well as statutory power to authorize "signals intelligence."[32] Gonzales noted at Georgetown University several weeks later, "The leadership of Congress, including the leaders of the Intelligence Committees of both Houses of Congress, have been briefed about this program more than a dozen times since 2001."[33]

The Justice Department continued to press its arguments, sending a letter to the chairs of the House and Senate Intelligence Committees, followed by an exhaustive legal brief that laid out the administration's case. "There is undeniably an important and legitimate privacy interest at stake," Assistant Attorney General William E. Moschella wrote, but it must be balanced "against the government's compelling interest in the security of the nation." Because FISA procedures (although they constituted "a very important tool" that the government makes "full use" of) were cumbersome, the president needed "speed and agility for the early warning system" and had to go beyond these procedures. To ask Congress for additional authority, Moschella pointed out, "would have tipped off our enemies concerning our intelligence limitations and capabilities."[34]

Subsequently, in a brief for a case before the FISA appeals court, the Justice Department argued that "the Constitution vests in the President inherent authority to conduct warrantless intelligence surveillance (electronic or otherwise) of foreign powers or their agents, and Congress cannot by statute extinguish that constitutional authority."[35] In another brief it argued that "the Government's overwhelming interest in detecting and thwarting further [al-Qaida] attacks is easily sufficient to make reasonable the intrusion into privacy," indicating that this intrusion was covered under the president's "inherent constitutional authority as commander in chief."[36]

The government argued that "FISA expressly contemplates that the Executive Branch may conduct electronic surveillance outside FISA's express procedures if and when a subsequent statute authorizes such surveillance." It then claimed that Congress had done so, through its passage after 9/11 of the Authorization for the Use of Military Force (AUMF).[37] The text of that congressional resolution authorized the president to "use all necessary and appropriate force against those nations, organizations, or persons he determines planned, authorized, committed, or aided the terrorist attacks" of September 11 in order to prevent "any future acts of international terrorism against the United States."[38] The government referred to the Supreme Court's decision in the *Hamdi* case, in which it held that the AUMF was an "act of Congress" sufficient to satisfy requirements in federal law that no U.S. citizen may be detained by the government "except pursuant to an act of Congress."[39] The Court held that the AUMF satisfied that requirement, even though it did not refer to detention; similarly, the AUMF would satisfy the FISA requirements, even though it did not specifically mention surveillance.[40]

The government then referred again to its original argument about presidential prerogative power, that "if FISA could not be read to allow the President to authorize the NSA activities during the current Congressionally authorized armed conflict with [al-Qaida], FISA would be unconstitutional," since such a reading of the statute would constitute an interference with the president's powers as commander in chief. Since the president has "inherent constitutional authority to conduct warrantless searches and surveillance within the United States for foreign intelligence purposes," the Justice Department asserted, there would be a "serious constitutional" question as to whether such spying "is such a core exercise of commander in chief control over the Armed Forces during armed conflict that Congress cannot interfere with it at all."[41]

THE ARGUMENT OF ADMINISTRATION CRITICS

Civil liberties watchdog groups challenged each of the administration's claims. The American Civil Liberties Union (ACLU), in a letter to Alberto Gonzales, requested appointment of an outside special counsel for investigation and prosecution of those involved in a conspiracy to violate criminal laws against warrantless wiretapping of Americans. It called it a "constitutional crisis" involving "serious felonies."[42] The letter observed that the FISA procedures were the only method Congress had authorized and that intercepting communications involving U.S. persons without judicial warrant or approval from the FISA court was expressly prohibited.[43] It pointed out that the statute contained an emergency authorization process, permitting surveillance for seventy-two hours prior to obtaining a court order.[44] It also noted that FISA governs surveillance "during time of war" and allows the attorney general to use warrantless taps for only fifteen days after a declaration of war by Congress.[45] The AUMF therefore could not have provided authorization nor could it have waived the fifteen-day provision, nor could it have waived the criminal liability provisions.[46] It noted that although the *Hamdi* decision did legitimize commander in chief powers involving detentions, *Hamdi* referred to battlefield detentions and was limited to a theater of war. In *Hamdi* the Court held unacceptable any executive effort to "condense power into a single branch of government," contrary to the checks and balances on power required by the Constitution.[47] The ACLU also noted that when the USA PATRIOT Act was passed it contained twenty-five provisions involving electronic surveillance that revised FISA rules.[48] None changed the requirements for a warrant or recognized any loopholes involving an emergency or war. None modified the language stating that FISA warrants "shall be the *exclusive* means by which electronic surveillance . . . and the interception of domestic wire, oral, and electronic communications may be conducted."[49]

The American Bar Association, at its annual convention in Chicago on February 13, 2006, denounced the administration's actions and claimed the president did not have constitutional authority to authorize such surveillance. "To prevent the very human temptation to abuse power," ABA president Michael Greco said, "there must be checks and balances in the form of oversight by the courts and Congress."[50]

Michael Ratner of the Center for Constitutional Rights charged that warrantless surveillance might have been used to conduct surveillance against lawyers representing detainees, thus subverting lawyer-client privilege. "By spying on me, my colleagues, and other attorneys who challenge them," he wrote, "the administration can learn our legal strategies, end our relationship of trust with our clients, and in essence make us into agents of the government: We ask questions of clients, and the government, listening in secretly, gets the answers."[51]

A group of distinguished constitutional law scholars, including many former government officials, wrote a letter on January 9, 2006, addressed to the chairs and ranking members of the Judiciary and Intelligence committees of Congress. They stated that "the Justice Department's defense of what it concedes was secret and warrantless electronic surveillance of persons within the United States fails to identify any plausible legal authority for such surveillance." They did not agree that the president as commander in chief had authority, in gathering "signals intelligence," to override FISA restrictions within the United States. Similarly, Harvard professor Laurence Tribe, in a letter to Representative John Conyers (D-Mich.) released January 6, 2006, noted that when the conference committee drafted the final version of FISA, it assumed that if a war began, the fifteen-day emergency period would "allow time for consideration of any amendment to this act that may be appropriate during a wartime emergency."[52] Tribe pointed out the contradiction in the administration's position expressed by Attorney General Gonzales in his December 19 briefing: the attorney general claimed congressional authorization through the AUMF but admitted that the administration had not gone to Congress to ask approval for a warrantless program because Congress would have denied it.[53]

The use of the AUMF went far beyond the language of the statute, according to some legal analysts. Congress had authorized the use of "appropriate force," which should be construed to mean that the president must comply with the law, including international law. The authorization was directed against those who "planned, authorized, committed, or aided" the 9/11 attacks or who "harbored such . . . persons." But the warrantless program extended far beyond that, to those with "known links" with al-Qaida or links with "an affiliated terrorist organization," or people who perhaps unintentionally communicate with those deemed to be terrorists.[54]

Leaders of some conservative groups also weighed in against the administration. Paul Weyrich, head of the Free Congress Foundation, said he was "troubled by what Bush could do," and Grover Norquist of Americans for Tax Reform said the administration should comply with the FISA requirements. Larry Pratt, executive director of Gun Owners of America, said court orders should remain part of the process. David Keene, chairman of the American Conservative Union, called on the administration to obtain congressional authorization rather than assert a presidential prerogative to bypass Congress in wartime. Robert Levy, affiliated with the libertarian Cato Institute, noted that "the president is acting contrary to the expressed will of Congress," rendering the program "most legally suspect."[55] The defection of some of the conservatives who formed the core of the Bush coalition would have its impact on the administration: rather than choose to confront Congress directly over presidential prerogative, the administration decided to work to obtain authorization that would legitimize its activities, a strategic decision to rely on "soft" rather than "hard" prerogative power.

Congress Responds

Democrats attacked the administration as soon as the existence of the program was made public. Senator Edward Kennedy sent a letter to Bush on December 22, 2005, urging him "to provide Congress and the American people with answers."[56] The following day Thomas Daschle, the former minority leader of the Senate, wrote an op-ed piece in the *Washington Post* taking issue with the idea that the AUMF could have authorized warrantless taps:

> Just before the Senate acted on this compromise resolution, the White House sought one last change. Literally minutes before the Senate cast its vote, the administration sought to add the words "in the United States and" after "appropriate force" in the agreed-upon text. This last-minute change would have given the president broad authority to exercise expansive powers not just overseas—where we all understood he wanted authority to act—but right here in the United States, potentially against American citizens. I could see no justification for Congress to accede to this extraordinary request for additional authority. I refused.[57]

Criticism was not limited to the Democrats. Republican Arlen Specter, chair of the Senate Judiciary Committee, announced that he would call congressional hearings because the program was "wrong, and it can't be condoned at all."[58]

INITIAL CONGRESSIONAL RESPONSES

One of the chief complaints of critics was that Congress had not been informed of the surveillance program. In fact, eight members of Congress were briefed—the leaders of the Senate and House and the heads of the Intelligence committees from both parties.[59] "It's been briefed to the Congress over a dozen times, and, in fact, it is a program that is, by every effort we've been able to make, consistent with the statutes and with the law," Vice President Cheney said December 18 in an interview with the ABC News program *Nightline*. "It's the kind of capability if we'd had before 9/11 might have led us to be able to prevent 9/11."[60] But briefings would be no substitute for congressional authorization. Members attend briefings without their staffers. Briefings are classified, so those briefed cannot discuss matters with other members of Congress or outside experts.[61] In any event, neither FISA nor any other law provided that any such briefings would be considered authorization.

Legislators requested that the Congressional Research Service (CRS) report on the legal issues. On January 5, 2006, analysts Elizabeth Bazan and Jennifer Elsea concluded that presidential authority to conduct the surveillance is "at its lowest ebb." They concluded that it was unlikely "that a court would hold that Congress has . . . authorized the NSA electronic surveillance operations here under discussion."[62] In late January the CRS issued two reports concluding that the National Security Act had been violated by the Bush administration, which had not kept Congress "fully and currently informed."[63] It turned out that Representative Peter Hoekstra (R-Mich.), former senator Bob Graham (D-Fla.), Senate Intelligence Committee ranking member John D. Rockefeller IV, and Senate Democratic leader Harry Reid (D-Nev.) had not received written reports from the White House on the surveillance operation, as required by the National Security Act.[64]

CONGRESSIONAL HEARINGS

Republicans in Congress did not defend presidential prerogatives in this program. On December 18, Senator Lindsey O. Graham (R-S.C.) said, "I don't know of any legal basis to go around" the requirement that the White House formally apply to the FISA court for a warrant to engage in domestic surveillance, while Senator John McCain (R-Ariz.) said it was a "legitimate question" to ask why "the president chose not to use FISA." Senate Judiciary Committee chair Arlen Specter announced there would be hearings. "They talk about constitutional authority," he predicted, referring to the administration, and added, "There are limits as to what the president can do."[65] Four Republican senators (including Specter) joined with the Democrats, providing a majority vote to proceed with hearings. Meanwhile, in the House, Heather Wilson (R-N.Mex.), a former Air Force officer and staff member of the National Security Council whose subcommittee on technical and tactical surveillance oversees the NSA, called for a full congressional inquiry.[66] The stage seemed set for significant oversight and, if necessary, new authorizing legislation.

On February 6 Attorney General Gonzales appeared before the Senate Judiciary Committee, and Specter, Graham, Michael DeWine (R-Ohio), and Sam Brownback (R-Kans.) all asked him why he would not want Congress to authorize the program. Gonzales responded that no change in FISA law was necessary and that the president had the constitutional power to authorize warrantless wiretapping.[67] The hearings lasted only a few days, with much sparring over the extent of presidential powers, but the committee did not subpoena key documents, witnesses did not face serious questioning, and, most significantly, there were no subpoenas for the testimony of telephone company executives. On February 16 the Senate Select Committee on Intelligence voted not to conduct hearings. Instead, its members concluded an "Agreement in Principle" with the White House whereby the Congress would be given more information by the administration. On March 7 the select committee voted along party lines to establish a seven-member oversight panel. Chair Charles "Pat" Roberts (R-Kans.) called on members "to reject confrontation in favor of accommodation."[68] The White House said the new subcommittee would be given the same briefings that in the past had been provided to the "gang of eight" congressional leaders—though the new group would not be allowed to share the information with other members of Congress.

Those who wished to put the program on a statutory basis also had leverage in the nominating process. The White House had nominated Michael Hayden to be director of the CIA. He told the Democratic Senate whip Richard Durbin of Illinois on May 11 that he would not oppose changes in the law if Congress thought it necessary. As of May 16 the White House dropped its objections to House and Senate Intelligence Committee reviews of the program. By early June a deal between Vice President Cheney and Senators Specter and Orrin Hatch (R-Utah) was concluded: the Bush administration would consider legislation to put the program under FISA procedures, and in return the Senate committee would postpone its efforts to have telecommunications executives testify about the existing program. Democrats denounced the deal: "Why don't we just recess for the rest of the year, and the vice president will just tell the nation what laws we'll have?" said ranking Democrat Patrick Leahy of Vermont.[69]

But in the House a coalition of Democrats and Republicans was pushing harder: on June 21, 2006, the House Judiciary Committee passed H.R. 819 (sponsored by Florida Democrat Robert Wexler) calling on the president and the Justice Department to disclose the massive telephone number databases maintained by the NSA. It requested "all documents in the possession of the President and Attorney General, including all legal opinions." The resolution even had the support of Republican Judiciary Committee chair Frank Sensenbrenner of Wisconsin. The following month, the Republican chair of the House Intelligence Committee charged that the Bush administration had not informed Congress about other secret intelligence programs. "I have learned of some alleged intelligence community activities about which our committee has not been briefed," said Representative Hoekstra. "If these allegations are true, they may represent a breach of responsibility by the administration, a violation of the law, and, just as importantly, a direct affront to me and the members of this committee who have so ardently supported efforts to collect information on our enemies."[70]

THE SPECTER BILL AND SOFT PREROGATIVE

At this point, with the administration's defense of prerogative power crumbling in Congress and with a federal district court decision declaring his program illegal (which was immediately appealed by the government, staying its execution), Bush turned to the "soft prerogative" strategy.[71] His goal was to forge a compromise with moderate senators on the Judiciary Committee. By mid-July Senator Specter had come up with S. 2453, the National Security Surveillance Act of 2006. The measure put the wiretapping program on a statutory basis, but its provisions provided the White House with great latitude. It provided retroactive legal immunity for the participants in both the disclosed and any undisclosed programs of wiretapping authorized since 9/11. Any legal challenges would be taken to the FISA Court of Review if the attorney general claimed grounds of national security. The court in turn "may dismiss a challenge to the legality of an electronic surveillance program for any reason." The bill recognized a unilateral presidential authority to conduct warrantless surveillance, even as it purported to establish procedures for judicial warrants: section

801 stated that "nothing in this Act shall be construed to limit the constitutional authority of the President to collect intelligence with respect to foreign powers and agents of foreign powers." In its proposed additions to section 9 of FISA, it would prohibit electronic surveillance except as authorized by statute—or "under the Constitution." It provided that electronic surveillance is authorized "under the constitutional authority of the executive or the Foreign Intelligence Surveillance Act of 1978," thus eliminating the FISA provision that had prescribed FISA as being the "exclusive means" of electronic surveillance.[72] Section 102 of the bill permitted warrantless "electronic surveillance programs" for a ninety-day period, indefinitely reviewable if the attorney general declared that the program could not be performed under FISA procedures. (This would have changed FISA's section 1811, which allowed warrantless surveillance for up to fifteen days after a declaration of war; under the new measure no declaration of war would be necessary, and the program could continue for a year instead of fifteen days.) Surveillance could be conducted against a broader range of targets, including: (1) a foreign power that is engaged in international terrorism activities or in preparation therefor; (2) an agent of a foreign power that is engaged in international terrorism activities or in preparation therefor; or (3) a person reasonably believed to have communication with or be associated with a foreign power that is engaged in international terrorism activities or in preparation therefor or an agent of a foreign power that is engaged in international terrorism activities or in preparation therefor. This expanded coverage would have sidestepped the Fourth Amendment's requirement that warrants must be issued to search and seize individuals, not classes of people.

Critics complained that Specter's bill acknowledged a presidential prerogative and did nothing to limit it. "They are wrong," Specter replied, adding, "the bill does not accede to the president's claims of inherent presidential power; that is for the courts either to affirm or reject. It merely acknowledges them, to whatever extent they may exist."[73] Some Republicans believed the measure provided the administration with too much latitude: Senators Larry Craig (R-Idaho), John Sununu (R-N.H.), and Lisa Murkowski (R-Alaska) proposed removing the language referring to the president's inherent constitutional authority, providing that FISC approval of a *program's* legality would not provide authorization to conduct surveillance without a warrant and adding that a warrant would be required if the attorney general could not certify a "reasonable expectation" that any warrantless surveillance authorized would not involve a U.S. citizen.

By mid-September the House had passed the Electronic Surveillance Modernization Act (H.R. 5825), sponsored by Heather Wilson, which authorized and expanded the time limits for warrantless surveillance.[74] The House bill was approved along party lines, 232 to 191, with only 18 Democrats crossing over to support it and only 13 Republicans defecting. Subsection 105(e) permitted emergency surveillance for seven days without a warrant. Section 14 made it easier to tap against imminent attacks for ninety days, provided the president notified selected members of Congress within five days and extensions would be allowed without a declaration of war. Section 102A provided that a warrant would not be required for up to one year if surveillance occurred outside the United States, even if a U.S. citizen was involved in a call into the United States. And section 102B greatly expanded the ways in which telecommunications companies were required to assist the government, and it also eliminated their liability from lawsuits. A new subsection 108(1)(b) required the attorney general, on a semiannual basis, to "fully inform the Permanent Select Committee on Intelligence of the House of Representatives and the Select Committee on Intelligence of the Senate on electronic surveillance conducted without a court order." An immunity provision was also included: section 10(a) limited liability for the period after September 11, 2001. Finally, and section 10(b)would transfer jurisdiction of lawsuits from any state court to a federal court.

A BILL BECOMES A LAW

As Congress shifted to Democratic control in 2007, there were fair prospects for a new measure that would reaffirm FISA procedures and curtail warrantless surveillance. But in order to overcome a Senate filibuster, such a bill would likely have to include some language providing (1) loopholes for the president in the form of certifications or waivers that would allow such surveillance, (2) expansion of the scope of targets, (3) an immunity clause, and (4) the transfer of existing lawsuits to the FISA courts.

Under White House pressure (with President Bush insisting that Congress stay in session to work on antiterrorism measures), a bipartisan coalition (all but two Republicans and forty-one Democrats in the House) passed the Bush administration's proposal for a six-month extension of FISA that expanded presidential surveillance powers. In doing so, the coalition sidetracked a more moderate version supported initially by the Democratic leadership. The bill provided expanded authority for the NSA to conduct surveillance on both foreign and domestic calls and e-mails without going through FISA procedures so long as the surveillance "concerned" al-Qaida and approval had been obtained from the attorney general and the director of national intelligence. Any FISA review would be after the fact and would deal only with policies, not individual surveillance authorizations. The new law had the effect of retroactively legitimizing, and providing a legal framework for, warrantless surveillance activities conducted by the NSA since 2001 and would give the government more legal authority to obtain cooperation from telecommunications companies. The law expanded the warrantless "intelligence" covered to include business records and physical searches of Americans in the United States, so long as the government could assert that they were needed in connection with an investigation of someone overseas.[75]

As of late fall 2007, the Democratic House had passed a revision of the law to roll back much of what the White House had won. With President Bush threatening to wield a veto on such a measure and with strong Republican opposition to the bill, it was doubtful anything much would be rolled back through the end of his term.

The Missing Backlash

It is a federal crime, punishable with a prison sentence and/or a fine, to violate the FISA statute. President Bush is the first president in American history to admit openly that he violated such a statute. Why has this admission not produced a "backlash" effect in which Congress checks the exercise of the power, the White House staff or the departments are rocked with investigations and resignations, public opinion turns against the president, his own party deserts him, and he and his administration are paralyzed while these events play out?

One of the obstacles faced by critics of the president's actions was that defenders could argue that they were just trying to ensure national security. The public would then consider it at worst a case of excessive zeal (as it did with the Iran-Contra affair), rather than a case of abuse of power (as it did with Watergate). At first public opinion was divided, but it gradually swung toward the administration. An IPSOS poll in early January 2006 indicated that 56 percent of the public thought a warrant should be required; three-fourths of Democrats and one-third of Republicans felt that way. By February 9, 2006, in another IPSOS poll, there was a 50–50 split, with only 18 percent of Republicans insisting on warrants. By May 10, 2006, only 35 percent of the public thought warrants were necessary, according to a *Washington Post*–ABC News poll. The issue was framed primarily as one of ensuring national security, rather than ensuring privacy and Fourth Amendment rights.

Unlike Watergate or the Iran-Contra affair, there was no dramatic story arc, no cast of characters, no cover-up that was gradually peeled away, no cathartic moment in congressional hearings. The president acknowledged he had authorized the program from the start. A seemingly colorless spymaster, Michael Hayden, deftly handled inquiries about the program, and the Senate confirmed him to head the CIA by a vote of 78 to 15, which was a good indication that there was no "traction" in this story. The Senate Intelligence Committee did what it could to limit its oversight to a select group of senators, and under Arlen Specter the Senate Judiciary Committee concentrated its efforts on producing a lengthy new intelligence bill whose detailed technical provisions would not easily become the focus of media or public attention.

The most vociferous critics of the administration made a strategic blunder by pursuing the possibility of censuring the president or other administration officials. This avenue was popular with the Democratic rank-and-file: two-thirds in various polls supported the idea, according to a *Washington Post*–ABC News poll that month. But most members, looking toward the midterm elections, backed away from the idea. They did so in the aftermath of a *Newsweek* poll of March 16–17 that found 50 percent of Americans opposing censure, 42 percent supporting it, and a considerable minority of Democrats (40 percent) opposed.

The Republicans were ready to call the Democrats' bluff on this issue. On March 13, Senate majority leader William Frist (R-Tenn.), on the floor of the chamber, said that if Wisconsin Democrat Russell Feingold brought up a resolution of censure, he would call for an immediate vote.[76] The Democratic leadership, responding to its membership, crafted a strategy to have most members vote *against* the censure amendment, to inoculate the party against charges that it was moving recklessly and unfairly against the president.

Democrats in the House not only were not prepared to vote for censure against the Bush administration; they played catch-up with the Republicans on the national security card: in the aftermath of the *New York Times* disclosure of a separate Treasury program to track terrorist financing, the House voted 227 to 183 for a resolution that condemned those who disclosed the program. While most Democrats voted against this resolution, they introduced one of their own that expressed concern about the leaks involving national security.

Impeachment was out of the question. It could occur only if the scandal had a "Watergate" dimension: it would have to involve revelations that the spying had been conducted against politicians, especially the Democratic opposition. As of early 2007, no such charges had been made or evidence produced to suggest that that had occurred. Nor was there evidence administration critics could adduce of a cover-up or of perjury in sworn proceedings. This was not a scandal in which "the cover-up is worse than the crime." Public opinion throughout ran strongly against the impeachment option against the president: only 32 percent in favor, with 58 percent opposed in a Rasmussen Reports survey (December 9–10, 2005) just after the program's existence was revealed. It was opposed by 84 percent of Republicans and 55 percent of independents and backed by only 49 percent of Democrats. Moreover, 52 percent of the public said they would be *less* likely to vote for a congressional candidate who supported impeachment. There were very few cosponsors for various impeachment and censure resolutions.

Warrantless surveillance programs in the war on terrorism formed part of a pattern of "parallel governance," in which the executive takes on legislative and judicial functions to create and maintain a "state within a state." In this case it involved bypassing a framework law and congressional intent and substituting an executive order and presidential fiat, then bypassing a statutory court (FISC) with judicial oversight in favor of a warrantless program with no oversight. Republican control of the House and Senate (until the November 2006 elections) ensured not only that there would be no serious hearings but also that any measures crafted to authorize the program would provide the president and other officials with more power (and immunities)—not less. Not until partisan control passed into the hands of the Democrats in 2007 was there any possibility that the warrantless presidency might be checked and balanced, and even then, the prospects of meaningful investigation and checking legislation remained slim. In the politics of presidential prerogative, public opinion would ultimately determine where the opposition party would hunt for political advantage. In the case of warrantless surveillance, it turned out that political pickings were too slim to make such efforts worthwhile.

Notes

1. Alberto Gonzales, Department of Justice, to Senator Patrick Leahy and Senator Arlen Specter, January 17, 2007, http://graphics8.nytimes.com/packages/pdf/politics/20060117gonzales_Letter.pdf (accessed May 27, 2009).

2. *Authorization to Use Military Force Act* (AUMF), Public Law No. 107–40, 115 *U.S. Statutes at Large* 24 (2001).,

3. Quoted in Eric Lichtblau and David Johnston, "Court to Oversee U.S. Wiretapping in Terror Cases," *New York Times,* January 18, 2007.

4. David Stout, "Gonzales Testifies on Eavesdropping Changes," *New York Times,* January 18, 2007.

5. Peter Baker, "Bush Retreats on Use of Executive Power," *Washington Post,* January 18, 2007.

6. Terry Eastland, *Energy in the Executive: The Case for the Strong Presidency* (New York: Free Press, 1992); John Yoo, *War by Other Means: An Insider's Account of the War on Terror* (New York: Atlantic Monthly Press, 2006).

7. James Madison, "Federalist Nos. 47, 51."

8. *Katz v. United States,* 389 U.S. 347 (1967).

9. Title III, *Omnibus Crime Control and Safe Streets Act,* Public Law 90–351, 82 *U.S. Statutes at Large* 197, 42 *U.S. Code* § 3711 (June 19, 1968).

10. *United States v. United States District Court for the Eastern District of Michigan et. al.,* 407 U.S. 297 (1972).

11. U.S. Senate, Select Committee to Study Government Operations with Respect to Intelligence Activities, Final Report, Book III, *National Security Agency Surveillance Affecting Americans* (Washington, D.C.: U.S. Government Printing Office, 1976).

12. Christopher Pyle, *Military Surveillance of Civilian Politics* (New York: Garland Press, 1986).

13. David Garrow, *The FBI and Martin Luther King Jr.* (New York: Norton, 1981).

14. *Halperin v. Kissinger,* 452 U.S. 713 (1981).

15. 50 *U.S. Code* 1801 et seq. (1978). On NSA activities, see U.S. Senate, Select Committee to Study Government Operations with Respect to Intelligence Activities, "Supplementary Detailed Staff Reports on Intelligence Activities and the Rights of Americans," April 23, 1976, Final Report, Book III, *National Security Agency Surveillance Affecting Americans.*

16. Congressional Research Service, *The Foreign Intelligence Surveillance Act: An Overview of the Statutory Framework and Recent Judicial Decisions,* CRS Report RL30465 (February 15, 2007.)

17. Executive Order 12,139, sec. 1–105 (May 23, 1979).

18. National Security Agency, U.S. Signals Intelligence Directive 18.

19. Executive Order 12,949 (February 9, 1995).

20. Lt. General Michael V. Hayden, USAF, NSA director, "Statement for the Record" to the House Permanent Select Committee on Intelligence, 106th Cong., 2nd sess., April 12, 2000.

21. Shane Harris, "NSA Sought Data before 9/11," *National Journal,* November 2, 2007

22. *Newsweek,* May 2, 2006.

23. *Foreign Intelligence Surveillance Act of 1978,* codified at 18 *U.S. Code* § 2511(2)(f).

24. U.S. Department of Justice, Office of Assistant Attorney General, Report to House Speaker Nancy Pelosi, 110th Cong., 1st sess., April 27, 2007.

25. Matthew Rothschild, "Authority and Mendacity," *Progressive,* March 2006; "President Discusses Patriot Act," speech delivered by George W. Bush in Columbus, Ohio, June 9, 2005, www.whitehouse.gov/news/2005/06/print/20050609–2.html.

26. Carol D. Leonnig, "Gonzales Is Challenged on Wiretaps," *Washington Post,* January 31, 2006.

27. Sidney Blumenthal, "The Law Is King," *www.salon.com,* December 23, 2005.

28. James Risen and Eric Lichtblau, "Bush Secretly Lifted Some Limits on Spying in U.S. after 9/11, Officials Say," *New York Times,* December 15, 2005.

29. George W. Bush, "The President's Radio Address, December 17, 2005," http://www.presidency.ucsb.edu/ws/index.php?pid=65075 (accessed May 27, 2009).

30. White House news conference, December 18, 2005, transcript at http; //www.nytimes.com./2005/12/19/politics/19text-bush.html (accessed May 27, 2009).

31. Among other documents, the president relied on a September 21, 2001, classified memorandum prepared by John Yoo, at that time deputy director of the Office of Legal Counsel in the Department of Justice. Yoo had argued that in a national emergency the government could use "electronic surveillance techniques and equipment that are more powerful and sophisticated than those available to law enforcement agencies in order to intercept telephonic communications and observe the movement of persons but without obtaining warrants for such uses." He added that "the government may be justified in taking measures which in less troubled conditions could be seen as infringements of individual liberties." Quoted in James Risen and Eric Lichtblau, "Bush Let U.S. Spy on Callers without Courts," *New York Times,* December 16, 2005, A1. See also Yoo, *War by Other Means.*

32. "White House News Briefing on Legal Issues Relating to the NSA Authorizations, as Released by the White House," December 19, 2005.

33. "Prepared Remarks for Attorney General Alberto R. Gonzales at the Georgetown University Law Center," January 24, 2006.

34. U.S. Department of Justice, Office of Legislative Affairs, Assistant Attorney General William Moschella to Hon. Pat Roberts, Chairman, Select Committee on Intelligence, December 22, 2005.

35. Quoted in David Johnston and Neil A. Lewis, "Defending Spy Program Administration Cites Law," *New York Times*, December 23, 2005, 20.

36. U.S. Department of Justice, "Legal Authorities Supporting the Activities of the National Security Agency Described by the President," January 19, 2006, 1, http://www.fas.org/irp/nsa/doj011906.pdf (accessed June 2, 2009).

37. Ibid., 2.

38. *Authorization for Use of Military Force*, Public Law 107–40, § 2(a), 115 *U.S. Statutes at Large* 224, 224 (September 18, 2001).

39. *Hamdi v. Rumsfeld*, 542 U.S. 507, 519 (2004).

40. U.S. Department of Justice, Office of Legislative Affairs, Moschella to Roberts, December 22, 2005.

41. U.S. Department of Justice, "Legal Authorities Supporting the Activities," January 19, 2006, 3.

42. ACLU to Attorney General Alberto Gonzales, December 21, 2005, http://www.aclu.org/safefree/general/23184/eg20051221.html (accessed June 2, 2009).

43. *Foreign Intelligence Surveillance Act of 1978*, 50 *U.S. Code* 1802(a)(1)(B).

44. Ibid., sec. 1805(f).

45. Ibid., sec. 1811.

46. Ibid., sec. 1809.

47. *Hamdi v. Rumsfeld*, 542 U.S. 507 at 535–36 (2004).

48. Public Law 107–56, 115 *U.S. Statutes at Large* 272 (2001) (Title II).

49. U.S. 18 *U.S. Code* § 2511(2)(f) (emphasis added).

50. Quoted in Abdon M. Pallasch, "Bar Opposes Warrantless Surveillance Programs," *Chicago Sun-Times*, February 11, 2006.

51. Michael Ratner, with Sara Miles, "Above the Law," *www.salon.com*, March 31, 2006.

52 House Conference Report 95–1720, at 34 (1978), ftp://cnss.org/rpt95–1720.pdf (May 27, 2009).

53. "We had discussions with Congress in the past—certain members of Congress—as to whether or not FISA could be amended to allow us to adequately deal with this kind of threat, and we were advised that that would be difficult, if not impossible," Gonzales said at his December 19, 2005, Department of Justice press briefing, http://www.whitehouse.gov/news/releases/2005/12/20051219–1.html (accessed May 27, 2009).

54. Jordan Paust, "Not Authorized by Law: Domestic Spying and Congressional Consent," *Jurist Forum*, December 23, 2005.

55. All quoted in Charlie Savage, "On Eve of Hearing, Split on Spying," *Boston Globe,* February 5, 2006.

56. Text of Senator Kennedy's letter available at http://kennedy.senate.gov/newsroom/press_release.cfm?id=595d0b6b-07d2–4e6a-bc9a-3a374f706389 (accessed May 27, 2009).

57. Thomas Daschle, "The Power We Didn't Grant," *Washington Post,* December 23, 2005.

58. Quoted in *Chicago Tribune,* December 17, 2005.

59. U.S. Senate, Committee on Intelligence, *Hearing 2: National Security Threats,* 109th Cong., 2nd sess., 2006.

60. Quoted in Hope Yen, "Lawmakers Demand Domestic Spying Probe," Associated Press, December 19, 2005.

61. Suzanne Spaulding, former general counsel for the Senate and House Intelligence committees and assistant general counsel at the CIA, "Power Play," *Washington Post,* December 25, 2005.

62. Elizabeth B. Bazan and Jennifer K. Elsea, "Memorandum: Presidential Authority to Conduct Warrantless Electronic Surveillance to Gather Foreign Intelligence Information," *Congressional Research Service,* January 5, 2006.

63. Alfred Cumming, Memorandum, *Congressional Research Service,* January 6, 2006.

64. The requirement for written reports was included in 2001 amendments to the National Security Act of 1947 to require the executive branch to provide more specificity briefings about continuing intelligence activities. President Bush signed the measure into law on December 28, 2001, but in his signing statement he indicated that he would interpret it "in a manner consistent with the president's constitutional authority" allowing him to withhold information on grounds of national security.

65. All quoted in Hope Yen, "Probe Sought on NSA Surveillance," Associated Press, December 19, 2005.

66. Eric Lichtblau, "Republican Who Oversees NSA Calls for Wiretap Inquiry," *New York Times,* February 8, 2006.

67. U.S. Senate, Committee on the Judiciary, *Wartime Executive Power and the National Security Agency's Surveillance Authority: Hearing before the Senate Committee on the Judiciary,* 109th Cong., 2nd sess., 2006.

68. Quoted in Walter Pincus, "Senate Panel Blocks Eavesdropping Probe," *Washington Post,* March 8, 2006.

69. Quoted in John Diamond, "Senators Won't Grill Phone Companies," *USA Today,* June 8, 2006.

70. All quoted in Eric Lichtblau and Scott Shane, "Ally Warned Bush on Keeping Spying from Congress," *New York Times,* July 9, 2006.

71. *ACLU et al. v. NSA et al.*, case no. 06-CV-10204, August 17, 2006.

72. 18 *U.S. Code* 2511(2)(e).

73. Arlen Specter, "Surveillance We Can Live With," *Washington Post,* July 24, 2006, A19.

74. Congressional Research Service, "H.R. 5825 (109th Congress): 'Electronic Surveillance Modernization Act,'" September 8, 2006.

75. Congressional Research Service, "P.L. 110–55, the Protect America Act of 2007: Modifications to the Foreign Intelligence Surveillance Act," CRS Report RL 34143 (August 23, 2007).

76. *Congressional Record,* March 13, 2006, S2010–S2019 (Senate).

Aiding and Abetting

Congressional Complicity in the Rise of the Unitary Executive

BRYAN W. MARSHALL AND PATRICK J. HANEY

The sequence in the U.S. Constitution establishing Congress as the "First Branch" of the three branches of government is much more than numerical organization. Congress is "First" for a reason.[1] The framers placed the legislature at the center of the republic. The legislative branch not only provided the vital link to the varied interests of the people but more importantly tied the collective interests of the institution to the promotion of the public good. In order to preempt the dangers associated with the accumulation of power, the framers divided powers between the institutions with overlapping jurisdictions. Although the powers vested with the executive and judicial branches would provide an important check on legislative power, Congress's only real principal would be the people.

With the legislative branch at the forefront of the people's business, it is no surprise that Congress's constitutional powers overshadow those of the other branches. Among other significant powers, the Congress can amend the Constitution, change the size and jurisdiction of the Supreme Court, and impeach and remove members of the executive and judiciary. As the lawmaking body, Article I gives Congress a formidable legislative horizon. Congress has monopoly rights over the making of all laws necessary and proper for carrying out its powers and all other powers vested by the Constitution. In contrast, the president owns the rather unexceptional power to provide information and make recommendations, call special sessions, and schedule adjournments when Congress is unable to agree upon such times. Even the president's most notable legislative power—the veto—is far from absolute, being subject to congressional override.

And although the framers divided powers in foreign affairs more evenly between the branches, the most important of these—the war power—was placed almost entirely in the hands of Congress. Here, Congress has the power (among other powers) to raise and maintain the armed forces, make the rules governing those forces, suppress insurrections, repel invasions, and most importantly to declare war. The framers' intent was to favor Congress's collective control over war as opposed to control by one individual. During proceedings of the Constitutional Convention in 1787, James Madison wrote to Thomas Jefferson, "We have already given in example one effectual check to the Dog of war by transferring the power of letting him loose from the Executive to the Legislative body, from those who are to spend to those who are to pay."[2] The president's constitutional authority to repel sudden attacks and role as commander in chief were limited as compared to those of Congress.

Clearly, Congress was given claim to the leash controlling the "Dog of War," albeit its grip would be loosened over time. Early presidents were quite careful not to tread upon congressional authority. For example, President Thomas Jefferson maintained the important distinction between the executive's defensive power to repel attacks and the legislature's authority over offensive campaigns. Under the former, he ordered the navy to the Mediterranean to protect American trading ships from attack by the Barbary pirates. But when he became convinced of the necessity for offense, he openly recognized Congress's exclusive offensive jurisdiction and dutifully asked permission.[3] And indeed, just a few years later, with President John Adams's order in 1804 that the navy to seize U.S. merchant ships sailing to or from French ports, which expanded the congressional authorization to seize only ships sailing *to* French ports, the Supreme Court easily sided with Congress. The Court reasoned, in *Little v. Barreme,* that Congress had legislated clearly on this matter in a 1799 act to suspend commerce with France and that the president could not rewrite or expand that legislation just because the expansion perhaps made better sense.[4]

By the early twentieth century, presidential power to make war had grown considerably beyond the parameters recognized by early presidents like Jefferson. The Monroe Doctrine, Theodore Roosevelt's corollary thereof, and military excursions in Mexico, Central America, the Caribbean, and the Philippines provided numerous opportunities for presidents to define new contexts in which their power could apply. And there has been seemingly little respite from the continuing expansion of authority by modern presidents into the twenty-first century.

The Iraq war resolution of 2002 illustrates just how loose Congress's grip over the war power has become since the days of the Barbary pirates.

With the passage of the Iraq war resolution, Congress delegated immense authority to President George W. Bush, the likes of which had not been seen since 1964, when President Lyndon Johnson was granted wide discretion in Vietnam. Section 3 of the resolution authorizes the president "to use the Armed Forces of the United States as he determines to be necessary and appropriate in order to (1) defend the national security of the United States against the continuing threat posed by Iraq; and (2) enforce all relevant United Nations Security Council Resolutions regarding Iraq."[5] Congress asked only for the Speaker and the president pro tempore of the Senate to be informed within twenty-four hours of the onset of war and for a report at least every sixty days on what the president is doing pursuant to the resolution. In sharp contrast to Jefferson's duty-bound bequest of offensive power, the Iraq war resolution virtually gave President Bush a free hand to use preemptive actions. Perhaps more importantly though, Congress seemingly undermined its own oversight role by not establishing any serious review procedures once conflict began and by setting no expiration date for such executive powers. As one notable source characterized congressional behavior, "Congress voluntarily removed itself from the debate over Iraq and went up into the cheap seats with the reporters and the pundits."[6]

Still, even this was an upgrade from the war resolution that followed the 9/11 attacks. In that case, Congress authorized the president "to use all necessary and appropriate force against those nations, organizations, or persons he determines planned, authorized, committed, or aided the terrorist attacks that occurred on September 11, 2001, or harbored such organizations or persons, in order to prevent any further acts of international terrorism against the United States by such nations, organizations or persons."[7] Ron Suskind notes, though, that Congress did stick up for its prerogatives in one way on that resolution, rebuffing a last-minute effort by the White House to insert the phrase "in the United States," after "use all necessary and appropriate force," essentially granting the president a blank check both abroad *and* at home.[8]

We are thus left with a puzzling situation. In spite of the fact that Congress was given the dominant constitutional powers on war and spending—which, as Louis Fisher notes in his authoritative book on the subject, is recognized by nearly all scholars of the subject with the notable exception of Professor John Yoo—the legislative branch is now nevertheless clearly positioned on the losing end of a zero-sum struggle for power with the president.[9] Through both complacent omissions and by willful abetting, Congress has ceded its grip on its own constitutional powers and has steadily given way to the executive. The bedrock principle of separation of powers is thus at some risk. Our focus is to attempt to explain why the pendulum of institutional power has swung away from the First Branch and toward the presidency. In our view, the recent debates surrounding the unitary executive represent another important development in the ongoing struggle for power between the executive and legislative branches. We argue that Congress, through sins of omission and commission, has played a key role in the expansion of executive power and has significantly fueled the rise of the unitary executive.

After a brief literature review focusing on the president's unilateral and institutional advantages over Congress, especially in foreign affairs, we examine two contrasting perspectives explaining Congress's role in the expansion of presidential power. For example, William Howell and Jon Pevehouse argue that partisanship largely explains the extent of Congress's influence over the use of presidential war powers.[10] However, Thomas Mann and Norman Ornstein are concerned with a more general decay of congressional power, not just in the politics of war but across the spectrum of domestic and foreign policy that has allowed presidents to exert extraconstitutional authority.[11] Although partisanship is an important factor in their argument, they point to broader factors at work, including what they see as Congress's loss of institutional identity and independence. From these perspectives, we put forward an argument using collective action as a lens to view the role Congress has played in the rise of the unitary executive and the expansion of presidential power. We offer tentative evidence supporting our arguments in the areas of foreign policy and appropriations. The empirical patterns illustrate both the expansion of presidential powers across issue areas and the congressional penchant for tepid responses that seemingly occur irrespective of party control. Overall, the evidence supports our main argument that Congress has aided and abetted the rise of the unitary executive and expansion of executive power. Finally, we conclude by discussing the implications of our findings for understanding the continuing struggle for power between branches and by offering some direction for future research.

How the Politics of Unilateralism Trumps Congress's Constitutional Power

For decades, scholars have sought to understand presidential power and the conditions explaining its variation over time.[12] Although the president's formal constitutional powers are substantial, they leave presidents precariously dependent upon the goodwill of others—most notably Congress—to achieve their ends. Richard Neustadt's perspective elevated the status of presidential politics in understanding executive power. His notion of the personal presidency argued that a president's power was rooted in the ability to bargain and persuade.[13]

However, the literature on presidential power has begun to expand beyond Neustadt's dominant framework by focusing on unilateralism. Modern presidents have increasingly relied upon unilateral tools not penned in the Constitution, especially when the president's ability to persuade or cajole Congress has been diminished.[14] Presidents can use such tools to "go it alone" in order to change the policy status quo in the face of congressional gridlock. For example, this new literature has shown that presidents increasingly use unilateral actions like executive orders, proclamations, national security directives, executive agreements, and signing statements to achieve their policy objectives.[15]

The tools of unilateral action offer presidents advantages in power that are quite different from the powers derived from Neustadt's framework. For one, unilateral action allows the president to act alone by initiating new policy commitments without congressional cooperation.[16] By doing so, the president is able not only to establish a new policy status quo but also to frame the debate surrounding such policy moves. Once a new policy commitment is made through unilateral action, Congress is faced with the choice of acquiescing or taking on the collective burden of a statutory response. The latter is, more often than not, very difficult for Congress to do, given the limited time and resources that must be dedicated to an ever-more demanding agenda. Of course, if Congress takes the path of least resistance by acquiescing, then the president succeeds in not only moving the policy status quo but also (re)creating the precedent of expanded presidential power.

The recent rise of the unitary executive in American politics is another important wrinkle in the ongoing struggle for power between the executive and legislative branches. At its heart, the theory of the unitary executive is a president-centered theory. It is a theory advocating for and legitimizing the powers of the institution. The "unitarian" view of presidential power is both expansive in its breadth and depth.[17] In terms of the former, executive power is not limited to the general powers subscribed under the Constitution. In terms of the latter, the unitarian view suggests that presidential power is the ultimate arbitrator of executive functions, even when such functions are shared. Although the inception of the modern unitary executive theory begins with the Reagan Justice Department, the underlying dynamic reflects the competition for power between the branches that goes back to the founding. The theory of the unitary executive is importantly linked to the study of unilateral action. That is, the unitary executive theory offers presidents a valuable rhetorical rationale to argue for more power while the unilateral tools provide presidents with the means to establish precedents on such arguments.

The tools of unilateral action are extremely valuable to presidents because not only do they affect policy outcomes but Congress's political weakness usually makes them too costly to overcome. So politics is a key driver of unilateral action and in this way offers an important complement to the Neustadtian framework. The political standing of the president can make strategies of unilateralism more attractive, and at the same time, such strategies are often beyond congressional challenge because of politics. But constitutional ambiguity and institutional advantages also provide the president with the capacity to outmaneuver Congress in policymaking, and these types of advantages can vary across the foreign and domestic policy realms.

Clearly, the powers such as those found in Article I were not intended to make Congress a rubber stamp for presidential actions. One might even reasonably conclude that the Constitution stacked power in favor of Congress. However, the necessary compromise forged by the framers left considerable ambiguity in the Article II powers of the executive. Leaving uncertainty regarding the exigencies in which congressional authority ends and executive authority begins has set into motion a continuous interinstitutional struggle for power. The outcomes of such interbranch rivalry are determined by the ongoing practice of politics.[18] But in this struggle, presidents have been dealt the stronger political hand. Presidents are more inclined and better suited to take advantage of constitutional ambiguity as compared to the other branches. Presidents enjoy significant advantages in terms of expertise and informational resources that flow from their control over the bureaucracy. Such resources significantly enhance the president's operational independence in executing the office's executive functions. The president's executive authority and independence also provide the means to unilaterally shift the policy status quo or to block such moves by the legislature.[19] Moreover, the executive nature of the office provides the presidency with the ability to effectively act with unified purpose and a single voice to expand the scope of power at Congress's expense.

While the Constitution gives both the executive and legislative branches some power to determine foreign policy, it is obvious that the political incentives to utilize such powers differ significantly between the institutions. For example, because Congress's primary constraint is in its reelection imperative, it is less inclined to delegate authority to the president in domestic policy, where it can claim significant reelection benefits. In the area of foreign policy, where the reelection benefits tend to be far removed and more uncertain, Congress has a greater incentive to delegate authority to the executive.[20] In addition, the political costs of pursuing foreign policy rather than reelection have proven to be very real even for many prominent statesmen. Senators J. William Fulbright (D-Ark.), Frank Church (D-Idaho), and Charles Percy (R-Ill.) were all defeated at least in part because of their focus on foreign policy instead of reelection.[21] This trade-off even became rooted in the decision rules of the House and Senate Committees on Foreign Affairs and Foreign Relations.[22] On these committees, rampant individualism tended to trump the pursuit of collective policymaking so much so that committee quorums were historically problematic. In fact, Senator Fulbright, chair of Senate Foreign Relations Committee from 1959 to 1966, once remarked that "this is the kind of committee that Senators like to be on, but they don't like to do anything."[23]

Even in the most important of foreign policy areas, congressional power and intentions may be suspect. Despite the grand symbolism associated with the passage of the War Powers Resolution in 1973, there remains a general consensus that this policy action has fallen short of its stated purpose of reining in unilateral executive actions. Yet there is a persuasive case to be made that even here Congress has traded away some authority to feed its hunger for reelection. Seen in this light, the resolution allows Congress the opportunity to achieve electoral gain by using its role to sanction the executive depending on the popularity of the foreign conflict. Joshua Lee Prober makes this very argument: "Congress can use the war resolution to force the president to end an unpopular military operation, or it can criticize presidential failure to comply with the procedural requirements of the resolution when public opinion is supportive or divided. Either way, Congress cannot lose."[24]

In terms of institutional resources, presidents clearly dominate the foreign policy environment. In the making and implementing of policy, presidents enjoy advantages in expertise through the departments of State and Defense, the NSC, and the entire intelligence community, to name a few. The resources that Congress has at its disposal pale in comparison, so Congress largely becomes the consumer of executive expertise and information. Moreover, the cost of independent congressional oversight in foreign affairs is considerably greater than in the area of domestic policy.[25] This obviously works to the president's advantage as well. The relative lack of codification and regulation in foreign policy (as compared to domestic) offers presidents greater latitude to exercise their powers independently of Congress.[26] Also, during times of perceived international threat—such as during the cold war or following the attacks of 9/11—there was a general consensus regarding national interests, so presidents could pursue their policies backed by relatively unified support of Congress. Thus, presidents are more likely to assert authority and subsequently achieve more in foreign affairs than on the domestic policy front.[27]

Thus, countervailing political incentives as well as constitutional and institutional differences all play an important role in explaining the powers Congress and the president use to establish public policy. While Congress frequently defers to the institutional expertise and resources of the executive in international politics, this does not mean Congress abandons foreign policy entirely. Yet most research in American politics seriously questions the significance of Congress in foreign affairs.[28] Indeed, conventional scholarly wisdom holds that when it comes to foreign policy, the invitation to struggle embedded in the Constitution has led to presidential dominance and congressional weakness.

Contrasting Perspectives and a Resolution

Next, we contrast two important arguments examining the role of Congress in the expansion of presidential power. Howell and Pevehouse argue that "there is considerable evidence that checks and balances, though diminished, persist nonetheless."[29] They agree with Louis Fisher's view that Congress has abdicated considerable responsibility for warmaking and that the president has claimed more power. But they part ways with others in their view that Congress still retains significant powers to restrain the executive, although Congress's willingness to exercise those restraints is conditioned by the partisan composition on Capitol Hill. They suggest that party allies in Congress provide the president with valuable political cover. The more numerous the members of the president's party are in Congress, the less constrained presidents will be in exercising war powers. In the post–World War II era, they suggest that the president's willingness to use force has always been conditioned on the president's party strength in Congress as opposed to any fear of Congress exercising institutional power.[30]

In their book *The Broken Branch,* Mann and Ornstein paint a different view. They discuss a wider range of public policy areas than just uses of force. Their argument is that although party is important as a conditioning factor for times when Congress might try to restrain an aggressive or noncompliant executive, there has also been a broader degrading of institutional power that has allowed, in a zero-sum context, the president to expand executive power at the expense of Congress. Mann and Ornstein thus posit that congressional willingness to subordinate its collective power to that of the president has occurred across domestic politics and foreign affairs. They argue that a variety of factors are at fault for this trend, including the loss of institutional identity, the willingness to abdicate responsibility to the president, the demise of "regular order," and most importantly that Congress has lost its one key advantage as a legislative body—the decay of the deliberative process. Thus, they do recognize that party politics has played an important role in the degrading of congressional power, but they see a larger dynamic at work, one that reaches beyond partisanship.

While we agree with Howell and Pevehouse that Congress retains important mechanisms for constraining the president, we tend to agree with the Mann and Ornstein view that there has been a significant and sustained decline in Congress's willingness to use these mechanisms to challenge presidential power. This tendency has been more prevalent in foreign affairs but has occurred noticeably across the spectrum of public policy issues. Building from both of those perspectives, and others, we argue that it is helpful to understand the pattern of congressional complicity in the rise of presidential power by viewing Congress's aiding and abetting as the logical outcomes of a collective action problem.[31]

By constitutional design, the legislative branch is in competition with the president for institutional power, yet Congress is less than ideally suited for such a political conflict. Congress's comparative disadvantage begins with its 535 "interests" that are very rarely aligned, and if so, only momentarily. Because individual reelection overshadows all other goals, members of Congress naturally seek to take as much credit and avoid as much blame from their constituencies as possible.[32] The dilemma this creates for members is how to use or delegate its collective powers in order to maximize credit and minimize blame in the making of public policy. Congress can choose to delegate power internally to committees and party leaders or externally to the executive branch. One can conceptualize the strategic situation of members of Congress in terms of a prisoner's dilemma.[33] If members cooperate (that is, in Mann and Ornstein's parlance, if members identify with the institution), they could maintain and advance Congress's institutional power. But they would have to bypass some potential individual payoffs that could come from defection, such as "running against Congress" as an electoral strategy. A stronger institution should make all members of Congress better off, but it also makes them responsible for policymaking. If members defect from the institution, they thus seek to maximize constituency interests either by simply allowing power to fall by the wayside or by simply delegating it to the president. As more and more members choose to defect over time, the "public good" of a strong Congress is not provided for or maintained—and Congress's institutional authority erodes and presidential power fills in the gap. Why, in other words, is congressional activism so often "less than meets the eye," as Barbara Hinckley maintained in her book by that title? Or why has the "culture of deference" that Stephen Weissman identified developed as it has?[34] We argue that the collective action problem that exists in Congress leads to the development of these trends away from meaningful congressional stewardship of foreign policy and spending.

We have argued that presidents have both the opportunity and incentive to exploit constitutional ambiguity in pursuit of power and that unilateral action represents a significant means to carry out such ends. Although Congress commands significant constitutional power, the First Branch often lacks the political strength to exert its power and challenge the president. Our theoretical argument suggests that Congress's political weakness is largely driven by the problems of collective action. As we have suggested, members of Congress face a dilemma in which they tend to trade away or delegate their powers as a strategy to avoid blame and curry more favor with their constituency. The equilibrium result of such a long-run strategic game is that Congress's collective power has been severely compromised and characterized by a long-term decay. The reward for individual member defection is relatively safe reelection to a weaker and weaker institution. We do not dispute Mann and Ornstein's assertion that Congress's loss of institutional identity explains much of Congress's decline as a powerful and independent branch of government. However, we view the symptoms of the broken branch as being driven by Congress's underlying strategy to delegate authority to the president. Indeed, we would suggest that

Congress is free-riding on its institutional power in order to serve its immediate reelection interests.

Based on this argument of collective action, we expect to see patterns of behavior at the institutional level that are consistent with congressional defection. That is, congressional defection should be associated with a decay in Congress's willingness to participate in policymaking or challenging presidential power. In addition, though, there is ample evidence to suggest that presidents use unilateral strategies more aggressively in some areas of public policy than in others.[35] No doubt presidents are aware of Congress's relative political strength and try to exploit issues on which Congress is politically weak. Thus, there will likely be variation in this dynamic across issue areas as presidents may push for more power in areas where ambiguity and the lack of Congress's political will are the greatest. For this reason, we expect patterns of decay (congressional defection) to be more prevalent in foreign affairs as compared to domestic policy. To empirically investigate this argument, we utilize international agreements and appropriations policy. These two areas provide us with a broad range of policy issues we can use in assessing our argument that Congress has delegated much of its institutional power to the executive.

International Commitments and Appropriations

Constitutional ambiguity extends to many areas of foreign affairs and provides ample opportunity for institutional conflict. The making of international commitments is one such area, an area where presidents have advanced their power and influence over time relative to that of Congress. One of the most important examples of executive expansion in the area of international commitments occurred at the outset of World War II. With the fall of France in 1940, President Franklin Roosevelt issued an executive agreement in an effort to bolster Great Britain in the face of an imminent German military onslaught. The executive agreement traded fifty outdated destroyers for key British naval bases in the Western Hemisphere.[36] This established an important precedent in the use of executive agreements for future presidents who would use such tools to chip away at Congress's constitutional authority.

Congress has largely been unable to collectively recover from the presidency's assault on its power. The two most noteworthy instances when Congress did attempt to counter presidential discretion in international commitment making occurred with the Bricker revolt in the early 1950s and the passage of the Case-Zablocki Act at the end of the Vietnam War.[37] Senator John W. Bricker (R-Ohio) led a congressional attempt to amend the Constitution so that all executive agreements would be overseen by Congress and require congressional action before they could take effect. President Dwight Eisenhower won the political battle, however. He successfully beat back the Bricker legislation by using the bully pulpit to turn the debate into one revolving around the necessity to preserve federal sovereignty and unity in foreign affairs in order to protect national interests and maintain peace.

The second congressional attempt to recover some of its power in international commitments was the passage of the Case-Zablocki Act. Reacting to the president's disastrous military foray in Vietnam, a powerful coalition of neo-isolationists formed, making "no more Vietnams" their rallying cry. The coalition was held together out of the fear of unchecked presidential discretion to initiate military operations in regions of the world not vital to U.S. national interest. Senator Church pointedly articulates this concern: "Our gravest mistakes in the last twenty years have come from the assumption that we have the wealth and power to mold the world to our own liking."[38] By the 1960s, presidents were issuing so many executive agreements that Congress often did not even know of their existence. But in 1972, Congress passed the Case-Zablocki Act, which required the State Department to report all statutory and executive agreements to Congress within sixty days. Although the Case-Zablocki Act was much less ambitious than the Bricker amendment, the reporting requirement of the act did restore some power to Congress. Still, the extent of policy leverage that the reporting requirement provides Congress remains an open question. James McCormick, drawing on data from the Congressional Research Service, shows that about 20 percent of executive agreements are not reported until after the sixty-day window.[39] Moreover, as McCormick suggests, the late reporting of an executive agreement regarding water supply to an American base might not detract from congressional oversight or influence in any appreciable way. But late reporting on one that bears on intelligence activities with other countries certainly could.[40]

If the Constitution provides an environment ripe for struggle over war powers, it provides no such obvious atmosphere in the area of appropriations. The Constitution gives clear power to Congress with respect to spending. Article I, section 8, gives Congress power over taxation, duties, borrowing on the credit of the United States, and coining money and regulating its value. Article I, section 9, states that no money may be drawn from the Treasury except through appropriation passed by Congress. The "power of the purse" was clearly vested in Congress as the "people's representative," as Fisher puts it. And Madison makes it clear in "Federalist No. 48" that Congress "alone has access to the pockets of the people."[41] Appropriations, in this sense, ought to be the *last* place we would see Congress delegate power to the executive. But that is exactly the pattern we have seen over time as Congress has ceded its responsibility and constitutional position relative to spending to the president—who has wanted more authority in this area and who has gladly accepted it.

Fisher tracks this trend toward delegation of appropriations power as gaining momentum with the reaction to the Smoot-Hawley Tariff Act of 1930. So unpopular was this attempt by Congress to control tariff policy that it delegated authority over tariffs to the executive (in what would later become the U.S. International Trade Commission). Raymond Bauer, Ithiel de Sola Pool, and Lewis A. Dexter, in their classic study of this episode, note that it was here that legislators learned that "responsibility involves blame," and thus Congress sought to get out of the way.[42] This trend to delegate authority over spending to the president continued through the Congressional Budget Act of 1974, and since then, he argues, Congress has exercised even less institutional control relative to the president. The Budget and Accounting Act of 1921, which shifted the locus of responsibility for budgeting to the executive, and other changes to budgeting that followed such as the line item veto, the Gramm-Rudman-Hollings balanced budget legislation, and the increasing use of omnibus appropriations bills are other mechanisms by which Congress has essentially transferred budget authority to the White House. As the United States rose to a position of global leadership and the size and scope of the federal government steadily increased from the Depression years forward, members of Congress increasingly found there are significant political advantages to delegating policy responsibility to the president. And it is worth noting that these changes did not take place over Congress's objection—quite the contrary. Members of Congress have been more than willing to step forward and join the president in calling the Capitol a house of profligate spenders.

Analysis

We now turn to empirical analysis to assess the general argument about the president's increasing reliance on unilateral tools and Congress's unwillingness to challenge presidential power. The first part of the analysis considers patterns over a number of years in the making of international commitments. We also consider Congress's willingness to debate and oversee international affairs policy more generally by assessing congressional hearings. In particular, we look at the president's use of executive agreements relative to the Senate's treaty-making authority in making compacts with foreign nations. The second part of the analysis considers patterns over a number of years in the area of appropriations. Here, we focus on the president's use of signing statements that challenge Congress's authority in appropriations legislation. And, as we do with the first part, we also consider Congress's willingness to debate and oversee policy through appropriations hearings.

We think these two areas provide a broad spectrum of evidence on which to base our argument that Congress has largely delegated its institutional power to the presidency and given the executive a free rein to effectively fill the power void. Based on the earlier argument of collective action, we expect to see patterns of behavior at the institutional level that are consistent with defection. That is, the result of such continuous defection by individual members should be associated with patterns that reflect decay in Congress's power and in its willingness to participate in directing policy or challenging presidential authority.

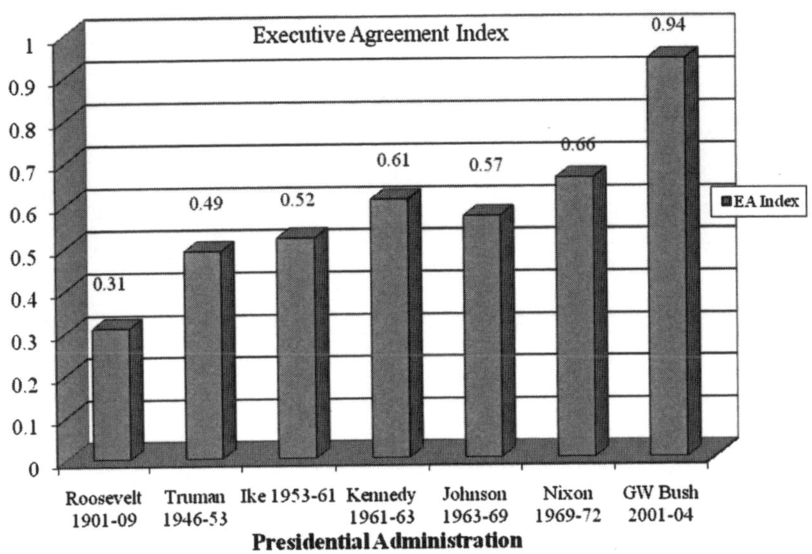

FIGURE 1. The rise in the use of executive agreements relative to treaties in the making of international commitments

The analysis begins with figure 1, which provides a snapshot of international commitment making over time. Much of the data we use on commitment making comes from Loch Johnson's classic study.[43] His work offers some of the most extensive and systematic analyses of changes in commitment making as well as the role of Congress and the president over time. Johnson's work suggests that statutory commitments and executive agreements have largely replaced the use of treaties in the making of foreign compacts since the post–World War II era. In fact, his study illustrates a significant increase in the presidential use of executive agreements over time. Figure 1 shows how the use of treaties in relation to the president's unilateral use of executive agreements in international commitment making has changed over time. In particular, the executive agreement index denoted by the bars represents the proportion of executive agreements used relative to the total number of executive agreements and treaties, by presidential administration.[44] The trend shows that presidents have increasingly relied upon executive agreements and thus have circumvented possible constraints that would be imposed by working with the Senate in treaty making.

The next relevant issue from our argument is to consider in a general way how Congress has reacted to the expansion of presidential authority in foreign affairs. Admittedly, we do not have a perfect indicator of Congress's willingness to be an active participant in the foreign policy process and act as a coequal branch or of its willingness to challenge the president. However, for this analysis we use hearings data as a rough indicator of Congress's willingness to play its part in the policy process and to protect its powers in foreign policy. In doing so we want to acknowledge that those who argue that Congress's role in foreign policy is more substantial than the conventional wisdom would suggest often point to the ability of the legislative branch to shape policy in indirect ways, such as through hearings and oversight, and through appropriations.[45] Given the clear trend in the president's increasing reliance on executive agreements to influence foreign policy, the relevant question becomes how has Congress responded or tried to keep pace? Figure 2 provides a broad assessment of congressional foreign policy activity by reference to congressional hearings. The data in figure 2 are drawn from the Policy Agendas Project, which codes all congressional hearings into a general topic area.[46]

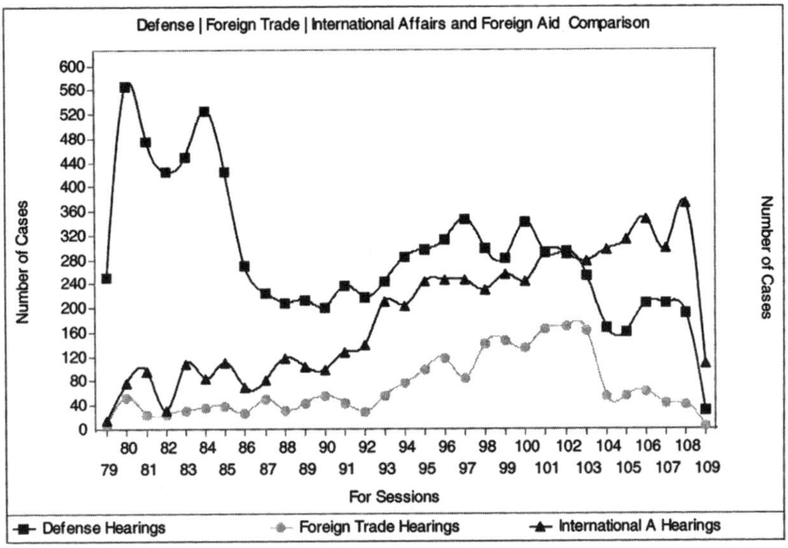

FIGURE 2. Defense, foreign trade, international affairs, and foreign aid hearings, 79th through 109th Congresses

Figure 2 shows all hearings that have been coded as dealing with the three topic areas that we see as falling into the general area of "foreign and defense policy," coded by the Policy Agendas Project as: (1) defense, (2) foreign trade, and (3) international affairs and foreign aid. The data cover the 79th through 109th Congresses. A couple of caveats are in order. First, it is possible that some congressional hearings that one would want to include as "foreign policy" are not included in this figure. Topics that deal with airline security, for example, are coded into a subsection of the "transportation" topic area and also may not be coded as defense or international affairs (though we found only one such example for the period since 2001). Still, the vast majority of what we would call "foreign policy" hearings are covered by this graph, certainly well enough to see the overall trend. Second, it is important to note that the data for the 109th Congress are not complete. Rather than discard it, however, since it seems to run through the first session of that Congress, we include it for reference, since even if we doubled the number of hearings for the 109th Congress, it appears unlikely that the number of hearings will increase over the number in the 108th Congress, so the trend toward decline from the 108th to the 109th Congresses would seem correct, although it would not be as steep a decline as the graph depicts.

The trend for hearings on foreign trade and defense seem in line with the expectation that Congress has delegated authority to the president in these areas. As discussed above, the rate of presidential foreign policy activity has been steadily increasing, but congressional activity has been lagging behind, including its oversight activity. Beginning around the time of the start of the first Clinton term, congressional activity in foreign trade and defense issues starts to decline and has been in general decline ever since. This is perhaps especially startling because during this period we witnessed an explosion of attention to foreign trade, including the North American Free Trade Act, the emergence of the World Trade Organization, and an increasing number of free trade deals with other countries and regions. And there has been no lack of defense activities during this period—the rapid expansion of NATO; major uses of force in Bosnia, Afghanistan, and Iraq; and several other significant uses of American military power. And yet congressional hearings in both of these content areas have been in decline.

The trend of hearings in the international affairs and foreign aid topic area in figure 2 is more curious, as it shows a rather steady increase in congressional activity from the Truman administration through the 108th Congress, so maybe there is this one sign of life. First, after looking at the data, we are confident that hearings coded in the past as "defense" or "foreign trade" have not been shifted to this category; rather, the number of hearings on general international affairs issues has in fact increased (that is, the upward trend is not just an artifact of the coding scheme). We think that much of this increase is being driven by the pride that the Senate Foreign Relations Committee takes in being the most active committee in the Senate.[47] The House International Relations Committee is also a busy major policy committee. And certainly part of the story here is Congress trying to keep up with developments around the world, developments often driven by the White House. So while the one trend line is in an upward direction, in general the trend here, especially around "war" issues that would fall in the defense topic area, is downward and consistent with congressional defection from policy responsibility in these areas.

Moving to the realm of appropriations would seem to be a real test of Congress's resolve as to whether or not it would choose to cede its authority in arguably the most important facet of public policy. Indeed, seats on the Appropriations committees have long been one of the most sought-after prizes by members of Congress because of the panels' unique power across the spectrum of public policy.[48] In addition, the Appropriations committees' internal decision rules emphasized consensus as a way to protect and promote its powers within the chamber and in relation to the president.[49] And although partisanship has become rampant throughout Congress, the Appropriations committees resisted the extreme partisan rancor for longer than other committees.[50] Despite the importance of appropriations to Congress, it is certainly not beyond encroachment by the executive. Presidents have plenty of incentive to challenge congressional authority here. The appropriations process provides the president with an important venue to shape the federal bureaucracy and, ultimately, public policy outcomes.[51]

Signing statements provide an important mechanism to shape appropriations policy. In a recent analysis of fiscal year 2006 appropriations bills, the Government Accountability Office (GAO) found from their sample that about 30 percent of the legislative provisions challenged through presidential signing statements were not executed according to Congress's statutory requirements.[52] The data in table 1 show how often Presidents Reagan through George W. Bush issued signing statements on appropriations legislation. The table is derived from Christopher Kelley and Bryan Marshall's data base on presidential signing statements, and it extends patterns they found in prior analysis.[53] Analysis of table 1 indicates that presidents have actively issued signing statements on appropriations legislation and that the number of challenges contained in such statements seems to have increased, especially under the most recent Bush administration. If the GAO findings are at all representative, Congress's authority in the appropriations process may be significantly undermined through the use of signing statements.

The operative question becomes how Congress has responded to the president's use of signing statements that can challenge Congress's authority over the purse strings. As before, the analysis utilizes congressional hearings to assess the extent of Congress's willingness to actively participate in the appropriations process and challenge executive encroachment on its authority. Figure 3 is also constructed from data taken from the Policy Agendas Project. The data include all hearings that have to do with appropriations across all possible topic areas, foreign and domestic. As we discussed above, because of the powers granted to Congress in the Constitution we should see ample congressional activity in this area. But contrary to that expectation, and consistent with our argument (and Louis Fisher's) that Congress has delegated substantial authority to the president concerning spending, we see a general decline in activity, from the start of the Reagan administration through the 109th Congress (which again,

TABLE 1

Presidential use of constitutional signing statements on appropriations bills from the Reagan to George W. Bush administrations

Congress	*% Appropriations bills prompting constitutional signing statements*	*Total no. challenges on appropriations*	*Average no. challenges per constitutional signing statement*
97th (1981–82) Reagan	4.0	1	1.00
98th (1983–84) Reagan	14.3	12	3.00
99th (1985–86) Reagan	15.8	4	1.33
100th (1987–88) Reagan	25.0	12	2.40
101st (1989–90) Bush I	26.8	19	1.73
102nd (1991–92) Bush I	33.3	19	1.46
103rd (1993–94) Clinton	20.0	11	1.57
104th (1995–96) Clinton	10.3	4	1.33
105th (1997–98) Clinton	17.6	12	2.00
106th (1999–2000) Clinton	17.0	20	2.50
107th (2001–2002) Bush II	50.0	50	3.13
108th (2003–2004) Bush II	44.4	225	18.75
109th (2005–2006) Bush II	60.9	252	18.00
Total divided	22.2	153	2.19
Total unified	38.8	488	14.79
TOTAL	25.9	641	6.22

includes only partial data for that Congress). While there are a couple of upturns since then, the general downward trend in figure 3 is striking. While hearings on spending consistently increased during the Nixon administration, which included very contentious issues about budget rescissions, for example, since the Reagan administration the trend has been downward. We see this as consistent with Fisher's argument about the power of the shift to automatic spending cuts in the Gramm-Rudman-Hollings law, the flirtation with the line-item veto, and the general shift of the locus of activity on spending from Congress to the White House. Indeed, we are at a loss to explain this trend in any other way.

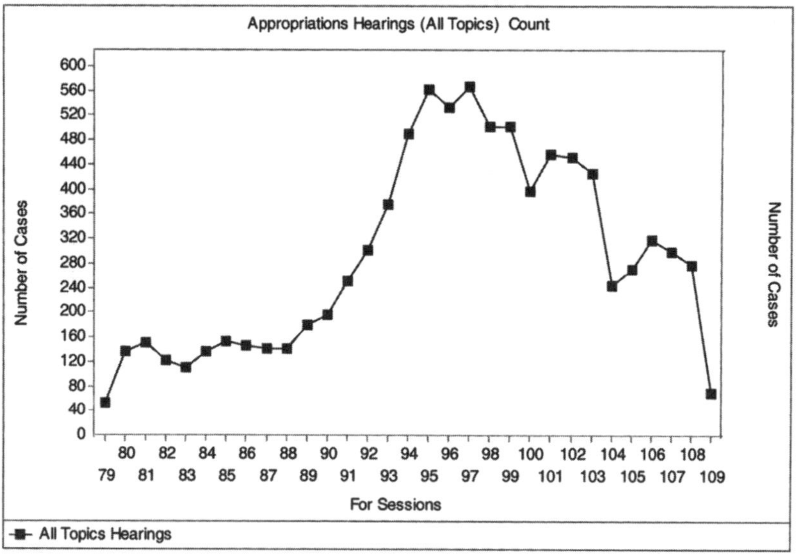

FIGURE 3. Appropriations hearings, 79th through 109th Congresses

Given that the power of appropriations is central to Congress's constitutional strength, we do offer up one additional anecdotal example to drive home the point about Congress's penchant to defect by delegating its prized power to the executive. In late 2003 the House and the Senate both included identical language in the 2004 appropriations bill for the departments of Treasury and Transportation. This language would have banned any money from being spent to enforce the ban on travel to Cuba. Momentum to end the travel ban had been building, and the House vote of 227 to 188 and Senate vote of 59 to 38 seemed likely to draw a presidential veto (which would have been Bush's first and which would probably have been sustained in the House). Normally a conference committee would not return to the portion of a bill that had passed both houses with identical language, but in this case the House leadership would do the president's work for him. House majority leader Tom DeLay (R-Tex.), a strong supporter of the embargo, stacked the committee, giving ten of the seventeen slots for the House to those in favor of the ban. The composition of Senate conferees led the conference committee to be about evenly divided on the travel ban.[54] At a late-night meeting of the committee staff, the Cuba travel provision was struck from the bill—a move that caused bipartisan irritation. A Democrat staffer said, "The fact that it could be undermined is mind-blowing, and more reminiscent of the Politburo than Congress."[55] Senator Michael Enzi (R-Wyo.) complained, "There is something out of whack with how the Cuba language was removed. It was stripped by staffers even before members of the committee formally met. There was no vote taken. Poof, it just disappeared into the congressional ether."[56]

Implications and Conclusion

Although the legislative body is the First Branch in terms of constitutional powers, Congress has been at a relative disadvantage in political scuffles with presidents. Congress seems trapped in a prisoner's dilemma in which more and more members choose to delegate (defect) their authority to the executive. In return, members of Congress can secure reelection by their constituencies by deflecting blame and maximizing credit. Moreover, presidents have been more than willing to expand their powers at Congress's expense. The trends toward greater unilateral activity provide presidents with the means to accrue such power, and the theory of the unitary executive has provided the rationale. The equilibrium result of such strategic interaction seems to be a continual diminution in Congress's authority and independence with respect to the president. Our analysis illustrates that presidents have used tools such as executive agreements and signing statements to expand their influence across foreign and domestic policy. The empirical patterns in the hearings data suggest that Congress's collective response to executive incursions has been weakening over time. This precipitous decline in congressional willingness to serve as a coequal branch holds in foreign affairs as well as in Congress's most prized area, the power of the purse.

While we think the weight of the evidence shown here and discussed by others such as Mann and Ornstein suggests reason to be concerned that

Congress is increasingly delegating its authority over foreign policy and appropriations to a presidency eager for more power, we have seen some signs of congressional life. The number of hearings in the international affairs and foreign aid topic area seems to be generally increasing over time, though it is not at all clear that these hearings are culminating in effective oversight of the president or the kind of procedural legislation for which a new institutionalist would hope. And Thomas Mann, Molly Reynolds, and Peter Hoey showed in a 2007 *New York Times* article some evidence to suggest that the 110th Congress had reasserted itself, at least with respect to oversight hearings and the number of votes held.[57] Even more, there was some bipartisan support from the chair and ranking minority member of the House Intelligence Committee, who brushed back an attempt by the Department of Justice to slow the congressional investigation of the destruction of the CIA's tapes of two suspected terrorists being "waterboarded." The House Intelligence Committee subpoenaed CIA officials with a demand to learn more about the destruction.[58] These types of actions would seem consistent with Howell and Pevehouse's expectation that, with a return to divided government, partisanship will permit a reemergence of congressional activism to restrain the president.[59]

We would like to be more optimistic but fear that these are just blips against the long-term secular decline of Congress acting as the First Branch on foreign policy and spending. Howell and Pevehouse, for example, point to a properly motivated Congress's ability to restrain the warmaking power of the president by "restricting the scope or duration of a conflict or by establishing reporting requirements" and through the appropriations process.[60] They argue that even by raising concerns through the media, Congress can affect the timing, size, and scope of military deployments. They show with past evidence that the circumstances in which Congress is more likely to restrain the president's warmaking ability include when congressional opposition is large and cohesive or when military operations are about to grow in size.[61] And they expect, writing before the 110th Congress started work, that that Congress would in fact show greater efforts to restrain President Bush's policy in Iraq. While it may be the case that Congress's signaling (and a new National Intelligence Estimate) helped slow the pace to war with Iran, it has had no real impact on military operations in Iraq. The 110th Congress came to the Hill with emboldened majorities and public support behind a change in policy in Iraq, but we saw instead an increase in the size of the deployment to Iraq and the continued funding of the war—with no strings attached—far into the future. The House passed an omnibus spending package that included the $70 billion the president had requested for military operations in Iraq and Afghanistan, which Representative Jim McGovern (D-Mass.) made clear was a "blank check."[62]

The 110th Congress's funding of the Iraq war follows our argument in that members of Congress preferred to avoid the political blame that would have resulted from voting against funding and not supporting the troops. In return, the president received all the spending he asked for while members of Congress were able to take home to their constituencies about nine thousand pet projects. We recognize that Iraq is only one case, but it is a central case, emphasized by Democratic candidates in the 2006 elections and one that Howell and Pevehouse seemed to expect to see the new Congress address. The pattern here would seem to support our view that Congress has ceded its authority to the executive. Individual members who might want to restrain the president have been unable to stem the tide of defections transferring authority to the White House.

The evidence about compliance with the Case-Zablocki Act on reporting executive agreements also seems to support our view that the long-term trend toward defection from policy responsibility outweighs any short-term resurgence in congressional activism. Passed so as to make sure Congress had the information it needed about executive agreements so that it could meaningfully oversee the president and intervene if necessary, presidential reporting under the act has been consistently late, with little or no response from Congress. As it has accepted its (bad) fortunes from the War Powers Act and abandoned any meaningful role in the Base Closure and Realignment Commission so as to protect its reelection chances, so too Congress seems to have accepted its fate here; it finds out late, if at all, about executive agreements. "Better than nothing" is not what Madison had in mind or what defenders of the institution of Congress would hope for.

Further investigation of these trends in the divided government of the 110th Congress is surely warranted. Another avenue for future research is to watch executive agreements. Since Congress can respond to unilateral actions by the president, such as executive agreements, presidents may be less likely to use them when faced with significant opposition.[63] Here, the 110th Congress may be an interesting test case: will there prove to be any difference in Bush's use of executive agreements under divided government than there was under unified government?

And what of the next president, and the next Congress? If our most recent experience provides some clue, it is that unified government can exacerbate congressional defection in maintaining itself as the First Branch, let alone a coequal branch. House Speaker J. Dennis Hastert, playing the role of loyal lieutenant, readily subordinated Congress to President Bush's agenda. According to Mann and Ornstein, "He proclaimed that his primary responsibility was not to lead and defend the first branch of government but to pass the president's legislative program."[64] Thus, party leaders chose not to let regular order get in the way of presidential priorities, so unified party control was allowed to trump the very essence of Congress's advantage as a legislative body—its deliberative process. Will this be the case in the 111th Congress, with Democrats in control of both the White House and the Congress? One curious indication that it may not is the news that Vice President Joseph Biden will not be a regular member of the Senate Democrats' strategy sessions, a departure from Vice President Richard Cheney's strong presence at those meetings.[65] In fact, congressional observers suggested that Cheney's presence stifled any inclination for Senate Republicans to exercise independence from the will of the White House. According to Ross Baker, "He [Cheney] was the Bigfoot that came into those meetings. If someone got out of line, he would put a thumb in their eyes."[66] Whether or not the move to exclude Vice President Biden from inner Senate deliberations represents a significant brush-back designed for the sake of that great chamber's independence, only time will tell.

Are we being alarmist about Congress aiding and abetting the rise of a more powerful unitary executive? Maybe we should think about it the way unitary executives think about it. After the 9/11 attacks, Vice President Cheney laid out his "1 Percent Doctrine," arguing that if there were even a 1 percent chance of something disastrous happening, the Bush foreign policy machinery must act as if it were an absolute certainty.[67] Madison reminds us of the stakes in "Federalist No. 47" as he quotes Montesquieu: "There can be no liberty where the legislative and executive powers are united in the same person." If there were even a 1 percent chance of this happening, then perhaps members of Congress should act as if it were an absolute certainty and reclaim their role as an active, authoritative, deliberate, coequal branch. We certainly do not see any evidence that such a reclamation lies ahead.

Notes

1. Thomas E. Mann and Norman J. Ornstein, *The Broken Branch: How Congress Is Failing America and How to Get It Back on Track* (New York: Oxford University Press, 2006).

2. Quoted in Frank Church, "Of Presidents and Caesars: The Decline of Constitutional Government in the Conduct of American Foreign Policy," *Idaho Law Review* 6, no. 1 (1969): 7. Even strong proponents of executive power such as Alexander Hamilton sanctioned the president's secondary role as commander in chief.

3. Church, "Of Presidents and Caesars," 7.

4. *Little v. Barreme,* 6 U.S. 170 (Cranch) 1804.

5. H.R. J. Res. 114, *Joint Resolution to Authorize the Use of United States Armed Forces against Iraq,* 107th Cong., 2nd sess., 2002, http://www.whitehouse.gov/news/releases/2002/10/20021002–2.html.

6. Quoted in Helen Fessenden and John Cochran, "Congress Seeks to Find Its Voice as Iraq War Rages," *Congressional Quarterly Weekly Reports,* March 22, 2003, 677.

7. H.R. J. Res. 64, *Authorizing Use of United States Armed Forces against Those Responsible for Recent Attacks against the United States,* 107th Cong., 1st sess., *Congressional Record,* September 14, 2001, H5638.

8. Ron Suskind, *The One Percent Doctrine: Deep Inside America's Pursuit of Its Enemies since 9/11* (New York: Simon & Schuster, 2006), 17.

9. Louis Fisher, *Congressional Abdication on War and Spending* (College Station: Texas A&M University Press, 2000), 14.

10. William G. Howell and Jon C. Pevehouse, "When Congress Stops Wars," *Foreign Affairs,* September–October 2007.

11. Mann and Ornstein, *The Broken Branch.*

12. See, e.g., Pendleton Herring, *Presidential Leadership: The Political Relations of Congress and the Chief Executive* (New York: Farrar and Rinehart, 1940); Richard E. Neustadt, *Presidential Power* (New York: John Wiley & Sons, 1960); Clint Rossiter, *The American Presidency* (New York: Harcourt, Brace, 1956); and Aaron Wildavsky, ed., *The Presidency* (Boston: Little, Brown, 1969).

13. Neustadt, *Presidential Power.*

14. See William G. Howell, "Unilateral Powers: A Brief Overview," *Presidential Studies Quarterly* 35, no. 3 (2005): 417–38.

15. See Phillip J. Cooper, "George W. Bush, Edgar Allan Poe, and the Use and Abuse of Presidential Signing Statements," *Presidential Studies Quarterly* 35, no. 3 (2005): 515–32; Loch K. Johnson, *The Making of International Agreements: Congress Confronts the Executive* (New York: New York University Press, 1984); and Kenneth R.

Mayer, *With the Stroke of a Pen: Executive Orders and Presidential Power* (Princeton: Princeton University Press, 2001).

16. Howell, "Unilateral Powers."

17. Jess Bravin, "Judge Alito's View of the Presidency: Expansive Powers," *Wall Street Journal,* January 5, 2006, A1.

18. Terry M. Moe and William G. Howell, "Unilateral Action and Presidential Power: A Theory," *Presidential Studies Quarterly* 29, no. 4 (1999): 850–73.

19. See ibid.; and Howell, "Unilateral Powers."

20. James M. Lindsay, *Congress and the Politics of U.S. Foreign Policy* (Baltimore: Johns Hopkins University Press, 1994).

21. Charles W. Kegley and Eugene R. Wittkopf, *American Foreign Policy: Pattern and Process,* 5th ed. (New York: St. Martin's Press, 1998).

22. Richard F. Fenno, *Congressmen in Committees* (Berkeley, Calif.: Institute of Governmental Studies Press, 1973), 187–89.

23. Quoted in David R. Mayhew, *Congress: The Electoral Connection* (New Haven: Yale University Press, 1974), 123.

24. Joshua Lee Prober, "Congress, the War Powers Resolution, and the Secret Political Life of a Dead Letter," *Journal of Law and Politics* 7 (fall 1990): 229.

25. Joseph White, "Decision Making in the Appropriations Subcommittees on Defense and Foreign Operations," in *Congress Resurgent: Foreign and Defense Policy on Capitol Hill,* ed. Randall B. Ripley and James M. Lindsay (Ann Arbor: University of Michigan Press, 1993), 183–206.

26. Steven S. Smith, "Congressional Party Leaders," in *The President, the Congress, and the Making of Foreign Policy,* ed. Paul E. Peterson (Norman: University of Oklahoma Press, 1994).

27. David W. Rohde's findings suggest that presidential advantage on foreign and defense policy compared to domestic policy continued well into the 1980s (this support for the president occurred primarily in the House of Representatives) and thus did not characterize only the early cold war era. See Rohde, "Presidential Support in the House of Representatives," in *The President, the Congress, and the Making of Foreign Policy,* ed. Peterson, 101–28.

28. See Fisher, *Congressional Abdication on War and Spending;* Joanne Gowa, "Politics at the Water's Edge: Parties, Voters, and the Use of Force Abroad," *International Organization* 52, no. 2 (1998): 307–24; Lee H. Hamilton, "The Making of U.S. Foreign Policy: The Roles of the President and Congress over Four Decades," in *Rivals for Power: Presidential-Congressional Relations,* ed. James A. Thurber, 2nd ed. (Lanham, Md.: Rowman & Littlefield, 2002), 207–28; and Barbara Hinckley, *Less Than Meets the Eye: Foreign Policy Making and the Myth of the Assertive Congress* (Chicago: University of Chicago Press, 1994).

29. William G. Howell and Jon C. Pevehouse, *While Dangers Gather: Congressional Checks on Presidential War Powers* (Princeton: Princeton University Press, 2007), 6.

30. Howell and Pevehouse, "When Congress Stops Wars"; Howell and Pevehouse, *While Dangers Gather.*

31. Moe and Howell, "Unilateral Action and Presidential Power."

32. Mayhew, *Congress: The Electoral Connection.*

33. Moe and Howell, "Unilateral Action and Presidential Power," 861.

34. Stephen R. Weissman, *A Culture of Deference: Congress's Failure of Leadership in Foreign Policy* (New York: Basic Books, 1995).

35. See Lawrence Margolis, *Executive Agreements and Presidential Power in Foreign Policy* (New York: Praeger, 1986); Mayer, *With the Stroke of a Pen;* Bryan Marshall and Richard L. Pacelle Jr., "Revisiting the Two Presidencies: The Strategic Use of Executive Orders, *American Politics Research* 31 (2005): 1–25; Howell, "Unilateral Powers"; and Christopher S. Kelley and Bryan W. Marshall, "Like Father, Like Son? The Presidents Bush and the Presidential Signing Statement," *White House Studies* 7, no. 1 (2007): 141–62.

36. Winston Churchill suggests that the agreement was of great import in that it committed the United States to war. Churchill argued that the agreement provided Germany with the legal grounds necessary for declaring war on the United States. See Church, "Of Presidents and Caesars."

37. Johnson, *The Making of International Agreements.*

38. Quoted in ibid., 117.

39. Congressional Research Service, Report for the Senate Foreign Relations Committee, *Treaties and Other International Agreements: The Role of the United States Senate* (Washington, D.C.: U.S. Government Printing Office, January 2001).

40. James M. McCormick, *American Foreign Policy and Process,* 4th ed. (Belmont, Calif.: Thompson and Wadsworth, 2005), 298–99.

41. Fisher, *Congressional Abdication on War and Spending,* 7; James Madison, "Federalist No. 48," http://thomas.loc.gov/home/histdox/fed_48.html (accessed May 27, 2009).

42. Raymond Bauer, Ithiel de Sola Pool, and Lewis A. Dexter, *American Business and Public Policy: The Politics of Foreign Trade* (New York: Atherton Press, 1963), 37.

43. Johnson, *The Making of International Agreements.*

44. The executive agreement index is a measure developed by Johnson in *The Making of International Agreements.* The Truman (1946–53) through Nixon (1969–72) years of figure 1 are based on analysis from Johnson, *The Making of International Agreements.* The Theodore Roosevelt (1901–1909) and George W. Bush (2001–2004) data are based on analysis from Brandon C. Prins and Bryan W. Marshall, "Senate

Influence or Presidential Unilateralism? An Examination of Treaties and Executive Agreements from Theodore Roosevelt and George W. Bush," *Conflict Management and Peace Science* 26 (April 2009): 191–208.

45. Lindsay, *Congress and the Politics of U.S. Foreign Policy;* Christopher J. Deering, "Alarms and Patrols: Legislative Oversight in Foreign and Defense Policy," in *Congress and the Politics of U.S. Foreign Policy,* ed. Colton C. Campbell, Nicol C. Rae, and John F. Stack Jr. (Upper Saddle River, N.J.: Prentice Hall, 2003).

46. Policy Agendas Project, http://www.policyagendas.org/index.html.

47. See, e.g., Shailagh Murray, "Foreign Relations at Center Stage," *Washington Post,* March 28, 2007, A13.

48. Kenneth Shepsle, *The Giant Jigsaw Puzzle* (Chicago: University of Chicago Press, 1978).

49. Richard F. Fenno, *The Power of the Purse: Appropriations Politics in Congress* (Boston: Little, Brown, 1966).

50. Bryan W. Marshall, Brandon C. Prins, and David W. Rohde, "Partisanship and the Purse: The Money Committees and Procedures in the Postreform Congress," *Politics and Policy* 29, no. 2 (June 2001): 291–315.

51. Roderick D. Kiewiet and Mathew D. McCubbins, "Appropriations Decisions as a Bilateral Bargaining Game between President and Congress," *Legislative Studies Quarterly* 10 (1985): 181–201.

52. U.S. Government Accountability Office, *Presidential Signing Statements Accompanying the Fiscal Year 2006 Appropriations Acts,* June 18, 2007.

53. Kelley and Marshall, "Like Father, Like Son?"

54. Frank Davies, "Cuba Travel Battle Looms," *Miami Herald,* October 31, 2003, 14A.

55. Quoted in Christopher Marquis, "Bush's Allies Plan to Block Effort to Ease Ban on Cuban Travel," *New York Times,* November 13, 2003.

56. Quoted in Frank Davies and Nancy San Martin, "GOP Leaders Kill Provision to End Ban on Travel to Cuba," Knight-Ridder Newspapers, November 13, 2003.

57. Thomas E. Mann, Molly Reynolds, and Peter Hoey, "A New Improved Congress?" *New York Times,* August 26, 2007, 11.

58. Matt Apuzzo, "White House Faces Hearing on CIA Tapes," Associated Press, December 21, 2007.

59. Howell and Pevehouse, *While Dangers Gather.*

60. Ibid., 10.

61. Ibid., 27., 33.

62. Quoted in Andrew Taylor, "House Approves $70 Billion More for War," Associated Press, December 19, 2007.

63. Howell and Pevehouse, *While Dangers Gather,* 47.

64. Mann and Ornstein, *The Broken Branch,* 139.

65. Lisa Mascaro, "Biden Unwelcome in Senate Huddles, Where Cheney Wielded Power," *Las Vegas Sun,* December 7, 2008, http://www.lasvegassun.com/news/2008/dec/07/biden-unwelcome-senate-huddles-where-cheney-wielde/

66. Quoted in ibid.

67. Suskind, *The One Percent Doctrine,* 62.

PART III

CONCLUSION

Going Forward

The Unitary Executive, Presidential Power, and the Twenty-first Century Presidency

RYAN J. BARILLEAUX AND CHRISTOPHER S. KELLEY

In his first week in office, President Barack Obama took several actions emblematic of his power as chief executive. He issued executive orders that changed policy on funding international organizations that provide abortion counseling, on the detention and trial of prisoners held at Guantánamo Bay as suspects in terrorist activities, on the adoption of environmental regulations by states, and on ethics guidelines for his administration.[1] Moreover, in a meeting with congressional leaders to discuss his plans for a package of measures intended to stimulate the sagging economy, Obama rejected appeals from Republican legislators to include more tax cuts in the legislation to serve as an economic stimulus. Using words that observers were too polite to compare to the language of the previous president ("I'm the decider"), Obama justified his position by stating flatly, "I won."[2] Within only a few days of taking office, he had made it clear that he intended to be an assertive president.

As the contributors to this volume have shown, such assertiveness by President Obama is consistent with a larger trend in the American presidency. While he campaigned for the White House in 2008 by promising to change the tone in Washington and while he was critical of several aspects of the use of executive power by George W. Bush, he did not sketch a vision for his presidency that suggested anything less than a chief executive as a leader of his administration, public policy, and public opinion. He intended to be an energetic and activist president.

Not only did he assert executive power, but Obama also organized his administration to centralize greater power in the White House by appointing a number of powerful "czars" to coordinate administration policy in areas such as health care, energy and the environment, and the economy. This centralization was also consistent with the four-decade trend of extending White House control over the executive branch.[3] President Obama's first days in office demonstrated that he had come to power intending to compete successfully in the interbranch competition that characterizes national policymaking.

George W. Bush's Executive Unilateralism

American politics is distinguished by competing forces—the presidency against Congress, the two major parties in contention, constitutional flexibility tugging against constitutional strictures, centralization and decentralization, as well as others. These competitions should not surprise any student of a system designed around the concept of checks and balances. One of these competitive dynamics is the struggle between the need for a strong chief executive and the need to "tame the prince" (in the words of Harvey Mansfield), that is, to keep executive power in constitutional check.[4] The debate over presidential power in the early twenty-first century, especially as it developed during the administration of George W. Bush, is but the latest example of this dynamic.

When Bush assumed the presidency in 2001, a struggle over presidential autonomy from congressional limitations had been under way at least since the Watergate crisis in the early 1970s. Indeed, one of the major themes of American politics in the decades since the New Deal had been the rise of the presidency as the dominant force in national politics (and even in American political consciousness). The New Deal was followed by World War II and then the national security state of the cold war, and the federal government acquired even greater size and scope as a result of the Great Society programs.

By the time Richard Nixon took office in 1969, the presidency had been firmly established as the center of the political system. Nixon took advantage of that fact to promote his foreign policy agenda, but he also continued to build on presidential power in other areas. He used administrative tools, such as impoundment, reorganization, tentative moves into White House oversight of executive regulation, budgetary oversight, a larger presidential staff, and executive orders to enhance the power of his office. He also employed less conventional power strategies, including "going public," "dirty tricks" against political opponents, and the promotion of sympathetic career officials in the bureaucracy (a tactic that Richard

Nathan called the "plot that failed").[5] Arthur Schlesinger Jr. characterized both the Lyndon Johnson and the Nixon administrations as "imperial" for their aggressive assertions of presidential power.[6]

Nixon was brought down by the Watergate scandal, and in the years that followed the American presidency appeared to retreat from the heights of power (some would argue, abuses of power) it had achieved under Johnson and Nixon. Indeed, the conventional reading of the presidencies of Gerald Ford and Jimmy Carter was that they represented a time in which the presidency was severely weakened and Congress was dominant. Several commentators and scholars in that period argued that Congress had taken charge, and they characterized the period as one of an "imperiled presidency," a "post-imperial presidency," an "imperial Congress," and an "impossible presidency."[7]

This conventional view, however, was mistaken. As Barilleaux and Zellers demonstrate in this volume, presidential unilateralism not only existed during the Ford and Carter presidencies but both presidents undertook assertions of presidential power. Some of these, such as use of the veto and international diplomacy, conformed to traditional and settled understandings of the president's constitutional authority. Other actions they took, including some now associated (critically) with George W. Bush (e.g., signing statements—which came into use before Bush's presidency), were more innovative (read controversial). Furthermore, Kelley demonstrates that the so-called abusive powers of the unitary executive exercised by Bush had been forged in the administrations before him, most importantly that of his Democratic predecessor, Bill Clinton. Thus, the unitary executive had been developing long before George W. Bush took office in 2001, despite what the press and critics of the Bush administration have otherwise argued. As we take great pains to demonstrate in the first part of this book, the unitary executive is much bigger than any one person, and so long as we reel back in horror as each new president acts according to its tenets, we will be missing the forest for the trees.

The second part of this book focused on the actions of the forty-third president. George W. Bush certainly put his own stamp on presidential power and asserted the broadest interpretation of that power in decades, but this assertion of wide-ranging power is not unique in American history, nor were Bush's claims for the origins and extent of this power as unprecedented as his critics claimed. There is a good case to be made (see our introduction) that Bush used the language of the unitary executive theory while going beyond it in his exercise of unilateral presidential power, but his exercise of power was distinguished mostly by its sweep and by the unapologetic way in which he did it. Bush claimed very broad power to act unilaterally (most emphatically in his comment "I'm the decider") and—while noting the legitimacy of Congress's role in making national policy—he was a veritable apostle of a strong president as national guardian. Recent presidents had claimed and exercised broad executive powers, but they tended to use language that was more deferential toward Congress even as they were acting unilaterally. Bush was more willing to defend publicly the positive good of a strong chief executive for national security, stability, and progress.

For most observers of the Bush presidency, the unitary executive seemed to materialize from thin air in the wake of the 9/11 attacks. The contributors to this volume have shown how that view is inaccurate and why the theory is not going to evaporate now that George Bush has left the stage. Despite rhetoric from the Bush administration justifying its actions in the name of the unitary executive, actions by administration officials suggest that something else was afoot. As Harold Krent has argued, President Bush's view of the unitary executive was different from that of his immediate predecessors in that it was fully unilateral in both the foreign and domestic spheres, cutting the Congress out of its shared administrative role in domestic politics.[8] For Krent, President Bush may not have behaved according to the dictates of the unitary executive theory as much as he tested its limits. In the end, for all of the administration's initial bravado in 2001 about restoring the privileged place of the presidency, it may actually have acted in a way that could limit presidential action by drawing so much attention from the press, the public, and the Congress.

On the other hand, we can view President Bush's assertion of the unitary executive as but a thoroughgoing example of a dynamic that has characterized the presidency throughout its history. This is the phenomenon of *venture constitutionalism.*[9]

Venture Constitutionalism and Presidential Power

Venture constitutionalism refers to assertions of constitutional legitimacy for presidential actions that do not conform to settled understandings of the president's constitutional authority. It is a form of constitutional risk-taking, a gamble that the president's action will be accepted, or at least acquiesced to, by other key actors in the political system. As Barilleaux has explained,

> "Venture constitutionalism usually occurs when the president takes an action (including negative actions, such as claims of executive privilege or immunity, impoundment, etc.) that 'stake out' a claim to authority not already accepted as within the chief executive's constitutional orbit. It has occurred throughout American history and in a wide range of cases, but it has been especially common in foreign affairs, and it has been responsible for much of the expansion of presidential power. It is has been a series of exercises in 'pushing back the frontiers' of presidential constitutional authority."[10]

Venture constitutionalism can be divided into three main types. Type 1 actions are those intended to protect the institutional interests of the presidency, such as claims of executive privilege or the long battle presidents waged with Congress over the removal power. Type 2 actions are intended to promote U.S. security and advance the national interest, and these include assertions of presidential autonomy to use force (presidential war), employ sweeping emergency powers, terminate treaties, and detain foreign combatants. Type 3 actions enhance the president's influence in shaping policy and include such developments as the growing White House control over executive branch rulemaking, control over budgeting and implementation, and the use of signing statements as instruments of policy. President Bush engaged in a number of actions that can be characterized as venture constitutionalism, and the theory of the unitary executive branch is itself both a form of this constitutional venturing (both Type 1 and Type 3) and a theory to justify more specific exercises in venture constitutionalism.

According to Barilleaux's analysis of venture constitutionalism, the cumulative effect of presidential assertions of greater constitutional authority has resulted in the "enlargement of the presidency" that analysts have seen over the course of American history. The accretion of precedents, built up from presidential victories in having Congress, the courts, and other political actors acquiesce to these assertions, have increased presidential power over time. President Bush's assertion of a justification for broad White House authority over the executive branch should be seen in this light. In that sense his actions represent some of the most critical developments in a long series of presidential actions to push back limits on the chief executive's power. To that extent, while the unitary executive may (or may not) be an innovation in itself, it is fairly characteristic of other forms of constitutional venturing.

Looking Forward

Placing George Bush's unilateralism and the unitary executive theory in this larger context, we can see that the record of previous presidential power assertions provides clues to the sort of dynamic that is likely to play out in the future to determine the fate of the unitary executive. Four points are relevant to predicting the future of the unitary executive:

Assertive presidential unilateralism is here to stay. Presidential candidates get elected promising to do things with the office, and presidents in office want to put their stamp on national policy. The prevailing theme of the presidency since World War II has been assertiveness, and at least since the Ford presidency unilateralism has been an important element in that assertiveness. During the 2008 presidential campaign, Democratic candidates Hillary Clinton and Barak Obama found much to criticize in George W. Bush's actions as president, but neither was willing to forswear the use of signing statements as an instrument of policy. Republican candidate John McCain said he would not use signing statements (though he later equivocated and claimed he would not use signing statements to make policy), but there was no evidence that he would otherwise refrain from unilateralism (even if he kept that promise, which circumstances might cause him to reconsider). With Obama as president, we can expect that he will employ signing statements if he finds them useful for promoting his objectives. Given that Obama promised much in the 2008 campaign and faced enormous problems even before entering office, there is no reason to think that he will refrain from using these tools. He demonstrated in his first days in office that he is willing to act assertively with regard to executive power; other actions attendant to presidential unilateralism are likely to follow. Even if he refrains from employing the language of the unitary executive theory (although there is no reason to suppose that his administration will not ever use it), the record of recent history and the dynamics of American politics suggest that the substance of unitary executive thinking will influence President Obama.

Presidents of both parties have resorted to unilateralism for the same reason: it is a way to put one's stamp on policy in the face of resistance or inaction from Congress or the bureaucracy. It is a fact that institutional forces within the executive branch push the president into acting unilaterally despite statements on the campaign trail not to do so. In this regard, the examples of recent presidents are instructive. Jimmy Carter, Bill Clinton, and George W. Bush all dealt with a Congress controlled by their own parties, but each found unilateralism useful for shaping policy. Sometimes this unilateralism takes a traditional form (e.g., vetoes or executive agreements), but at other times it takes a more innovative form (e.g., signing statements and other actions).

There is much to criticize in presidential unilateralism, but first we must understand it. At least since Richard Nixon, every president has engaged in unilateralism as an instrument of policy and of power. This is true despite differences of party, ideology, partisan control of Congress, or even personality. There is an underlying dynamic to the unilateral presidency that cannot be ignored.

The underlying dynamic is as old as the republic, but it has been accelerated by developments in American politics since 1970. In "Federalist No. 51," Publius (James Madison) wrote that "ambition must be made to counteract ambition." Presidents have long made forays into the constitutional weeds to expand the limits of their authority, practicing venture constitutionalism. In the twentieth century, particularly since Franklin Roosevelt, the presidency has been an assertive and expansive institution, driven by the ambition of the incumbent to shape national policy and/or to meet the obligations imposed by the office. The Oval Office has been both the prize of the ambitious and their operating base—candidates have not sought the presidency just to enjoy prestige but to accomplish something.

Congress, following the logic of Daniel Patrick Moynihan's "Iron Law of Emulation" (which holds that what one branch of government does will be emulated by another), responded to the enlargement of the presidency and its powers by undertaking a number of actions in the 1970s to enable itself to be a more active and assertive player in the making of national policy.[11] It gave itself a large professional staff, reformed its budget process, developed tools for more oversight of the executive, passed legislation to gain more information about the conduct of foreign policy and influence over it (the Case-Zablocki Act, the War Powers Resolution, and other laws), and at times acted aggressively to challenge presidential policy (in the mid-1970s and again in the late 1990s and after the 2006 midterm elections). In less than forty years, Congress has moved toward impeaching one president (Nixon, whom it ultimately drove from office), legislated an end to the Vietnam War, prohibited American intervention in the civil war in Angola (1975), impeached another president (Clinton), shut down the government in a duel with the White House over the federal budget (1995), investigated the Iran-Contra affair and other incidents, passed a bill to require a timetable for withdrawing U.S. forces from Iraq (2007), tried several times to bring the president to heel on the use of force, and balked when the Bush administration tried to have its first financial industry bailout plan passed summarily in 2008. These and other incidents have made the legislature a full player in the separated system of American government, but they have also stimulated presidents to seek greater autonomy from legislative constraints.

The unilateral presidency is the result of this stimulation. Barack Obama follows in this line of presidents seeking to accomplish something in office and feeling the urgency of their task. In his victory speech on election night in 2008, he told the assembled crowd that "this is our time—to put our people back to work and open doors of opportunity for our kids; to restore prosperity and promote the cause of peace; to reclaim the American Dream and reaffirm that fundamental truth—that out of many, we are one; that while we breathe, we hope, and where we are met with cynicism, and doubt, and those who tell us that we can't, we will respond with that timeless creed that sums up the spirit of a people: Yes We Can."[12] There is no reason to think that he or any subsequent president will be passive in the conduct of office.

Congressional responses to executive unilateralism will be too late and too strong and will in turn stimulate a new round of executive assertiveness. In the 1960s and 1970s Congress bridled at the growth of presidential power but acquiesced to it until legislators finally decided that they had seen enough. Beginning in the mid-1970s, Congress reacted with a spate of president-curbing legislation (the War Powers Resolution, the Case-Zablocki Act, the Budget and Impoundment Act), the near-impeachment of Richard Nixon, a legislated end to the Vietnam War, an investigation of the CIA, and other actions to restrict presidential autonomy. The consequence, to some extent described in this volume, was the rise of executive unilateralism as a way to circumvent Congress.

Congress is likely to respond to signing statements and other forms of executive unilateralism in a similar way. Members will complain about various presidential actions, but institutional action will come only after a long series of precedents have been laid. Then Congress will try to curb the presidency through new legislation or a court challenge, which in turn will stimulate a new round of presidential actions designed to circumvent the legislature. However, if recent congressional responses to the signing statement are any guide to future action, then we should be worried about Congress's inability to mount nothing more than a symbolic challenge to presidential unilateralism.

The long-term dynamics of venture constitutionalism favor the expansion of presidential power and therefore the consolidation of the unitary executive. One characteristic of venture constitutionalism is that precedents are generally cumulative. As Barilleaux notes, "Perhaps the most significant lesson to be gleaned from understanding the dynamics of this venturing is that the first precedent is the most important one. Consider, for example, Jimmy Carter's initial use of PUPDs [parallel unilateral policy declarations] in 1978 to extend the life of the expiring SALT I agreement."[13] Barilleaux states that

> the president's action was initially denounced in the Senate as a usurpation of the upper chamber's constitutional authority as regards treaties, a violation of the Arms Control and Disarmament Act of 1961, and a dangerous precedent for unilateral executive control over a vital area of national security policy. But the Senate did not act to challenge Carter's action, in part because influential Members of the House were uninterested in the issue, and the precedent was set. Within a few years, PUPDs had become part of the governmental landscape: by the time of Ronald Reagan, it was now taken as a matter of course that the president alone would decide whether or not the United States should abide by the (unratified, but implemented by PUPDs) SALT II agreement. . . . Successful risk-taking begets further risk-taking, and the overall trend of venture constitutionalism is in the direction of enlarged presidential power.[14]

George W. Bush repeatedly asserted his authority to control the unitary executive branch. Over time, if subsequent presidents do likewise (and there is no reason to suppose that others will not, even if it does not occur for several years), they will point to Bush's assertions as precedents. Along with the general trend of executive unilateralism, the unitary executive theory will eventually become part of the conventional wisdom. Unless there were to be some decisive challenge to the president that would result in a resounding rebuke by the Supreme Court (and at least for the foreseeable future, this is a pro-executive Court), the long-term prospects for institutionalizing the unitary executive theory are good.

Some form of the "unitary executive" theory will not only remain but will eventually become the prevailing view. This conclusion follows from all of the preceding. The situation is similar to that of presidential war: it went from being almost unthinkable, to being controversial, to being more common but still not quite normal, to being the way things are done. Over time, the unitary executive theory is likely to become the prevailing theory of presidential power over the executive branch. The president is a unitary actor with an incentive to push for greater control and autonomy; Congress is a collective body with a less compelling incentive to reply to every assertion of unilateralism by the president. Future presidents will find this theory useful for justifying their unilateral actions, perhaps in the name of slowing global warming, promoting ethics in government, increasing diversity in the federal workforce, or preventing Congress from undoing a key presidential initiative. Time and precedent are more likely to favor the president than Congress, and in time the unitary executive theory may well become the accepted view of the relationship between the president and the executive branch.

The relevant dynamic here is that of George Bush's successors finding the unitary executive theory useful, compounded by the tendency of government officials to protect the power claims of their predecessors, even when they soften those claims. Consider what happened in January 2009, shortly after Barack Obama took office: lawyers for his administration prepared to go to court to defend the claims made by Bush administration lawyer John Yoo (Bush's head of the Justice Department's Office of Legal Counsel) that authorized American interrogators to employ methods that were denounced by candidate Obama and other Bush critics as torture. Despite the fact that Obama had publicly attacked John Yoo's interpretations of presidential power as wrong and dangerous, Obama administration lawyers were not going to reject his interpretation of the law or governmental power. As explained by Bradford Berenson, who served as associate White House counsel during George W. Bush's first term, the reason for this defense of Yoo is simple: "The dirty little secret here is that the United States government has enduring institutional interests that carry over from administration to administration and almost always dictate the position the government takes."[15]

In addition to all of the other political dynamics discussed above, there is this final reality that "enduring institutional interests" favor the continuation of ideas and practices over time. Presidents will still desire autonomy from congressional control, and the unitary executive theory—in one form or another—will help to serve that interest. Moreover, presidential unilateralism, however it is justified, will continue to mark the behavior of the officials who work in the White House.

Both critics and advocates for the unitary executive theory may be surprised at our conclusions, but what will also be surprising (or ironic) will be what happens in the future. At some point, the unitary executive theory is likely to be employed by a president with very different goals than George W. Bush, and that president's supporters will be happy to rely on this theory to support their leader, while those who oppose that president will regret that Bush started down this path. The unitary executive is likely to be with us for a long time, but perhaps not for the purposes that its original advocates intended.

Notes

1. "A Look at Obama's Latest Executive Orders," *Washington Post,* January 22, 2009, http://www.washingtonpost.com/wp-dyn/content/article/2009/01/22/AR2009012201761.html (accessed January 28, 2009).

2. Quoted in Jonathan Weisman, "Obama to GOP: 'I Won,'" *Wall Street Journal,* January 23, 2009, http://blogs.wsj.com/washwire/2009/01/23/obama-to-gop-i-won/ (accessed January 28, 2009).

3. See Ryan J. Barilleaux, *The Post-Modern Presidency* (New York: Praeger, 1988).

4. Harvey Mansfield, *Taming the Prince: The Ambivalence of Modern Executive Power* (Baltimore: Johns Hopkins University Press, 1993).

5. See Samuel Kernell, *Going Public: New Strategies of Presidential Leadership,* 4th ed. (Washington, D.C.: CQ Press, 2006); and Richard Nathan, *The Plot That Failed* (New York: Wiley, 1975).

6. Arthur Schlesinger Jr., *The Imperial Presidency* (New York: Houghton Mifflin, 1975). Schlesinger described many actions by Nixon and Johnson as abuses of power, although he was unconvincing in distinguishing their conduct of power from the assertive uses of presidential power by Franklin Roosevelt and John Kennedy (of which he approved). Schlesinger's book coined the famous phrase, but it is more name-calling than useful analysis.

7. For a discussion of this period, see Barilleaux, *The Post-Modern Presidency,* especially chaps. 2 and 3.

8. Harold J. Krent, "From a Unitary to a Unilateral Presidency," *Boston University Law Review* 88 (2008): 523–60

9. For a systematic exposition of venture constitutionalism, see Ryan J. Barilleaux, "Venture Constitutionalism and the Enlargement of the Presidency," in *Executing the Constitution,* ed. by Christopher Kelley (Albany: State University of New York Press, 2006), 137–52.

10. Ibid., 142.

11. Daniel Patrick Moynihan, "Imperial Government," *Commentary*, June 1978.

12. Barack Obama, "Obama's Victory Speech," http://www.huffingtonpost.com/2008/11/04/obama-victory-speech_n_141194.html (accessed December 12, 2008).

13. Barilleaux, "Venture Constitutionalism," 49. Parallel unilateral policy declarations are devices by which the United States and another country (in this case, the Soviet Union) issue parallel statements with uniform language pledging adherence to a common policy (e.g., force levels in an arms-control agreement that has expired or is not yet ratified). This action is not technically an executive agreement and thus allows the president to circumvent a provision of American law that would otherwise require congressional action. For more information, see Ryan J. Barilleaux, "Parallel Unilateral Policy Declarations: A New Device for Presidential Autonomy in Foreign Affairs," *Presidential Studies Quarterly* 18 (1987): 107–17.

14. Barilleaux, "Venture Constitutionalism," 49.

15. Quoted in "Obama Lawyers Set to Defend Yoo," *Politico.com*, January 28, 2009, http://www.politico.com/news/stories/0109/18063_Page2.html (accessed January 29, 2009).

CONTRIBUTORS

RYAN J. BARILLEAUX is professor of political science at Miami University, Oxford, Ohio. He is the author or editor of seven other books on the presidency and American politics, including *The Post-Modern Presidency* (Praeger, 1988), *Power and Prudence: The Presidency of George H. W. Bush* (with Mark Rozell, Texas A&M University Press, 2004), and *Presidential Frontiers* (Praeger, 1998). From 2001 to 2009 he was chair of the Department of Political Science, and he previously served on the staff of the U.S. Senate.

LOUIS FISHER is a senior scholar in the Law Library of the Library of Congress. He is the author of more than a dozen books on the Constitution, the presidency, and Congress. His recent work includes *In the Name of National Security* (University Press of Kansas, 2006) and *Military Tribunals and Presidential Power* (University Press of Kansas, 2005).

MICHAEL A. GENOVESE is professor of political science at Loyola Marymount University, where he also holds the Loyola Chair of Leadership and is director of the Institute for Leadership Studies. He is the author of sixteen books on the presidency and politics and is a frequent political commentator on local and national television.

PATRICK J. HANEY is professor of political science at Miami University, Oxford, Ohio. He is the author of *Organizing for Foreign Policy Crises* (University of Michigan Press,1997, 2002) and *The Cuban Embargo* (with Walt Vanderbush, University of Pittsburgh Press, 2005). From 2003 to 2009 he was assistant chair and director of undergraduate studies for the Department of Political Science

CHRISTOPHER S. KELLEY is an adjunct assistant professor of political science at Miami University, Oxford, Ohio. He is the editor of *Executing the Constitution: Putting the Presidency Back into the Constitution* (State University of New York Press, 2006) as well as a number of shorter studies of the presidency and politics. His research on presidential signing statements has been widely cited by scholars and journalists.

MELANIE MARLOWE is an instructor of political science at Miami University, Oxford, Ohio. She is a doctoral candidate in government at

Claremont Graduate University and conducts research on executive orders and the Constitution.

BRYAN W. MARSHALL is associate professor of political science at Miami University, Oxford, Ohio. He is the author of *Rules for War: Procedural Choice in the U.S. House of Representatives* (Ashgate, 2005) as well as many articles in professional journals. He is also a 2009 Congressional Fellow of the American Political Science Association.

RICHARD M. PIOUS is Adolph and Effie Ochs Professor of Political Science at Barnard College, Columbia University. He is the author of *The American Presidency* (Basic Books, 1979), coauthor of *The President, Congress, and the Constitution* (with Christopher H. Pyle, Free Press, 1984), and author of *The War on Terrorism and the Rule of Law* (Roxbury Press, 2006).

MARK J. ROZELL is professor of public policy at George Mason University. He is the author of many books on American politics, including *Religion and the Bush Presidency* (with Gleaves Whitney, Palgrave Macmillan, 2007) and *Power and Prudence: The Presidency of George H. W. Bush* (with Ryan J. Barilleaux, Texas A&M University Press, 2004). He is a widely cited authority on executive privilege.

MITCHEL A. SOLLENBERGER is a visiting assistant professor in the Department of Public and International Affairs at George Mason University. He is the author of *The President Shall Nominate* (University Press of Kansas, 2008).

DAVID ZELLERS is a research associate with Susquehanna Polling and Research in Harrisburg, Pennsylvania. He is a graduate of York College (Pennsylvania) and received an MA in political science from Miami University, Oxford, Ohio. He was an intern with the Pennsylvania Department of State's Bureau of Commissions, Elections, and Legislation, and conducted research for the Center for Public Management and Regional Affairs at Miami University.

INDEX

Other Books in the Joseph V. Hughes Jr. and Holly O. Hughes Series on the Presidency and Leadership

The Politics of Shared Power: Congress and the Executive, Louis Fisher

Shaping and Signaling Presidential Policy: The National Security Decision Making of Eisenhower and Kennedy, Meena Bose

Games Advisors Play: Foreign Policy in the Nixon and Carter Administrations, Jean A. Garrison

The Managerial Presidency, James P. Pfiffner

Good Advice: Information and Policy Making in the White House, Daniel E. Ponder

Congressional Abdication on War and Spending, Louis Fisher

Vicious Cycle: Presidential Decision Making in the American Political Economy, Constantine J. Spiliotes

Presidents and the People: The Partisan Story of Going Public, Mel Laracey

The Opposition Presidency: Leadership and the Constraints of History, David A. Crockett

The Presidency, Congress, and Divided Government: A Postwar Assessment, R. S. Conley

The White House World: Transitions, Organization, and Office Operations, Martha Joynt Kumar and Terry Sullivan, eds.

Between Law and Politics: The Solicitor General and the Structuring of Race, Gender, and Reproductive Rights Litigation, Richard Pacelle Jr.

The Presidency and Women: Promise, Performance, and Illusion, Janet M. Martin

Out of Touch: The Presidency and Public Opinion, Michael J. Towle

Power and Prudence: The Presidency of George H. W. Bush, Ryan J. Barilleaux and Mark J. Rozell

The Character Factor: How We Judge America's Presidents, James P. Pfiffner

The Nerve Center: Lessons in Governing from the White House Chiefs of Staff, edited by Terry Sullivan; foreword by James A. Baker III

Nixon's Business: Authority and Power in Presidential Politics, Nigel Bowles
Saving the Reagan Presidency: Trust Is the Coin of the Realm, David M. Abshire
Policy by Other Means: Alternative Adoption by Presidents, Steven A. Shull
Institutionalizing Congress and the Presidency: The U.S. Bureau of Efficiency, 1916–1933, Mordecai Lee
Scripted for Change: The Institutionalization of the American Presidency, Victoria A. Farrar-Myers
The American Campaign: U.S. Presidential Campaigns and the National Vote, Second Edition, James E. Campbell
Running against the Grain: How Opposition Presidents Win the White House, David A. Crockett
Intelligence and National Security Policymaking on Iraq, James P. Pfiffner and Mark Phythian
The Leadership of George Bush: An Insider's View of the Forty-first President, Roman Popadiuk
Bridging the Constitutional Divide: Inside the White House Office of Legislative Affairs, Russell L. Riley